R RETURN

Patriots, Settlers, and the Origins of American Social P

Patriots, Settlers, and the Origins of American Social Policy offers a pathbreaking account of the pivotal role played by entitlement policies during the first hundred years of the United States' existence. Contrary to the story of developmental delay contained in the standard historiography, Laura Jensen reveals that national social policies not only existed in early America, but also were a major instrument by which the fledgling U.S. government built itself and the new nation. From 1776 on, Federal pensions and land entitlements figured prominently in the growth and empowerment of a unique American state, the consolidation and expansion of the country, and the political incorporation of a diverse citizenry. The book provides a rich account of how governing institutions, public expectations, ideas about law and legality, political necessity, and public policy gave shape to definitions of need, worth, and eligibility in late-eighteenth- and nineteenth-century America.

Laura Jensen is an Assistant Professor of Political Science at the University of Massachusetts, Amherst. Her Ph.D. dissertation, "The Entitlement Mentality: American Expectations of the State," won a 1993–4 Dissertation Award from the National Endowment for the Humanities. Prior to joining the faculty at the University of Massachusetts, Professor Jensen served for almost a decade in elected municipal office in Connecticut.

Patriots, Settlers, and the Origins of American Social Policy

LAURA JENSEN

University of Massachusetts, Amherst

CAMBRIDGE
UNIVERSITY PRESS

1004 092488 T

PUBLISHED BY THE PRESS SYNDICATE OF THE UNIVERSITY OF CAMBRIDGE
The Pitt Building, Trumpington Street, Cambridge, United Kingdom

CAMBRIDGE UNIVERSITY PRESS
The Edinburgh Building, Cambridge CB2 2RU, UK
40 West 20th Street, New York, NY 10011-4211, USA
477 Williamstown Road, Port Melbourne, VIC 3207, Australia
Ruiz de Alarcón 13, 28014 Madrid, Spain
Dock House, The Waterfront, Cape Town 8001, South Africa

http://www.cambridge.org

First published 2003

Printed in the United States of America

Typeface ITC New Baskerville 10/13 pt.   *System* LaTeX 2$_\varepsilon$ [TB]

A catalog record for this book is available from the British Library.

Library of Congress Cataloging in Publication Data
Jensen, Laura Smietanka, 1955–
Patriots, settlers, and the origins of American social policy / Laura Smietanka Jensen.
p.   cm.
Includes bibliographical references and index.
ISBN 0-521-81883-4 – ISBN 0-521-52426-1 (pb.)
1. United States – Social policy – History – 18th century.   2. United States –
Social policy – History – 19th century.   3. United States – Politics and government –
18th century.   4. United States – Politics and government – 19th century.   I. Title.

HN13 .J46 2003
361.6′1 – dc21   2002034799

ISBN 0 521 81883 4 hardback
ISBN 0 521 52426 1 paperback

To Rick

for everything

Contents

Acknowledgments

I have accumulated many personal and intellectual debts in the course of writing this book. While I can only hope to acknowledge some of the people and institutions that helped along the way, I offer my sincerest thanks for all of the assistance, encouragement, and patience that made this book possible.

I am especially indebted to the advisors who supervised the doctoral work that launched this project in the first place. Robert Gilmour, David Walker, and J. Garry Clifford provided the blend of enthusiasm and guidance that I needed to write a dissertation very unlike the one I originally planned. As I extended my research to produce this book, several colleagues at the University of Massachusetts kindly read portions or all of the manuscript and offered helpful comments and suggestions. John Brigham deserves special thanks for his engagement, encouragement, and appreciation of the constitutive. Alexandra Deschamps, Sheldon Goldman, John Hird, Kathyrn McDermott, Joya Misra, Leonce Ndikumana, Mary Deane Sorcinelli, and George Sulzner also offered valuable advice and a supportive presence. Students in the Department of Political Science and the Center for Public Policy and Administration provided thoughtful audiences as I developed some of the ideas found in this volume. The members of my fall 2001 graduate seminar on American welfare policy read the manuscript with care, offered helpful suggestions about what made sense and what didn't, and gave me new energy. Christine Barber also furnished valuable research assistance on the final draft of the book.

Many scholars generously shared their expertise at critical stages of this project. Several offered important insights as I began to formulate my ideas: Janet Blasecki, Joel Handler, Susan Silbey, and Tom Tyler. I am also grateful to a number of scholars who shared ideas,

read chapter drafts, and provided key suggestions and criticisms: Melissa
Buis, Christine Harrington, Ronald King, Eileen McDonagh, R. Shep
Melnick, Sidney Milkis, Richard Morgan, James Morone, Karen Orren,
Stephen Skowronek, Rogers Smith, and Robert C. Wood. My thanks
also go to several anonymous reviewers who provided incisive comments and suggestions and to John Resch, who kindly let me read his
fine book on Revolutionary veterans while it was still in page proof.
Deborah Stone read the penultimate draft of the manuscript with interest and enthusiasm, offering vitally important advice on substance and
style along with much-needed encouragement. She has shown me that
shaping and polishing a book really is a collegial affair, and I will always be grateful. I am particularly indebted to Stuart McConnell, who
over the years has extended his time and expertise with extraordinary
generosity. His appreciation of what I wanted to accomplish in this
project helped beyond measure, as did his intelligence, irreverence, and
friendship.

   For facilitating my research, I would like to thank the library staffs of
Connecticut College, the University of Connecticut at Storrs, the Uni-
versity of Connecticut School of Law, the University of Massachusetts at
Amherst, and Yale University. A number of librarians and archivists went
out of their way to help me locate documents and solve research myster-
ies. I am especially grateful to Erhard Konerding at Olin Library, Wesleyan
University; Rodney Ross and Nancy Melley at the Center for Legislative
Archives, National Archives and Records Administration; Ellen McAllister
Clark at the Society of the Cincinnati Library; William Thompson at the
DuBois Library, University of Massachusetts; and Deborah Pelletier at
Amherst College's Frost Library depository.

   Thanks are also due for the considerable organizational and institutional support that made this book possible. A 1993–4 National
Endowment for the Humanities Dissertation Award, #FD-20623, provided a crucial combination of financial support and uninterrupted time
to work in the early days of the project. I am also grateful for grants from
the University of Connecticut in the form of the Abraham Ribicoff and
G. Lowell Field fellowships, and for research funds and a Lilly Teach-
ing Fellowship from the University of Massachusetts. Thanks also go to
the Law and Society Association for inviting me to participate in its first
Summer Institute on Sociolegal Studies in 1992; the Wesleyan University
Center for the Humanities for a 1995 Senior Research Fellowship; and

the American Political Science Association for naming me the runner-up for the Schattschneider Award in 1997. For giving me the opportunity to present and test ideas as I prepared this book, I am particularly grateful to R. Shep Melnick, Morton Keller, Sidney Milkis, and Brandeis University; Betsy Traube and Wesleyan University; and Christopher Tomlins and the American Bar Foundation.

Lewis Bateman, editor extraordinaire, deserves my sincere thanks for his sustained interest in this project. I am very glad that I was able to work with him on this book. Thanks for editorial assistance are also due to Sarah Gentile, Helen Greenberg, and Louise Calabro. An early version of material now in Chapters 2 and 3 was published under the title "The Early American Origins of Entitlements" in *Studies in American Political Development* 10 (1996): 360–404. I am grateful to the editors for permission to reprint portions here.

Heartfelt thanks are due to the many friends who have provided encouragement, cheer, holiday celebrations, and home renovation adventures during my years of work on this book. Rhonda Domin, the late Jane Cobb Dow and Alva Morrison Dow, Anne and Will Emmet, and Miriam Kolodney and the late Harold Kolodney deserve special thanks for their many acts of kindness, good humor, and unflagging faith. Special thanks also go to Sandy Anglund for her insight, support, and appreciation of the ridiculous. Gail and Sal Catanzaro, Stenie and Steve Gullans, Sheila Suess Kennedy, Zyg Plater, Betty Smith, and Dara Wier also deserve thanks for the ways in which they helped me bring this book to fruition, as do the friends who have made Woods Hole such a wonderful place for the last ten summers: Charlotte, Bill, Max, and Fannie Bialek; Tera, Rob, Floor, Ninah, and Stan de Ruyter van Steveninck; and Karen, David, Alex, and Spencer Tank. Drs. Stuart Chipkin of Baystate Medical Center and John Heaney of Dartmouth Medical Center worked to ensure that I would finish this book, and I am enormously grateful for their intelligent care.

My greatest debt is to my family for sustaining me, and it is a particular pleasure finally to be able to thank them here. I am grateful for the special support of my parents, the late Leonard Lambert Smietanka, Marilyn Smietanka Ross, and William Ross; my grandmother, the late Estelle Anderson Carlson; and Patricia James Jensen, the late Roderick Emil Jensen, and the late Augusta James Wallace. Thanks also go to Ted and Jane Burnside Jensen and Ru and Suzanne Everson Jensen for good times and affirming e-mail. To my husband, Roderick V. Jensen, and our children, Kate and Rory Jensen, go my love and thanks for always being there. You have filled my years of working on this book with more joy than I could have imagined possible, and reminded me daily about what is truly important in life. In more ways than I can express, I am so blessed.

                                        L.S.J.
                                        Pelham, Massachusetts
                                        March 18, 2002

1

Entitlements in Law and History

As a legal idea, the concept of an entitlement is utterly mundane. But the substantive content and distributive effects of the range of legal entitlements are not matters of indifference, rather they reflect and enact distinct political values. Legal entitlements do not descend from the sky, but are created by human actors who make moral or philosophical decisions, explicitly or implicitly, about who is deserving or undeserving of reward within a chosen economic structure. The politics of race, gender, and class are filtered through these choices.

Lucy A. Williams, 1998[1]

In December 1817, sixty-six-year-old George McBeth of the Pendleton District of South Carolina, a veteran of the American Revolution, petitioned the United States Congress to grant him Federal income assistance. McBeth admitted that he had not received an injury in the service of the nation that would entitle him to disability benefits. Nonetheless, he hoped that he could rely upon the Government in his time of need. Aged, infirm, and incapable of supporting himself and his elderly wife, he had no relatives or connections upon whom to rely for support during "the short time that m[ight] remain of his frail existence." McBeth ascribed "no particular merit" to himself for having fought in the Revolution, but begged Congress to shelter him from "the pitiless storms of adversity" and "shield him from the chilling grasp of utmost poverty." As his acquaintances would attest, he was an "honest, honorable, sober upright man" who sincerely believed that he had "claims upon the bounty of his

---

[1] "Welfare and Legal Entitlements: The Social Roots of Poverty," p. 575, in *The Politics of Law: A Progressive Critique*, ed. David Kairys (New York: Basic Books, 3rd. ed., 1998), pp. 569–90.

country, whose liberties he fought for and whose independence he aided in establishing."[2]

McBeth was not alone in thinking that the United States should come to his aid, as the many petitions and claims sent to Congress in the late eighteenth and early nineteenth centuries demonstrated. Rawleigh Christian of Northumberland County, Virginia, another veteran of the Revolution, wrote to Congress in December 1817 to ask for "something for his immediate support and also such an annual pension as [Congress] m[ight] think just, taking into consideration his services and situation." He had devoted the prime of his life to the American cause, having fought in seven major engagements between 1774 and 1781 as a soldier in the army. Advancing in age, feeling the effects of his war wounds, and incapable of earning a living through his own labor, Christian "thr[ew] himself on the justice and bounty of the Congress of the United States under the most thorough assurance that they w[ould] not suffer the worn out Soldier of the Revolution to pine in want for that pittance which would be like a drop from the ocean of a great and wealthy country."[3]

Congress received the petition of Nathaniel Kinnard of Portsmouth, New Hampshire, in January 1818. It detailed Kinnard's decades of devotion to the United States, from his enlistment as a soldier in the revolutionary army in 1775 to his discharge as the commander of the cutter *New Hampshire* in 1815. He had "served the whole of two Wars, during which he ha[d] suffered more than five years imprisonment & captivity." Like McBeth and Christian, the sixty-three-year-old Kinnard felt "compelled to throw himself on the bounty, or the justice of his Government, for that decent support to which his own means [we]re totally inadequate." He prayed that Congress would add him to the pension list or otherwise provide for him so that "the few remaining days, or years, which m[ight] be allotted to him, [would] not be embittered with the reflection, that while he ha[d] devoted the best period of his life to his country, his services & sufferings should have resulted in the Poverty of himself and his family."[4]

On March 18, 1818, President James Monroe signed a bill establishing a Federal pension program for aged, impoverished veterans of the

---

[2] Petition of George McBeth, HR15A-G10.1, Records of the U.S. House of Representatives, Record Group 233, National Archives, Washington, DC.

[3] Petition of Rawleigh C. Christian, SEN 16A-G10, Records of the U.S. Senate, Record Group 46, National Archives, Washington, DC.

[4] Petition of Nathaniel Kinnard, HR 15A-G10.1, Records of the U.S. House of Representatives, Record Group 233, National Archives, Washington, DC.

American Revolution. The legislation had been passed by overwhelming majorities of both chambers of the Fifteenth Congress of the United States. According to its terms, surviving patriots who had served in the Continental Army or Navy until the Revolution ended, or for at least nine months during that war, and who were in need of their country's support because of reduced circumstances, became entitled to Federal pensions for life.[5]

The enactment of the Pension Act of 1818 was a watershed event. Most obviously, it committed the U.S. Government to playing an active and direct role in the alleviation of poverty. The Pension Act constituted a major departure from the uncertain and highly localized support provided under the poor laws, establishing a vital new source of national-level income assistance for thousands of citizens and a new partner for state and local entities charged with caring for the poor. In conferring entitlement status upon aged veterans, the act also constituted an expression of "enforceable virtue," which embodied new national standards for public morality and civic responsibility.[6]

In addition to inaugurating an important new Federal social role, the Pension Act entailed a critically important congressional turn toward a novel type of public policy: statutes entitling *groups* of citizens to Federal benefits via public benefit *programs*. Entitlement programs are such standard fare today that they seem to be an intrinsic part of public affairs. As a policy strategy, however, they were an invention of the early national period. An essentially new form of public law, entitlements proactively granted Federal largesse to citizens sharing certain designated characteristics. Such a device deviated radically from the tenets of representation and fiscal responsibility enshrined in the political and constitutional culture of early America, which obligated legislators to respond directly to the petitions and claims of citizens like McBeth, Christian, and Kinnard on an individual, case-by-case basis.

In creating pension entitlements in 1818, Congress acknowledged decades of struggle for recognition by the military veterans who had fought to establish the American nation. Yet, as many men petitioning for Federal aid soon learned, the Pension Act passed by Congress did

---

[5] *Annals of Congress*, 15th Cong., 1st sess. (Washington, DC: Gales and Seaton, 1834–), pp. 2518–19.

[6] John Resch, *Suffering Soldiers: Revolutionary War Veterans, Moral Sentiment, and Political Culture in the Early Republic* (Amherst: University of Massachusetts Press, 2000), p. 118.

not recognize or reward the efforts of all veterans.[7] Instead, it took an overtly selective approach in designating a category of eligibles, restricting benefits to a carefully delimited subset of the men who had served in the Revolutionary War. Many people who celebrated the Pension Act's enactment apparently were willing to overlook the selective perception involved in its establishment. Others, however, were appalled by the new law's selectivity, which seemed to violate contemporary legal norms barring legislation that operated "partially" upon particular classes of citizens, advancing inegalitarian conceptions of citizenship and distributive justice.

In embracing entitlements as a device for programmatically addressing the presumptively similar characteristics and circumstances of groups of citizens, Congress relinquished some of its legal authority and duty to determine the worthiness of individuals. This created a need for an administrative branch of government and invested it with significant powers over citizens' lives. At the same time, the American state gained the power to construct abstract categories of desert and reward, signaling what kinds of people and behaviors would be deemed virtuous and meritorious by the nation. America's original entitlements bound citizens and their loyalties to the government of the United States, but not in such as way as to engender passivity. Rather, Federal entitlements urged positive actions in the service of Government goals, by members of the military and civilians alike. Mobilizing the energies and imaginations of thousands of American citizens, entitlement programs allowed multiple thorny problems of national governance to be addressed simultaneously, be they conquest, territorial expansion, or the elimination of native peoples.

The scope of the 1818 Pension Act was unprecedented when its terms were inscribed in the statute books of the United States. In form, however, it was not entirely new, for it joined a set of earlier enactments that programmatically entitled other select groups of Americans to land and monetary benefits. Because the Federal government had extended the Continental and Confederation Congresses' commitments to provide for men injured in the service of the state, the pension program of 1818 was grafted onto an existing pension plan for disabled veterans. A set of

---

[7] There is no record that George McBeth or Nathaniel Kinnard ever received pensions under the Pension Act of 1818. Rawleigh Christian apparently died shortly after he petitioned Congress for aid, leaving his widow to seek a pension. Revolutionary War Pension and Bounty–Land–Warrant Application Files, Records of the Veterans Administration, Record Group 15, National Archives, Washington, DC.

land-related entitlement programs was also already in place. Federal law granted land to certain classes of veterans who had fought in national forces during the Revolution and the War of 1812, and bestowed special purchase rights upon select categories of civilians who had settled illegally on the public domain. New pension and land entitlements would soon be added to those on the books in March 1818, further extending the beneficence of the United States to particular "types" of citizens. Together, these early American entitlements constituted the United States' first "system of national public care."[8] The establishment of this early system of Federal social aid, and the coincident invention and legitimation of programmatic, legal entitlement as a Federal policy practice, had enormous consequences for the institutional development of the American state, the contours of American civic life, and the shape of future U.S. social policy.

Rethinking the American State and American Governance

The idea that an important system of national social provision came into being in the United States at the turn of the nineteenth century may confound readers steeped in the conventional wisdom that a Federal social role did not meaningfully exist in the United States until the 1930s. Even those acquainted with recent revisionist scholarship situating the origins of Federal social policy in the Civil War pension system may be perplexed to learn that major programs of public care existed well before the Civil War and Reconstruction. For many, the absence of an American "welfare state" before the late nineteenth or early twentieth century logically denies the existence of antebellum social programs of enduring significance. Theda Skocpol, most notably, ignores Federal land benefits in her account of the origins of social policy in the United States, and dismisses the establishment and expansion of Federal military pensions before the 1860s as "minimal" compared with what was to come later, even though she otherwise emphasizes that policies shape politics.[9]

Those who understand the early American state to have been a limited, underdeveloped, premodern shell may similarly be confounded by the notion of a significant early-nineteenth-century system of national

---

[8] Theda Skocpol's phrase. *Protecting Soldiers and Mothers: The Political Origins of Social Policy in the United States* (Cambridge, MA: Harvard University Press, 1992), p. 151.

[9] Ibid., p. 105.

social benefits. The preeminent works detailing American state formation postpone the evolution of genuine "stateness" until the middle to
late nineteenth century, when the exigencies of the Civil War and Reconstruction led to the development of wholly new forms of central authority
and capacity.[10] By the terms of these and other accounts, the insubstan-
tial, essentially frail entity that was the antebellum American state would
not have been capable of enacting and implementing Federal social policies and programs on behalf of the nation's citizens. Not until the victory
of the Union's forces, as Richard Bensel puts it, would the American
state gain the "fundamental attributes of territorial and governmental
sovereignty."[11]

It is unfortunate that some of the finest scholarship on American political development not only fails to account for the empirical realities
of early Federal institutions and social welfare policy but, moreover, effectively dismisses them, creating large blind spots in our field of vision.
These blind spots will not disappear until we begin to rethink the qualities
of the early American state and its policies, elucidating the attributes that
it possessed and the goals it could and did achieve, instead of focusing
upon the features that it lacked and the tasks it could not and did not
accomplish.

A critical first step in this reconsideration is that of identifying the
scholarly tendencies that have worked to camouflage the true dimensions
of the American polity in its formative years. One of these tendencies is
the almost systematic inattention that has been paid to the institutional dimensions of early American governance during the past several decades,
even by scholars of a "new historical institutionalist" stripe, whose research focuses on the relations between institutions, social forces, and
political outcomes and their consequences. Richard John has attributed
this inattention to the emergence of new traditions in historiography
that discounted the role of state institutions in the early republic, effectively rendering analysis of the structural features of American governance passé.[12] Only very recently have scholars begun to redirect their

[10] Richard Franklin Bensel, *Yankee Leviathan: The Origins of Central State Authority in America, 1859–1877* (Cambridge: Cambridge University Press, 1990); see also Stephen Skowronek, *Building a New American State: The Expansion of National Administrative Capacities, 1877–1920* (Cambridge: Cambridge University Press, 1982).

[11] *Yankee Leviathan*, p. 2.

[12] "Governmental Institutions as Agents of Change: Rethinking American Political Development in the Early Republic, 1787–1835," *Studies in American Political Development* 11(2) (Fall 1997): 347–80.

focus toward the law, public policy, and public administration of the early national period in an effort to assess how governmental institutions, in combination with ideas and social circumstances, enduringly influenced the developing nation. Much more remains to be discovered about governance in the United States' early national period.

John has also diagnosed the myopia that results when early American governance is evaluated in terms of anachronistic understandings of state and "stateness," such as when the nation's original administrative apparatus is measured according to comparisons with the post–Civil War or even the twentieth-century administrative state. Such judgments render the state building and governance that took place before the 1860s prehistoric, effectively consigning them to an interesting but irrelevant past. This is regrettable, for meaningful and far more appropriate comparisons can and should be drawn between the institutional arrangements and policy outputs of the founding generation and those that existed immediately prior to the framing of the Federal Constitution.[13]

These insights of John's provide a valuable starting point for an inquiry into the true qualities of the early American state, but they need to be extended to reveal the ways in which our vision is also distorted when American "stateness" either is appraised in terms of inapt international comparisons or assessed solely in administrative terms. Federally organized, formally dedicated to the principles of popular sovereignty, representation, and citizens' rights, and curiously invested in both liberal and illiberal pursuits,[14] the early American state was in key respects a state like no other. The institution at the core of this unique state was not the executive, as is implied by studies measuring state strength according to central administrative capacity, but rather the nation's legislature. It was the U.S. Congress that was the key institutional player in establishing political stability, prosperity, and security while expanding the American nation and forging a national community – in no small part through the establishment of the entitlement programs chronicled in this book.

Just as incongruous assessments of the state and state capacity skew our vision of the realities of early American governance, so too do analyses predicated upon contemporary understandings of the welfare state.

---

[13] Ibid., p. 368. See also Richard R. John, *Spreading the News: The American Postal System from Franklin to Morse* (Cambridge, MA: Harvard University Press, 1995).

[14] Rogers M. Smith, *Civic Ideals: Conflicting Visions of Citizenship in U.S. History* (New Haven, CT: Yale University Press, 1997).

The welfare state is an extremely problematic standard for evaluating the national social programs of nineteenth-century America, because those programs were not necessarily enacted with the goal of constructing a deliberate, holistic system of care or even intended primarily as what we now think of as "social policy." This does not mean that they should be viewed as insignificant providers of welfare or classified as a different "type" of policy, such as military policy or land policy. Instead, they should be recognized as forms of governance established under changing conditions of democracy, which constituted systems of public benefits appropriate to particular historical circumstances. Like their counterparts in modern welfare states, these benefits were legal entitlements.

Calling eighteenth- and nineteenth-century Federal benefits "entitlements" may be fraught with some danger, since the term has strong modern associations, means strikingly different things to different people, and usually carries a strong political charge. Many who take the sign of that charge to be positive understand entitlement programs to indicate that a given nation-state recognizes certain basic commitments to its citizens, whether they take the form of universal guarantees for all (in T. H. Marshall's words, the "social rights of citizenship") [15] or more discretionary allocations. Those reading the sign of the charge to be negative, by contrast, typically comprehend entitlements to invoke the specter of welfare, or unearned, noncontributory assistance. To them, the word entitlement is either a term that signifies a welfare benefit per se or a label that contains the potential to invite social stigma, whatever program it might be applied to.

There is nonetheless an inherently neutral understanding of entitlements – the one relied upon in this book – that takes the term entitlement simply to identify a particular *form* of public law or policy: one that grants public benefits to groups of "like" individuals *programmatically*, on the basis of the statutory eligibility criteria of deliberately enacted legislation. [16] R. Shep Melnick has called attention to the formal, programmatic aspect of entitlements in order to demonstrate that such benefits have never

---

[15] See "Citizenship and Social Class" in *Class, Citizenship, and Social Development* (New York: Doubleday & Co., 1964), pp. 65–122.

[16] A form of public policy has been usefully defined by Deborah Stone as a particular strategy for "structuring relationships and coordinating behavior" toward the achievement of particular purposes. *Policy Paradox and Political Reason* (Glenview, IL: Scott, Foresman & Co., 1988), p. 208. This definition of entitlements is refined further in subsequent sections of this chapter.

achieved the status of constitutional guarantees in the United States.[17] Equally important, however, is the fact that it is the programmatic dimension of entitlements as a form of public law that distinguishes them from the sporadic acts of legislative generosity found in private law. This distinction admittedly is not vital to an understanding of the modern world of social policy, for public law is now at the core of the legislative process. However, it is absolutely essential to an understanding of American political development in the late eighteenth and nineteenth centuries, when the congressional agenda was dominated by private claims and private legislation. Early American legislators devised the programmatic entitlement of categories of citizens as a formal alternative to the one-time, ad hoc grants of aid or preferential treatment that were then their normal mode of response to citizens' individual and unpredictable claims of need and right.

To underscore this formal dimension of entitlements is not to suggest that their substance is unimportant. Entitlement programs distribute certain resources and impose certain burdens. They confer identities, encourage preferences, establish understandings, and enable experiences. The particulars of specific programs matter. Yet, the common structure shared by all entitlements is also significant. As the case studies of America's original entitlements found in the following chapters demonstrate, different programs tend to generate similar institutional processes, serve the same ideological functions, and produce the same kinds of political dynamics. In both form and substance, entitlements play a vital role in composing states and societies, as well as the institutions and characters that inhabit them.

This book explores how, why, and with what effects national legislative bodies selectively entitled groups of Americans to social benefits from the very beginning of the nation's existence, starting with land grants and disability and service pensions for veterans of the Revolutionary War. It shows that entitlements were a primary instrument by which the fledgling U.S. Government constituted itself and the new nation during the first century of the Republic's existence. First, and perhaps most obviously, there was a vital substantive link between entitlements and the concrete geographical development of the nation. The national-level pension and

---

[17] *Between the Lines: Interpreting Welfare Rights* (Washington, DC: Brookings Institution, 1994), pp. 16–18, 274–83; "The Courts, Congress, and Programmatic Rights," in *Remaking American Politics*, ed. Sidney Milkis and Richard Harris (Boulder, CO: Westview Press, 1989), pp. 188–212.

land entitlements legislated by the Continental and U.S. Congresses from 1776 on facilitated the establishment, consolidation, expansion, and reconstruction of the United States through military and civilian conquest, allowing the Revolution to be won and American sovereignty gradually to be extended over a continental republic of unprecedented size.

State building went hand in hand with these processes, and entitlement programs played a major role in the development of national institutions. To begin with, they allowed the new American state to build and sustain a capable national military – no mean feat in a country philosophically opposed to professional or standing armies. Entitlements also necessitated and justified the establishment of a national treasury and a public domain, even as they simultaneously required their use. They shaped the development of Congress, contributing to the establishment of the committee system and the emergence of modern legislative behavior rooted in programmatic responses to group demands. Early American entitlements also spurred the creation of a Federal bureaucracy, since government agents of various kinds were needed to process, verify, and police applications for programmatic benefits and organize their disbursement. The nation's first entitlement policies even affected the evolution of the federal courts by provoking conflicts over procedural justice and the distinction between legislative and judicial roles and functions.

Entitlements also figured prominently in the evolution of the U.S. Constitution's meaning and, more generally, in the development of law and legality in the United States. The creation of Federal pension and land entitlements involved the practical incarnation of foundational American legal concepts that were not self-executing, including the separation of powers, federalism, Congress's taxing and spending authority, property, the right of petition, and representation. Looking at the actual record of the first hundred years of U.S. governance through the lens of statutory entitlements, we learn that original understandings of institutional functions, derived from colonial legislative precedent, vested adjudicatory authority over certain kinds of claims in Congress rather than the courts.[18] The mechanism for conveying those claims to Congress was the petition, a form of political speech so vital as an expression of the will of the people, and as an instrument that structured politics and the processes of representative government, that the ability to petition became

---

[18] Christine A. Desan, "The Constitutional Commitment to Legislative Adjudication in the Early American Tradition," *Harvard Law Review* 111 (1998): 1381–90.

the capstone of the rights protected by the First Amendment.[19] Contrary to what the standard legal historiography would have us believe about pre–New Deal limits on Congress's authority, neither federalism nor the provisions of Article I of the Constitution prevented Congress from establishing new forms of property, including the pensions, land grants, and preemption rights that played a significant role in social provision from the early days of the nation's existence. The history of America's early entitlement programs indicates that much of the dialogue that took place about the meaning of the Constitution from the late eighteenth to the mid-nineteenth century took place in Congress, not the judiciary. It was a dialogue that was produced by the dynamics of the interaction between citizens and their representatives: one that demonstrated that America's original constitutional culture was produced as much in practice as in theory, and as much from the bottom up as from the top down.[20]

Because most of America's original entitlement programs were very selective, distributing benefits to relatively small subsets of the American people, they gave rise to debates both in and out of Congress about the meaning of distributive justice and redistributive obligation. Even in instances when the enactment of particular benefits was widely supported, there was significant concern about the *constitutive* effects of creating formal legal categories of citizen deservingness, or about the ways in which the practice of selective entitlement might reach into social and political life to affect everyday patterns of thinking and acting.[21] It was understood that beyond providing a substantive inducement for citizens to become invested in state endeavors like Indian removal and expansionism, entitlements also contributed symbolically to the formation of political and legal consciousness. Entitlements were a form of social knowledge. They suggested new avenues by which people could make claims and demands, generated new expectations about the Federal role, imparted an understanding of statutory benefits as rights, and shaped conceptions of identity and citizenship. Partisan, sectional, and electoral concerns as well as the politics of self-interest undoubtedly figured prominently in arguments

[19] Gregory A. Mark, "The Vestigial Constitution: The History and Significance of the Right to Petition," *Fordham Law Review* 66 (1998): 2153–2231.

[20] As Christine A. Desan has observed, "institutions conceived as matters of everyday practice are the relationships that incarnate the state." "Writing Constitutional History beyond the Institutional/Ideological Divide," *Law and History Review* 16(2) (Summer 1998): 392.

[21] John Brigham, *The Constitution of Interests: Beyond the Politics of Rights* (New York: New York University Press, 1996), pp. 2–3.

over program establishment, expansion, and retrenchment. Yet, citizens and their representatives in Congress also struggled with questions of principle, as can be seen in debates over the legal or political nature of claims of entitlement, the meaning of justice and honor, the extent to which Congress was to be guided by legislative precedent, and the kind of republic that the United States was intended to become.

The first American entitlements thus played a major role in the constitution of a distinctly American, exceptional state: one that largely was organized around neither universal social provision nor even social provision per se, but rather around the selective entitlement of certain citizens who advanced the diverse goals and purposes of the Federal government. Entitlements were designed both as retrospective rewards for past service to the nation and as prospective incentives for citizens to behave in ways that Congress deemed necessary for the achievement of national objectives. In essence, Congress created and disbursed particular entitlements in order to recruit people to do the Government's bidding, whether that was fighting foreign enemies, exterminating Native Americans, settling upon southern or western lands, or establishing certain forms of economic development on the frontier.

Congress's practice of selective legal entitlement, and the understandings it both sprang from and generated, simultaneously transformed particular individuals into virtuous citizens while ignoring others' claims of need and right, fashioned geographic and social communities around newly created, quasi-private property, and brought about the destruction of the communities and lives of indigenous peoples. This would have an enduring influence on the scope and direction of congressional authority, the contours of Federal social policy, and the meaning of American citizenship. Although land entitlements evinced a discernible shift toward universal provision during the homestead movement of the mid-nineteenth century, the Civil War and Reconstruction resulted in a return to Federal governance that enshrined selective entitlement as a standard operating procedure. That the American state of the late nineteenth and early twentieth centuries failed to incorporate citizens broadly and equitably into the polity is perhaps not surprising given this legacy.[22]

---

[22] Incorporation, or "the manner and extent to which people are included, consolidated, and organized" as members of a political community, is powerfully affected by governance. Suzanne Mettler, *Dividing Citizens: Gender and Federalism in New Deal Public Policy* (Ithaca, NY: Cornell University Press, 1998), p. 9.

This book portrays the early American state as it grew into the relatively cohesive and autonomous organization that claimed and exercised sovereignty over a signficant portion of the North American continent and its population during the late eighteenth and nineteenth centuries. Its specific focus is upon one way in which that state grew, through its development of a policy device that utilized the state's extractive and rhetorical capacities simultaneously to privilege particular interests and extend into ideological space to define American conceptions of identity and citizenship. The rest of this chapter explores that policy device in depth, drawing upon both historical examples and contemporary struggles to illustrate the kinds of contests over meaning and frames of meaning that entitlement programs have always engendered.

Rethinking Entitlement(s)

Entitlements work most obviously in a top-down way, establishing public benefits and burdens and shaping people's perceptions, attitudes, and behavior. Yet, they are also given meaning from the bottom up, in social relations and politics. The worthiness of citizens is constructed both by entitlement programs, as they are implemented via particular administrative arrangements, and by the ways in which societal norms and ideas about deservingness become part of the architecture of those programs. In analyzing any system of social provision, historic or contemporary, it is critical to look beyond the definitions of desert that emanate from formal institutional locations to consider how citizens' social identities and statuses, rights and obligations, relationships, and behaviors are influenced by entitlement programs and the ways those programs are understood. It is also important to identify the ways in which individuals and groups consciously invoke beliefs about entitlement in order to give shape to a state and its policies.

A rich and growing body of scholarship has emerged in recent years to examine the effects of legal practices, institutions, and language on social and political identity. Scholars have investigated how law is implicated in people's struggles to define themselves as individuals and as groups, and how legal processes influence and respond to those struggles. Of particular interest have been the processes by which people and things come to be recognized as differentiable, how difference is inscribed in and reified by legal categories, and how legal forms and categories work to direct and constrain people's preferences and construct their expectations.[23] This is because knowledge of the social world and the categories that make it possible "are the stakes, *par excellence*, of political struggle, the inextricably theoretical and practical struggle for the power to conserve or transform the social world by conserving or transforming the categories through which it is perceived."[24] Legal categories play a particularly critical role in constructing the social world, because law has particular force in shaping human decisions about what is natural and unnatural, normal and abnormal, legitimate and illegitimate, acceptable and unacceptable.[25]

Entitlements are an extraordinarily overt and powerful form of law. Their eligibility requirements reflect deliberate decisions about issues of social definition, made by state actors who have chosen at a particular historical moment to recognize certain citizens and mark them as deserving of tangible public benefits. This does not imply that entitlement programs necessarily represent a uniform political consensus, that the identities they endorse are solely the product of their making, or that those identities are not subject to resistance, contestation, and change. To the extent that entitlements stimulate and justify belief in the deservingness of certain citizens at the expense of certain communities, though, the stories they tell and the strategic suggestions they impart are central to a larger epistemological framework.[26] In the aggregate and over time,

---

[23] See, e.g., Carol J. Greenhouse, "Courting Difference: Issues of Interpretation and Comparison in the Study of Legal Ideologies," *Law & Society Review* 22 (1988): 688; William E. Connolly, *Identity\Difference: Democratic Negotiations of Political Paradox* (Ithaca, NY: Cornell University Press, 1991), especially pp. 64–94; Martha Minow, *Making All the Difference: Inclusion, Exclusion, and American Law* (Ithaca, NY: Cornell University Press, 1990); Brigham, *Constitution of Interests*.

[24] Pierre Bourdieu, "The Social Space and the Genesis of Groups," *Theory and Society* 14 (1985): 729. Bourdieu notes that it is "no accident that the verb *kategoresthai*, which gives us our 'categories' and 'categoremes,' means to accuse publicly."

[25] Zillah R. Eisenstein, *The Female Body and the Law* (Berkeley: University of California Press, 1988), p. 43. It must be noted that although complex social realities often seem to be simplified in terms of such dichotomous oppositions, they can be (and often are) ordered in other ways. One of the issues that legal entitlements have always raised is that of whether they create de facto categories of "*un*deserving" individuals diametrically opposed to those "deserving" of (or "qualified" to receive) benefits, or merely recognize those *most* deserving of benefits out of a *universe* of deserving citizens. The difference is not merely semantic. For a potent example of congressional arguments over this very issue, see the debate over the 1818 Pension Act chronicled in Chapter 2.

[26] See Jerome Bruner, *Actual Minds, Possible Worlds* (Cambridge, MA: Harvard University Press, 1986), pp. 11–43; Patricia Ewick and Susan S. Silbey, "Subversive Stories and Hegemonic Tales: Toward a Sociology of Narrative," *Law and Society Review* 29 (1995): 197–226; John Brigham, "Right, Rage, and Remedy: Forms of Law in Political Discourse,"

entitlements play a central role in the development and legitimation of nation-states. First and foremost, they are policy devices that engineer a large part of the terrain that is social and political reality.

Thinking about entitlements in this way is not intended to deemphasize the unique politics of particular programs, but rather to emphasize the ways in which the structure shared by all entitlement programs influences their politics and vice versa. This can be seen more clearly if we consider two potential methods of social provision, justified by political ideologies that are polar opposites.[27] One is social provision via "the market," under which no one is entitled to anything, and the state's role is minimal and noninterventionist (in essence, classic liberal capitalism). The other possibility is that of universal social provision, where by all citizens are entitled to, and the state charged with the distribution of, an array of nonrival, nonexclusive public goods.[28] Obviously, neither the market nor universal social provision has ever existed in anything close to pure form in practice, for the market would degenerate into anarchy without the legal and military apparatus of the state to sustain it, and universalism always requires the establishment of at least some basic categories of selection (for example, categories determining disability or old age). This is why the key to understanding any given system of social provision lies first in recognizing the *conscious programmatic action* that establishes its entitlements and then in carefully analyzing those entitlements' particular *categories of selection, degrees of selectivity or exclusiveness,* and *policy purposes* at relevant points in that system's historical development. Entitlements are not natural functions of governments, but rather reflect strategic choices between those policy alternatives that seem within the realm of the possible in specific jurisdictions at specific times.[29]

Studies in American Political Development: An Annual, vol. 2 (New Haven, CT: Yale University Press, 1987), pp. 303–16; Ann Swidler, "Culture in Action: Symbols and Strategies," *American Sociological Review* 51 (1986): 273–86; and Robert W. Gordon, "Critical Legal Histories," *Stanford Law Review* 36 (1984): 57–125. As Gordon observes (p. 111), the legal forms we use not only condition our power "to get what we want but what we want (or think we can get) itself."

[27] I am grateful to Stuart McConnell for valuable insights that contributed to this paragraph.
[28] To term a public good "nonrival" or "indivisible" means that a quantity of that good may be consumed by one citizen without in any way diminishing the consumption opportunities of others. A "nonexclusive" public good is a good that, when supplied to one citizen, cannot be denied to others.
[29] As suggested earlier, those policy alternatives may have little if anything to do with the conscious, deliberate construction of a "welfare state," yet they nonetheless may come to constitute a national system of care.

The case studies that form the core of this book demonstrate that the U.S. Government typically relied upon very selective entitlement programs for key groups of citizens as a dual means of social provision and state building during the first century of its existence. This shaped the people's notions of the kinds of political claims that could and should be articulated and by whom, encouraging certain behaviors while constraining others. In the formative years of the polity, Americans learned to argue over what reasons were adequate for winning particular entitlements. As time passed and additional selective benefits were legislated by Congress, they argued less and less about whether fighting for entitlements was the best use of their energies, or whether an array of highly selective entitlements was a proper foundation for a national system of care. Debates over the disposition of the public domain did engender consideration of the central state's basic obligation to provide during the 1830s, to the extent that arguments rooted in the natural rights of man were transformed into powerful new arguments about the social and political rights of citizens. However, the politics of section and race that culminated in the Civil War derailed that civic conversation. Only in principle would the Homestead Act of 1862 extend the nation's beneficence to all in need of home and farm. Congress's subsequent creation and expansion of an inegalitarian pension system benefiting only Union veterans of the Civil War dealt a major blow to nineteenth-century visions of a national system of social provision rooted in the guarantees of citizenship.

The E-Word in Contemporary American Politics: What's in a Name?

Many of the battles that historically have erupted over American social benefits have had to do with the details of particular entitlement programs. Thus it was something of an unusual development when entitlements per se became the focus of public attention in the United States in the late 1980s and early 1990s. Concern that entitlement spending was "threatening the nation's future" became so strong that a presidential commission was appointed and charged with making recommendations on entitlement and tax reform in late 1993.[30] Critics also warned that

---

[30] See, e.g., Peter G. Peterson and Neil Howe, *On Borrowed Time: How the Growth in Entitlement Spending Threatens America's Future* (New York: Simon & Schuster, 1988). President William Jefferson "Bill" Clinton established the Bipartisan Commission on Entitlement and Tax Reform by executive order in November 1993.

the nation was imperiled by an "entitlement mentality."[31] The situation seemingly offered a window of opportunity for the nation to consider the nature and uses of the policy device that undergirds its system of social provision, perhaps even to the extent of getting beyond fiscal concerns to consider the constitutive effects of America's highly categorical social programs and their skewed pattern of distribution. That window of opportunity rapidly closed, however, as it became apparent that no one really knew what an entitlement was. Prominent observers parsed the language of academics, presidents, and Federal statutes but were unable to determine who had coined the word entitlement, when it had come into common usage, or what precisely it meant.[32] Fixated on the policies and programs of the twentieth century, they failed to notice that laws informing people that they would "be entitled" to certain public benefits were as old as the nation itself.

Lack of definitional consensus was a key element in the endeavors of President Clinton's Bipartisan Commission on Entitlement and Tax Reform and in the public uproar that ensued over them. Despite months of effort, the commission's experts not only failed to reach accord on a plan to control the growth of entitlement spending, but, more fundamentally, were unable to agree on which public programs should be counted as entitlements. Rendered incapable of any sort of holistic deliberation on either the principles or practice of legal entitlement in the United States, they turned to debate various program-specific schemes, including raising the eligibility age for Medicare and Social Security benefits; indexing Social Security benefits to the average growth in wages rather than the Consumer Price Index; attaching means tests to Social Security, Medicare, unemployment compensation, and certain veterans' benefits; reducing food stamp and welfare benefits; and limiting income tax deductions for taxpayers with incomes above a certain level.[33] Although none of these ideas were agreed to, their proposal drew howls of protest from program beneficiaries and associated interest groups.

---

[31] See, e.g., George F. Will, "Who Would Kill Big Bird?" *The Washington Post*, 23 April 1992, p. A23, and "Freer, Richer, Healthier – and Entitled," *The Washington Post*, 18 January 1996, p. A25; Debra J. Saunders, "Work to Rule, A Lesson in Lucre," *The San Francisco Chronicle*, 25 November 1992, p. A18; Robert J. Samuelson, *The Good Life and Its Discontents: The American Dream in the Age of Entitlement, 1945–1995* (New York: Times Books, 1995).

[32] Samuelson, *Good Life and Its Discontents*, p. 46.

[33] Bipartisan Commission on Entitlement and Tax Reform, *Final Report* (Washington, DC: January 1995); Andrew Taylor, "Consensus Elusive for Panel in Plan to Cut Benefits," *Congressional Quarterly Weekly Report* 52 (18 June 1994): 1583.

One such group was the American Association of Retired Persons (AARP), in which alarm at the prospect of cuts in Social Security and Medicare benefits both spurred an intensified lobbying effort and led to fierce internal debate over the question of whether those programs could accurately be labeled as entitlements. AARP's leadership presented the Bipartisan Commission with a "blunt warning" against a "raid" on Social Security and Medicare through means testing or spending reductions. Meanwhile, AARP members sent hundreds of letters to Congress and to AARP's national headquarters complaining that their Social Security and Medicare benefits were needlessly at risk because they were being "confused" with entitlements, which they characterized as welfare programs as opposed to paid-in accrued benefits. AARP inadvertently fanned the flames of the controversy in an article in its April 1994 monthly *Bulletin*, which attempted to correct members' "misconceptions" about the nature of Federal social programs by distinguishing between entitlements in general and welfare, then classifying Social Security and Medicare as entitlements. The result was another volley of furious letters from AARP members contending that their benefits had unjustly been "smeared," and cautioning that the continued application of the term entitlement to Social Security and Medicare would delegitimize and endanger those programs in the future. The December 1994 *Bulletin* featured AARP Executive Director Horace Deets almost completely avoiding the e-word, declaring in his editorial that Social Security and Medicare must be protected as "earned benefits that our members need and deserve." Deets urged AARP members to "challenge elected officials to look beyond the myths and acknowledge the millions of middle-class Americans who contributed to and earned th[o]se benefits," and to "demand that Congress clearly differentiate among entitlements, in plain English."[34]

---

[34] "Social Security: Entitlement?"; "What's an Entitlement? Readers Speak Bluntly"; and "AARP Issues Blunt Warning to Panel," AARP *Bulletin*, April, July–August, and November 1994 issues, pp. 1, 10, 8–9, and 4–5, respectively; " 'Well-off' Enrollees Likely Target" and "Social Security Debate Needs Your Voice," AARP *Bulletin*, December 1994, pp. 2, 7, and 3, respectively. See also the November–December issue of AARP's magazine *Modern Maturity*, which also featured the entitlement question. In his editorial "Just What Is an Entitlement?", Deets told AARP members that "Social Security and Medicare *are* entitlements, and you should be glad they are. They are a good thing, something to plan and count on." AARP members, Deets said, were "right to be furious ... not for the description of [Social Security and Medicare] as entitlements, but for the attempt to perpetuate the myth that entitlement programs alone are responsible for the deficit and skyrocketing national debt" (pp. 6–7, emphasis in the original). I am grateful to the AARP *Bulletin*'s former managing editor, Robert P. Hey, for providing me with a copy of

AARP was by no means the only group to react negatively to the Bipartisan Commission's reform proposals or to contest the attachment of the label entitlement to particular benefit programs. Organized labor, U.S. military veterans, and the National Association of Retired Federal Employees (NARFE), to name but a few, also questioned the Commission's motives and proposed actions. Testifying at a Bipartisan Commission hearing that he would later call an "inquisition," NARFE President Charles W. Carter took exception to the Commission's inability to distinguish among "so-called 'entitlements,'" contending that the "earned, work-related retirement benefits of federal workers are not the same as entitlements provided on the basis of need and public policy goals." Carter insisted that the failure to articulate that distinction not only did "a great disservice" to those who served as employees of the United States, but also "undermine[d] forthright, honest debate." Even after the Bipartisan Commission disbanded without effecting any changes in Federal spending programs, NARFE continued to protest the association of work-related Federal pensions with what it termed "beneficent government welfare."[35]

Kindred arguments subsuming a moral opposition between "contributory" and "noncontributory" benefits were also put forth by a number of prominent government actors, including Bipartisan Commission member Daniel Patrick Moynihan, longtime chairman of the Senate Finance Committee.[36] Noting in AARP's magazine *Modern Maturity* that it had "become somewhat popular in the nation's capital ... to talk about the need to cut federal spending for entitlements," Senator Moynihan distinguished between the technical language of people he called "professional budgeteers" (presumably government financial analysts) and a "simpler, more surreptitious" definition of entitlement that was "a code word for

the April 1994 issue and for his willingness to discuss the controversy at AARP over the meaning of entitlement. Telephone interview, 20 December 1994.

35 "Attacks Begin on Proposal to Cut Entitlements," *The New York Times*, 10 December 1994, p. 30; "Do You Remember?" and "NARFE Provides Entitlement Commission the Facts Regarding Retirement System," *Retirement Life* 70 (November 1994): 3, 16; "Steadfastness and Bipartisanship to Face Political Winds of Change," *Retirement Life* 71 (March 1995): 45.

36 Public discourse and much of the scholarly literature on social policy in the United States tend to use the oppositional terms "contributory" versus "noncontributory" and "social insurance" versus "public assistance" to describe and contrast the structure and philosophy of different entitlements. Richard M. Titmuss similarly distinguished between "achievement"- and "nonachievement"-based benefits in *Social Policy: An Introduction* (New York: Pantheon Books, 1974), p. 31.

Social Security."[37] Labeling that program an entitlement seemed, to Moynihan, to "put all the emphasis on getting something and none on the obligations one must fulfill before rights are established . . . as if you have a right to something just because you were able to survive to 65 or 62." Moynihan asserted that while the term entitlement originated in "lawyerly conceptions of welfare," welfare is not the idea behind contributory "social insurance," for which citizens establish their eligibility through work and payroll deductions.[38] He thus disagreed "as a matter of principle" with "attaching the entitlement label to Social Security," because the term does not "capture the essence of the program, which is its contributory nature."[39]

Bipartisan Commission member Senator Alan Simpson took strong exception to his colleague Moynihan's classification scheme. Refusing to conflate entitlements and welfare, and denouncing the idea of a fundamental distinction between contributory and noncontributory entitlements, Simpson insisted instead upon "collective recognition that all Americans bear a responsibility to future generations." That responsibility is not met, he asserted,

> by seeking refuge in quaint nostrums about "foreign aid" and "welfare deadbeats" – problems that, real as they are, do not represent one-tenth the threat to our future that's embodied by [the nation's] largest entitlement programs. Either we agree to face the reality that Social Security, Medicare and Medicaid must be reformed, or we will be leaving posterity holding the check for our excesses that it is incapable of paying.[40]

These arguments illustrate the conceptual and ideological contests involved in contemporary American debates over entitlements. Senator Simpson's comments revealed him to be willing to apply the term entitlement generically to refer to any programmatic social benefit, because his

---

37 "You may ask," wrote Moynihan, "what exactly is an entitlement? Well, truthfully, I wondered myself and recently did a little noodling around to find out." "The Case Against Entitlement Cuts," *Modern Maturity*, November–December 1994, p. 13.

38 Moynihan specifically cited Charles A. Reich's 1965 article "Individual Rights and Social Welfare: The Emerging Legal Issues," *Yale Law Journal* 74 (1965): 1245–57. As Reich phrased it, the "idea of entitlement is simply that when individuals have insufficient resources to live under conditions of health and decency, society has obligations to provide support, and the individual is entitled to that support as of right" (p. 1256).

39 "The Case Against Entitlement Cuts," pp. 13–14. The senator noted that the "surreptitious" definition of entitlements as a "code" used by advocates of cutting Social Security was one he had "inferred, rather than found somewhere."

40 "Why We Need Entitlement Reform," *Modern Maturity*, November–December 1994, pp. 12, 14.

primary policy goal was to maintain the fiscal capacity of the United States. AARP, NARFE, and Senator Moynihan, by contrast, clearly were interested in preserving particular portions of the Federal social safety net. They were also sensitive to the political context of the early to mid-1990s, in which middle- and working-class Americans had joined the poor as potential targets of public retrenchment. As a consequence, they deployed the discursive strategy of invoking welfare pejoratively. Their aim was not to fuel the ongoing debate over welfare reform, but rather to distinguish the contributory, achievement-based, "deserved" entitlements of middle- and working-class citizens from all unearned forms of "undeserved" public assistance.

This distinction has long been encouraged by the Federal Government, which, despite programmatic reality, has nurtured the image of individually deposited, actuarially and contractually protected, contributory benefits via both statutory structure and political rhetoric.[41] Although both AARP's and NARFE's arguments can be read as a demand for privileged treatment for their groups' particular benefits *among* middle-class entitlements, they were primarily aimed at maintaining the primacy of middle- and working-class people as beneficiaries of the state by eluding the stigma that historically has attached to welfare and its recipients. To fail in that effort would be to facilitate the Government's ability to define and treat all entitlements in the same way, and possibly to invade what were (and still are) widely considered middle- and working-class rights.

It did not take long for these disputes over entitlement and tax reform to yield to debates over the "end of welfare as we knew it," which specifically signified revoking poor Americans' legal entitlement to cash public assistance under the sixty-one-year-old Aid to Families with Dependent Children (AFDC) program.[42] By the mid-1990s, the term entitlement had come to be associated rhetorically only with the legal right of poor people to receive AFDC, and was made to appear as an aberration or anomaly in American legal culture, despite the existence of thousands of other entitlements of one kind or another guaranteed by the nation's legal system.[43] The degree to which current arguments over the future of

[41] Robert M. Cover, "Social Security and Constitutional Entitlement," in *Social Security: Beyond the Rhetoric of Crisis*, ed. Theodore R. Marmor and Jerry L. Mashaw (Princeton, NJ: Princeton University Press, 1988), p. 83.

[42] President Clinton coined the phrase "end of welfare as we know it" in his 1992 campaign.

[43] Williams, "Welfare and Legal Entitlements."

American social policy obsess over the details of particular programs like Social Security and Medicare reveals the extent to which the e-word has been banished from the public lexicon since 1996, when the passage of national welfare reform legislation in the form of the Personal Responsibility and Work Opportunity Reconciliation Act[44] ostensibly solved the entitlement crisis.

As Senator Moynihan and many at AARP and NARFE were almost certainly aware, the Government's "professional budgeteers" indeed define entitlement programs generically, because their concern has less to do with the ideological politics of entitlement – that is, with establishing and/or maintaining the normative status of particular benefits – than with assessing the financial commitments of the U.S. Government. If a given public program is not subject to annual appropriations ceilings, then the various agencies of the Federal Government concerned with fiscal policy count it as an entitlement, even if it is a contributory program like Social Security, which is partly funded through citizens' payment of Federal payroll taxes. According to the Congressional Budget Office (CBO), "entitlements and mandatory programs" are those programs that "make payments to recipients – usually people, but occasionally businesses or state and local governments – who are eligible and apply for funds. Payments are governed by formulas set in law and are not constrained by annual appropriation bills."[45] The General Accounting Office's (GAO's) more technical language, emphasizing legal obligation, defines entitlements as

[l]egislation that requires the payment of benefits (or entitlements) to any person or unit of government that meets the eligibility requirements established by such law. Authorization for entitlements constitute[s] a binding obligation on the part of the Federal Government, and eligible recipients have legal recourse if the obligation is not fulfilled. Budget authority for such payments is not necessarily provided in advance, and thus entitlement legislation requires the subsequent enactment of appropriations unless the existing appropriation is permanent. Examples of entitlement programs are social security benefits and veterans compensation or pensions.[46]

---

44 P.L. 104–193, 110 Stat. 2105 (1996).
45 U.S. Congress, Congressional Budget Office, "The Economic and Budget Outlook: Fiscal Years 1995–1999 (Washington, DC: GPO, January 1994), p. 43.
46 U.S. General Accounting Office, "A Glossary of Terms Used in the Federal Budget Process and Related Accounting, Economic, and Tax Terms," (Washington, DC: GAO, 1981, 3rd ed.), p. 57.

Though widely utilized, definitions like these have not led to an absolute consensus as to precisely which spending programs count as entitlements, even among government budget experts.[47] Moreover, while these and other public finance–oriented definitions are illuminating with regard to the size and composition of the directly appropriated portion of the U.S. budget, their focus on the "payment" of entitlement benefits obscures the existence of other public policies that are the functional equivalent of direct expenditures: namely, tax expenditures. Also known as tax incentives, preferences, deductions, and "loopholes," tax expenditures are provisions of the U.S. Internal Revenue Code that strategically reduce the tax liability of certain individuals (or businesses) who meet statutory eligibility criteria. Such provisions can be a feature of any generally applicable broad-based tax, but the most significant ones in the United States are those found in the national income tax. Tax expenditures have been an integral part of the U.S. income tax, and thereby the U.S. budget, since the income tax's formative years during the Civil War.

The fact that the United States accomplishes much of its social spending through taxation seems counterintuitive, and, perhaps as a consequence, it is still less than universally acknowledged.[48] Nonetheless, the concept of tax "expenditures" is easily understood if the income tax is envisioned as consisting of two distinct components.[49] The first component

---

[47] For example, the entitlement or nonentitlement status of loan guarantees, revenue-sharing programs for subnational governments, commodity price supports, interest payments to federal debt holders, and the food stamp program have all been debated. *On Borrowed Time*, pp. 77–9.

Definitions similar to those of CBO and GAO tend to be relied upon in the small, budget-oriented literature focusing on entitlements. See Aaron Wildavsky, *The New Politics of the Budgetary Process* (New York: HarperCollins Publishers, 1992, 2nd ed.), p. 272; R. Kent Weaver, "Controlling Entitlements," in *The New Direction in American Politics*, ed. John E. Chubb and Paul E. Peterson (Washington, DC: Brookings Institution, 1985), p. 307; Joseph White, "Entitlement Budgeting vs. Bureau Budgeting," *Public Administration Review* 58 (1998): 510–21; Ronald F. King, *Budgeting Entitlements: The Politics of Food Stamps* (Washington, DC: Georgetown University Press, 2000). By contrast, the legal and sociolegal scholarship on entitlement(s) often tends away from such positivist or formalist definitions. See John Brigham, *Property and the Politics of Entitlement* (Philadelphia: Temple University Press, 1990), p. 4; Williams, "Welfare and Legal Entitlements."

[48] Some also object to the concept of tax expenditures because it seems to imply that without such beneficence, all income would belong to the government. Stanley S. Surrey and Paul R. McDaniel, "The Tax Expenditure Concept: Current Developments and Emerging Issues," *Boston College Law Review* 20 (1979): 231–3.

[49] The distinction drawn between these two components here is not intended to imply that the basic structural provisions of an income tax are in any way inherent. Established by human actors and political institutions, they may contain forms of inadvertent or

encompasses all of the basic, revenue-raising, structural provisions necessary for the implementation of an income tax (such as the definition
of net income, the specification of accounting periods and rules, the determination of entities subject to tax, and the specification of the rate
schedule and exemption levels). The second component, in turn, consists of the exceptions to (or departures from) that basic tax structure
designed to favor particular industries, activities, or groups of people.
These consciously legislated exceptions to the normal rules governing the
taxation of income, which result in the loss of tax revenue that would otherwise be generated by the normal rules, constitute government spending
"effected through the tax system rather than through direct grants, loans,
or other forms of government assistance."[50] Tax expenditures familiar to
many Americans include the individual income tax deductions allowed
for mortgage interest paid on homes and charitable contributions and
the child care and dependent care expense tax credit.

The provision of public benefits accomplished through these and
other programs embedded in the tax code is now so significant in terms
of cost alone – hundreds of billions of dollars per year, or from one-third
to one-half as much as is spent upon the vast array of directly appropriated programs – that it is accurately called the "hidden side of the
welfare state."[51] Perhaps even more significant is the structural similarity

deliberate bias, just as any other kind of legislation can. I am grateful to Stuart McConnell
for this observation.

[50] Stanley R. Surrey and Paul R. McDaniel, *Tax Expenditures* (Cambridge, MA: Harvard
University Press, 1985), p. 3; see also "The Tax Expenditure Concept and the Budget
Reform Act of 1974," *Boston College Industrial and Commercial Law Review* 17 (1976): 679–
88; and Surrey, *Pathways to Tax Reform: The Concept of Tax Expenditures* (Cambridge, MA:
Harvard University Press, 1973). Stanley Surrey was an ardent champion of tax reform
and was largely responsible for the enactment of legislation requiring the inclusion of a
tax expenditure analysis in the annual U.S. budget (see the Congressional Budget Act
of 1974). Yet he was by no means the first to recognize that special exceptions in the tax
code constituted a form of government spending. See, e.g., Arthur Pigou, *The Economics
of Welfare* (New York: Macmillan & Co., 1932, 4th ed.), p. 98; and Richard Titmuss, *Essays
on the Welfare State* (London: Unwin University Books, 1958), pp. 45–50.

[51] Christopher Howard, *The Hidden Welfare State: Tax Expenditures and Social Policy in the
United States* (Princeton, NJ: Princeton University Press, 1997); "The Hidden Side of the
Welfare State," *Political Science Quarterly* 108 (1993): 403–36. Howard's phrase comes
from Jeffrey P. Owens's reference to the "hidden welfare state" in "Tax Expenditures
and Direct Expenditures as Instruments of Social Policy," *Comparative Tax Studies*, ed.
Sijbren Cnossen (Amsterdam: North Holland Publishing Company, 1983), p. 177. See
also Jerry J. Jasinowski's observation that subsidies, including tax expenditures, have
"been allowed to exist in the shadows of public policy." "The Great Fiscal Unknown –
Subsidies," *American Journal of Economics and Sociology* 32 (1973): 1–16.

of the entitlement programs on the spending side of the U.S. budget and the benefits granted through the nontaxation of income. Tax expenditures not only operate exactly like direct outlays in their establishment of open-ended fiscal commitments that subvert budgetary control, but, first and foremost, as devices that *programmatically create legally circumscribed categories of entitlement.*

To acknowlege that entitlements may be structured either as direct expenditures or as tax expenditures is not to imply that the politics of spending and taxation are identical, any more than the politics of particular spending or taxing programs are identical. The point is rather that the failure to consider tax expenditures as entitlements results in views of American social provision that substantially underestimate coverage and expenditure levels and distort patterns of distribution among and between economic strata.[52] Our inability to agree on what counts as an entitlement has allowed powerful interests not only to secure resources, but also to have them delivered in forms that are not construed as public benefits.[53] What is sorely needed is a much more comprehensive and historically informed understanding of entitlements: one that acknowledges the full extent of the instrumental and constitutive roles that they play, whether they are structured as direct expenditures or tax expenditures.[54]

Entitlements as a Policy Device

Entitlements are public policies that create positive, substantive rights to public benefits for those citizens who satisfy eligibility criteria established by statute. Positive, substantive rights imply a legal duty on the part of the state to provide "right holders" with tangible benefits, a duty that is

---

[52] The inclusion of tax expenditures in a definition of entitlements points to the contemporary American state's skewing of benefits toward certain members of the middle and upper income classes. It also, as Howard has observed, indicates the extent to which ostensibly private benefit programs are subsidized by public monies, demonstrating that the line separating public and private realms of the welfare state is not a rigid barrier. *The Hidden Welfare State,* pp. 30–1.

[53] Linda Gordon, *Pitied But Not Entitled: Single Mothers and the History of Welfare* (Cambridge, MA: Harvard University Press, 1994), p. 288.

[54] The case studies contained in this book concentrate on direct expenditures because no broad-based tax upon individual citizens existed until the mid-nineteenth century, when a national income tax was first established. It is critical to recognize, however, that the origins of the entitlements found in the U.S. tax code lie in the provisions of the income tax of the 1860s. See Chapter 5.

enforceable by the courts.[55] Such rights also imply an obligation on the part of the state to procure what it intends to disburse, since, as Charles Reich observed, the state has no material resources of its own, but must "syphon" in revenue and power in order to "pour forth wealth."[56] In the case of most entitlements, this, in turn, implies an obligation on the part of citizens at large to submit to taxation or some other mode of state resource acquisition, such as the taking of private property.[57] The only alternative to such an internal redistribution scheme is the expropriation of the resources of other communities – an alternative that the United States relied upon heavily in its formative years in acquiring territory for settlement, as we shall see in the following chapters.

Arguably, any of the benefits emanating from the state might be thought of as entitlements, in the sense that they are intended to provide citizens with goods and services that satisfy a range of human physical and social-psychological needs. As Lucy Williams has observed, entitlement or right is the basic legal form utilized in a range of private law areas. Americans are legally entitled to recover certain damages for breach of contract, for example, or sue for certain kinds of injury under tort law. As the basis of private property allocations and contractual rights, these kinds of entitlements play a significant role in determining the prevailing distribution of wealth and income, favoring particular interests and disfavoring others. Neither natural nor neutral but chosen, they are the legal "background rules" against which the *programmatic* entitlements of public law are created.[58]

These programmatic benefits are the specific focus of this book. Only those public policies that create positive, substantive rights to benefits on a programmatic basis for groups or categories of putatively like citizens are defined as entitlements in this analysis. Importantly, entitlements are further classified here as programs granting individual-level, as opposed to collectively consumed, benefits. In economic terms, this distinguishes entitlements from other forms of public provision: specifically, from public

---

[55] Stone, *Policy Paradox*, pp. 265–71. Legislative decisions to "cap" or set expenditure ceilings on entitlement programs delimit this legal duty in ways that are both theoretically and practically problematic. See King, *Budgeting Entitlements*.

[56] "The New Property," *Yale Law Journal* 73 (1964): 733.

[57] Herein lies the essential tension that inheres in all entitlements: the need to square the positive rights of program beneficiaries with what might be considered the negative rights of citizens to be left alone if they are not interfering in the lives of others.

[58] "Welfare and Legal Entitlements," p. 575.

goods that are both nonrival in consumption and nonexclusive,[59] at least until points of congestion are reached (such as traffic jams due to increased vehicular traffic on public highways). Such "pure" public goods – what Paul Samuelson aptly termed "collective consumption" goods[60] – are plainly premised upon the equality of citizens and designed, to the greatest extent possible, to serve all the members of a community simultaneously in essentially the same manner.[61]

Entitlements, by contrast, are individually, rather than collectively, consumed, at least as they are originally disbursed. They are only implicitly nonrival in the short run, and become explicitly rival when program cutbacks or expenditure ceilings are threatened or imposed, even to the extent of pitting different programs and their recipients against each other.[62] (Witness the Bipartisan Commission's efforts and protests of program beneficiaries against the potential loss of *their* particular entitlements.) Moreover, entitlement programs are almost always somewhat exclusive, relying upon statutory eligibility criteria to direct benefits to subsets of citizens rather than to an entire population. Though a given program's degree of selectivity may vary widely (it may embrace a nation's entire population or cover only very restricted groups), most entitlements, even in Scandinavian "universal" welfare states, qualify recipients for benefits according to some criteria (for example, by age or by wealth).

---

[59] Classic examples include national defense, common schools, and roads.

[60] "The Pure Theory of Public Expenditure," *Review of Economics and Statistics* 36 (1954): 387–9.

[61] This does not imply that a pure public good that is equally available to all the members of a community is necessarily considered equally useful by all of them. In addition, one's ability to enjoy or consume the benefits of a large community (such as a nation) that would technically be considered pure public goods might be limited spatially. A Federally sponsored fireworks display launched over the Mall in Washington, DC, for example, might in theory be labeled nonrival and nonexclusive, but practically speaking, most citizens living in California are not likely to be able to travel to see it. See, e.g., Richard Cornes and Todd Sandler, *The Theory of Externalities, Public Goods, and Club Goods* (Cambridge: Cambridge University Press, 1986).

[62] The basic concept behind an entitlement program is that anyone meeting the terms of its statutory eligibility criteria has a legal right to its benefit(s), even if the U.S. Government does not have the resources on hand to provide it/them. In budgetary parlance, entitlements generally are understood not to have ceilings, or expenditure limitations. In recent years, however, the Federal government has experimented with ceilings or caps on certain welfare programs, contradicting the root concept of entitlement. Ronald King has aptly termed Federal expenditure caps "the expression of a hesitant fiscal conservatism, unwilling to adequately finance its welfare obligations yet equally unwilling to renege on them." *Budgeting Entitlements*, p. 9; see also White, "Entitlement Budgeting vs. Bureau Budgeting."

In essence, then, except in the relatively rare instances in which an entitlement accrues to all members of a polity without qualification, exception, or restriction of any kind, entitlements are quasi-private, individual-regarding goods that are overtly premised upon citizen differences or inequalities. This is despite the fact that many welfare state theories perpetuate an idealized view of entitlements as egalitarian, nonexclusionary social benefits.[63]

As numerous economists have long pointed out, the sharp theoretical dichotomy between pure public and private goods elaborated upon here is difficult to sustain in reality.[64] Most goods fall somewhere between the poles of the pure public and pure private labels because they lack the properties of strict nonrivalry (or rivalry) and nonexcludability (or excludability) that pure publicness (or privateness) requires. Nonetheless, the distinction between public goods that are intended to be collectively consumed and public goods parceled directly to individual members of a community is vitally important. Even if the latter are essentially universal in their distribution and can be expected to generate positive externalities that serve to enhance the well-being of the larger community,[65] the fact that they first accrue to individual citizens, as matters of individual right, means that they can be expected to generate different sets of citizen understandings and expectations, and lead to different social and political consequences, than collectively consumed benefits do.

Consider, for example, the relatively simple policy problem posed by a river bisecting a particular geographic area. For a variety of social and economic reasons, people from the local community want or need to cross the river. Although more than two potential policy solutions present themselves, there are two obvious alternatives that illustrate

---

[63] Note that what makes a "universal" welfare state universal is its calculated *combination* of programs aimed at providing citizens with social minima as their needs progress "from cradle to grave." This approach to social provision is what distinguishes the welfare states of Scandinavian countries from those of other nations. Bo Rothstein, *Just Institutions Matter: The Moral and Political Logic of the Universal Welfare State* (Cambridge: Cambridge University Press, 1998), p. 19.

[64] See, e.g., Julius Margolis, "A Comment on the Pure Theory of Public Expenditure," *Review of Economics and Statistics* 37 (1955): 347–9; Paul A. Samuelson, "Diagrammatic Exposition of a Theory of Public Expenditure," *Review of Economics and Statistics* 37 (1955): 350–6.

[65] A classic example of a positive externality is the decreased potential for illness that the larger community enjoys when a member of the community is vaccinated against disease. Clearly, while the greatest benefit is to the individual receiving the inoculation, there is a positive effect generated that works to the good of the community at large.

the theoretical distinction drawn previously. The first would involve the building of a bridge so that all citizens would be accommodated collectively, at least until the bridge became overcrowded (necessitating the construction of another bridge or some other new policy solution addressing the problem of congestion). In the second alternative, the state would entitle each citizen to receive a boat. Both policy options are practicable, since they would both enable all the members of the community to get to the area on the other side of the river. Yet they are by no means equivalent, for although both alternatives would enable all the members of the community to cross the river – they would both create universal benefits – the two alternatives would still constitute radically different approaches to solving the same problem, and thereby of constituting part of a normative social order. Where the first policy solution both assumes and promotes commonality, invoking the power of the state to treat citizens alike through a shared public facility, the second employs the power of the state to create a statutory scheme by which citizens may receive their "due" in the form of individual rights to newly created private property.[66]

When entitlements are selective, so that their eligibility schemes identify only certain subsets of a community's population as deserving of benefits, their role in shaping social and political reality becomes even more transparent. Here the state can be seen to discriminate actively among citizens as it categorizes them according to differences that are perceived to exist between them. These differences are not inherent, but are socially constructed through a process of purposeful comparisons among people, comparisons that invoke cultural norms and that both depend upon and reconfirm the importance of particular selected characteristics and associations.[67] This is not to suggest that meaningful differences between citizens do not exist. Rather, it is to observe that the state makes choices to recognize certain attributes while ignoring others as it creates and assigns rights to its benevolence.[68] In so doing, the state does not

---

[66] See Stone, *Policy Paradox*, p. 308.

[67] See Minow, *Making All the Difference*, pp. 50–60; Richard A. Shweder (with Joan G. Miller), "The Social Construction of the Person: How Is It Possible?", in Richard A. Shweder, *Thinking Through Cultures: Expeditions in Cultural Psychology* (Cambridge, MA: Harvard University Press, 1991), pp. 156–85; and George Lakoff, *Women, Fire, and Dangerous Things: What Categories Reveal about the Mind* (Chicago: University of Chicago Press, 1987).

[68] Deborah Stone has argued that public policy in general "is centrally about classification and differentiation, about how we do and should categorize in a world where categories are not given.... Policy arguments are convincing to the extent that they give a satisfying

merely characterize the target groups who are to benefit from public policies,[69] but also creates and employs a legal discourse of difference to determine their very existence in the first place.

This creative process can be seen to operate in the hypothetical river-crossing scenario sketched earlier if it is elaborated upon so that only those individuals owning land on the opposite side of the river are entitled to receive boats. The state's goal in such a policy of selective entitlement might be explained as the promotion of economic development: particular citizens need to be enabled to cross the river so that they can access their property to develop and manage it. Accordingly, a new, discrete legal category of "productive" members of society is created (and then reified) based upon their possession of the attribute of ownership (first of land, then of boats). While the members of that category and their ownership status are invested with new meaning (deserving), others who do not bear the requisite attribute are either implicitly or explicitly located outside the societal boundary that the category establishes as the undeserving. Whether or not the establishment of this particular category of citizens is the best means of enhancing the economy, it is clear that other points of similarity between citizens that might have also been meaningful to the community, and that might also have worked in some way toward its betterment, were either overlooked or not chosen as the social landscape became partitioned in a new and significant way.

An example of the creative role that entitlements play is provided by the contemporary category of those citizens labeled "blind" by the U.S. Government for social policy purposes. Blindness is undoubtedly a physical attribute of some Americans that limits their ability to function in society in ways that the sighted can. Yet, as Deborah Stone has pointed out, there is a difference between the physical condition of blindness itself and "legal" blindness, where a formal administrative category has been created to entitle certain citizens to public benefits on the basis of a particular attribute.[70] To admit this distinction is not to suggest that blind

---

account of the rightness of treating cases alike or differently," *Policy Paradox*, pp. 308–10. See also Roy G. D'Andrade, "Cultural Meaning Systems," in *Culture Theory: Essays on Mind, Self, and Emotion*, ed. Richard A. Schweder and Robert A. Levine (Cambridge: Cambridge University Press, 1984), p. 91.

[69] Anne Schneider and Helen Ingram, "Social Construction of Target Populations: Implications for Politics and Policy," *American Political Science Review* 87 (1993): 334–47.

[70] Deborah A. Stone, *The Disabled State* (Philadelphia: Temple University Press, 1984), p. 27. As Stone points out, there are also distinctions *among* those classified as legally blind, with some members of that category seemingly able to function better than others despite their eligibility for benefits. Thus, although such categories may be the result of searches

people do not really exist or that they are not deserving of public benefits, but rather to acknowledge that in establishing a category of the blind, the state has chosen to recognize and aid particular citizens out of the universe of possible beneficiaries.

The pension program established by Congress in 1818 for certain aged, impoverished veterans of the Revolution furnishes an original example of the selective perception involved in the state's creation of entitlements. Again, the issue is not the worthiness of that program's designated beneficiaries, who suffered from the infirmities of old age and poverty. Rather, the issue is why other military veterans and civilians, whose characteristics and circumstances may have been remarkably similar, were not also identified and entitled to receive pension benefits. The root question is not merely that of why instititutions respond to some individuals differently than to others,[71] but why institutions decide to grant benefits at all: a question that links the construction of entitlement categories with state building.

This discussion has begun to suggest ways in which the policy strategy of entitlement, or the structure of the programs that result from the deployment of that device, might be linked to social, political, and institutional outcomes. Before turning to the case studies analyzing the causes and consequences of America's original entitlement programs, however, this chapter will conclude by considering two sets of interrelated issues in more depth in order to explore the nexus that entitlements create between state and citizen. The first set of issues has to do with how citizens understand entitlements as public benefits. Given that such policies are rights-tendering, it is important to consider how the technically temporal, nonconstitutional status of those rights relates to the set of expectations, or rights consciousness, that entitlements engender. The second set of issues involves the questions of how entitlements might work to cause citizens to understand themselves and others, and how those understandings figure in beliefs about distributive justice.

Entitlements as "Rights at Work"

Strictly speaking, American entitlements have always been creatures of statute, and thereby of legislative discretion. According to long-standing

for "means of objectively determining who is deserving of social aid," they should also be understood to represent "politically fashioned compromise(s) at any given time and place about the legitimacy of claims to social aid."

[71] Stone, *Disabled State*, p. 21.

federal court doctrine, there is nothing in the U.S. Constitution, other than the congressional authority to tax and spend to provide a "general Welfare,"[72] to suggest that the Government has any responsibility to furnish Americans with substantive benefits. As a result, entitlements constitute what R. Shep Melnick has aptly termed "programmatic rights."[73] Benefits cannot be denied to claimants meeting the statutory eligibility criteria of extant programs, but there are no constitutional guarantees that any entitlements, including long-standing enactments such as Social Security, will continue to be dispensed ad infinitum. In essence, entitlements are still "privileges" that may be withdrawn or granted conditionally as the state sees fit,[74] a legal status reflecting the fact that the United States historically has not embraced a concept of national social citizenship that extends to the provision of social minima for all.

This situation did not result from a lack of effort on the part of many social workers, lawyers, judges, academics, and welfare rights advocates, who sought to transform the legal status of entitlements, particularly those entitlements that could be characterized as social minima or subsistence benefits, from matters of legislative and administrative whim into constitutional right.[75] Poverty lawyers and other activists involved in the welfare rights movement of the 1960s campaigned vigorously for a constitutional "right to life" that "would finally move America toward the fulfillment of

---

[72] Article I, section 8. Arguably, one might also cite the preamble, which stated that the people of the United States had established the Constitution in order to "form a more perfect Union, establish Justice, [and] insure domestic Tranquility."

[73] *Between the Lines*, pp. 16–18, 274–83. Melnick views contemporary entitlements as "the joint creation of the courts, Congress, and federal administrators," which "fall within a gray area between what is purely statutory and what is overtly constitutional." "The Courts, Congress, and Programmatic Rights," p. 189. The next two paragraphs draw upon Melnick's history of the technical legal status of entitlements in *Between the Lines*, pp. 41–61.

[74] Laura S. Jensen, "Federalism, Individual Rights, and the Conditional Spending Conundrum," *Polity* 33 (Winter 2000): 259–82.

[75] The story of the welfare rights movement and, in particular, the litigation strategy employed by welfare rights advocates is well documented elsewhere. See Martha F. Davis, *Brutal Need: Lawyers and the Welfare Rights Movement, 1960–1973* (New Haven, CT: Yale University Press, 1993); Susan E. Lawrence, *The Poor in Court: The Legal Services Program and Supreme Court Decision Making* (Princeton, NJ: Princeton University Press, 1990); Rand E. Rosenblatt, "Legal Entitlement and Welfare Benefits," in *The Politics of Law: A Progressive Critique*, ed. David Kairys (New York: Pantheon Books, 1982), pp. 262–78; Samuel Krislov, "The OEO Lawyers Fail to Constitutionalize a Right to Welfare: A Study in the Uses and Limits of the Judicial Process," *Minnesota Law Review* 58 (1973): 211–45; and Edward V. Sparer, "The Right to Welfare," in *The Rights of Americans*, ed. Norman Dorsen (New York: Pantheon Books, 1971), pp. 65–93.

the social rights of citizenship."[76] In the late 1960s and early 1970s, many federal courts, including the U.S. Supreme Court, handed down decisions that appeared to be moving in the direction of interpreting the due process and equal protection clauses of the Fourteenth Amendment to create a substantive constitutional right to social minima. Yet, despite such assertions as Justice William Brennan's famous pronouncement for the Court in 1970 that it might be more realistic to "regard welfare entitlements as more like 'property' than a 'gratuity,' "[77] the judicial vision of entitlements as constitutional guarantees gradually has faded from view. The federal courts have decided numerous contests over statutory interpretation in ways that broadened the eligibility standards and raised the benefit levels of many programs, but the concept of a constitutional entitlement to social support has failed to evolve from a recurring theme to a controlling legal principle as far as judicial enforceability is concerned.[78]

The judiciary's take on entitlements, however, is only part of the picture. To limit our understanding of entitlements as rights dependent upon constitutional politics and the doctrinal revelations of the courts is to acknowledge only one view of rights: the one that is centrally concerned with the formally articulated legal rules describing judicially enforceable claims of individuals or groups against the state.[79] That view reveals little about the set of beliefs and expectations, or *rights consciousness*, that entitlements as a form of public law may engender.[80] From

---

[76] Joel F. Handler, "Symposium: The Legacy of *Goldberg* v. *Kelly*: A Twenty Year Perspective: 'Constructing the Political Spectacle;' Interpretation of Entitlements, Legalization, and Obligations in Social Welfare History," *Brooklyn Law Review* 56 (1990): 900.

[77] *Goldberg* v. *Kelly*, 397 U.S. 254 (1970). See also the dissenting opinions in *Dandridge* v. *Williams*, 397 U.S. 471 (1970), and *Board of Regents* v. *Roth*, 408 U.S. 564 (1972). Justice Marshall's dissenting assertion in *Roth* that government employment is an individual, substantive, constitutional property right that cannot be denied to citizens without due process of law was particularly notable (pp. 588–9).

[78] Melnick, *Between the Lines*, pp. 54–60. See also Mark A. Graber, "The Clintonification of American Law: Abortion, Welfare, and Liberal Constitutional Theory," *Ohio State Law Journal* 58 (1997): 731–818.

[79] Martha Minow, "Interpreting Rights: An Essay for Robert Cover," *Yale Law Journal* 96 (1987): 1866–7.

[80] Patricia Ewick and Susan S. Silbey have usefully described legal consciousness as "part of a reciprocal process in which the meanings given by individuals to their world, and law and legal institutions as part of that world, become repeated, patterned, and stabilized, and those institutionalized structures become part of the meaning systems employed by individuals." "Conformity, Contestation, and Resistance: An Account of Legal Consciousness," *New England Law Review* 26 (1992): 741. See also Ewick and Silbey, *The Common Place of Law: Stories from Everyday Life* (Chicago: University of Chicago Press, 1998); and

the broader perspective of that consciousness, rights are "neither limited to nor co-extensive with precisely those rules formally announced and enforced by public authorities," but encompass articulations of "claims that people use to persuade others (and themselves) about how they should be treated and about what they should be granted."[81] This is the sense in which John Brigham defines entitlements, to "refer to the legitimate expectations people have about something that they believe to be rightfully and legally theirs."[82] To invoke Michael McCann's luminous phrase, entitlements are "rights at work": part of a "complex repertoire of discursive strategies and symbolic frameworks that structure ongoing social intercourse and meaning-making activity among citizens."[83]

A sense of entitlements as rights at work, and more generally of entitlements as constitutive elements in social life, is evident in Robert Cover's essay on the legal status of the Social Security system,[84] in which he maintained that Social Security could be understood to imply certain constitutional commitments even if the Supreme Court was disinclined to "discover a constitutional solution" to any of the major policy issues that the program raises. As Cover analyzed it, neither the failure of courts to establish an absolute claim in law to benefits nor the fact that the Social Security system effectively is subsidized could justify a failure on the part of the state to "keep faith" with the participants in the program, for the state had long made contract-like promises of permanent income security through an official rhetoric of paid-in, earned benefits and the "coerced payment" of wage deductions or "FICA" tax.[85] Such an argument recognizes law as a communal language that cannot be divorced from the social context in which norms are generated and given meaning, and where relationships among citizens (as well as between citizens and the

Sally Engle Merry, *Getting Justice and Getting Even: Legal Consciousness among Working-Class Americans* (Chicago: University of Chicago Press, 1990), pp. 5–11, for a discussion of legal consciousness as the "ways people understand and use law."

[81] Minow, "Interpreting Rights," pp. 1866–7.

[82] *Property and the Politics of Entitlement*, p. 4.

[83] *Rights at Work: Pay Equity and the Politics of Legal Mobilization* (Chicago: University of Chicago Press, 1994), p. 282. See also Stuart A. Scheingold, *The Politics of Rights: Lawyers, Public Policy, and Political Change* (New Haven, CT: Yale University Press, 1974); and Helena Silverstein, *Unleashing Rights: Law, Meaning, and the Animal Rights Movement* (Ann Arbor: University of Michigan Press, 1996).

[84] "Social Security and Constitutional Entitlement," pp. 69–87.

[85] FICA is the acronym standing for Social Security's euphemistic companion tax statute, the Federal Income Contributions Act.

state) are interpreted, negotiated, and reinterpreted.[86] As part of the normative universe Cover was concerned with, AARP's struggle to define and defend the Social Security benefits its members had "earned" and "deserved" against a "raid" by government reformers is as much a story of protest against incongruous patterns of power and authority as a classic tale of self-interested, latter-day, interest group liberalism.

An essential part of Cover's analysis was his claim that the benefits provided through the Social Security system "differ[ed]" from most transfer programs because their receipt is conditioned upon a substantial record of FICA payments over time. This "difference" made it "quite right to consider the government's obligation to Social Security participants as greater than the responsibility entailed in almost all other programs."[87] Cover's line of argument is important in that it points to the fundamental conceptual linkage that inheres in entitlements, particularly selective entitlements, between the rights to benefits they bestow and the statutory eligibility criteria that cite their reasons for bestowing them. All entitlements contain and convey this justificatory logic. As a consequence, they do not merely create rights, but *rights tied to reasons.*[88]

The psychological effects of this conceptual linkage between rights and reasons are quite significant and are related to the politics that entitlements generate. The pronouncement in law that people are deserving of benefits for particular reasons – that is, that they are somehow special, or *particularly deserving* – suggests that their claim to benefits may be of even higher standing than ordinary rights claims might be or, for that matter, the claims of others to *their* entitlements.[89] As politicians well

---

[86] Minow, "Interpreting Rights," pp. 1861, 1891–3. See also Brigham, *Constitution of Interests*; and Cover, "Nomos and Narrative" (1983), in *Narrative, Violence, and the Law: The Essays of Robert Cover*, ed. Martha Minow, Michael Ryan, and Austin Sarat (Ann Arbor: University of Michigan Press, 1992), pp. 95–172.

[87] "Social Security and Constitutional Entitlement," pp. 85–6.

[88] These reasons can of course be quite basic, as in the case of the entitlements of universal welfare states premised upon the social rights of citizenship. This is not to suggest, however, that such universal welfare states are immune to controversy over social benefits or that they are immune to change. Indeed, recent developments in the United Kingdom, Scandinavia, the Netherlands, and Belgium indicate that the "absolute" status of the social rights of citizenship may be yielding to a more contingent, negotiated one. Robert Henry Cox, "The Consequences of Welfare Reform: How Conceptions of Social Rights Are Changing," *Journal of Social Policy* 27 (1998): 1–16.

[89] To suggest that people are particularly deserving of certain rights is not, of course, to guarantee that those rights will really act as trumps. But to invoke rights is to invite the community's attention in a particular and potent way, one that tends to make those

understand, it also suggests that entitlements can never be legitimately taken away, even if the resources to provide those benefits diminish or disappear, as long as the reasons that established claims to them as "rightful" do not.[90] These understandings appear to work most forcefully in justifying visibly contributory or achievement-based benefits like the old-age pensions of the Social Security program that Cover described. However, they also are generated by arguably less contributory entitlements and can be imagined to operate in still others.

Consider, for example, the popular home mortgage interest tax deduction, a modern selective entitlement often justified as a benefit that increases the strength of American cities and towns through its encouragement of stable, owner-occupied neighborhoods. As Christopher Howard has observed, anyone who proposes cutting or eliminating this tax expenditure risks being labeled an enemy of the nation's housing industry and a threat to the American dream. Citizens factor the mortgage interest deduction into their calculations concerning the cost of purchasing a home, and count on its future availability as a right accruing to those who have made a social and financial commitment to home ownership.[91] Their belief in the continued existence of that right is inherently similar to Social Security participants' belief that FICA contributions tender contract-like promises of future income security. Such beliefs essentially

in power (and others) "at least listen." Minow, *Making All the Difference*, pp. 293, 299. Regarding rights as trumps, see Ronald Dworkin, *Taking Rights Seriously* (Cambridge, MA: Harvard University Press, 1978, new ed.). See also Scheingold, *The Politics of Rights*, concerning the "myth" of rights.

[90] President Clinton's 1993 proposal to create a "right" to comprehensive health benefits that could "never be taken away" demonstrated that political actors appreciate the rhetorical appeal of entitlements as rights, and often work to impart a view of such benefits as unassailable, sacred obligations of the state about which there can be no compromise and from which there can be no retreat. President Franklin D. Roosevelt's well-known remark about Social Security provides another case in point: "... those taxes were never a problem of economics. They are politics all the way through. We put those payroll contributions there so as to give the contributors a legal, moral, and political right to collect their pensions and their unemployment benefits. With those taxes in there, no damn politician can ever scrap my social security program." See Theda Skocpol, "From Social Security to Health Security? Opinion and Rhetoric in U.S. Social Policy Making," *PS* 27 (March 1994): 21–5; Luther Gulick, "Memorandum on Conference with Franklin D. Roosevelt ... Summer 1941," Roosevelt Foundation Papers, cited in Arthur M. Schlesinger, Jr., *The Age of Roosevelt: The Coming of the New Deal* (Boston: Houghton Mifflin, 1958), pp. 308–9; and, generally, Murray Edelman, *Constructing the Political Spectacle* (Chicago: University of Chicago Press, 1988).

[91] *The Hidden Welfare State*, p. 94.

rest upon an ownership paradigm that is fundamentally at odds with an understanding of property rights as social phenomena. When property rights are understood socially, as something that people "collectively define and construct,"[92] contract-like implications can be seen to issue from *all* entitlements. Even noncontributory, means-tested entitlements might be envisioned to justify rights claims if the primary goal of welfare policy in a given society is agreed to be that of guaranteeing social justice.

The logic of entitlements as "rights tied to reasons" feeds into the set of understandings that citizens have about themselves and others, for, as Beth Singer has written, people do not "have" rights, but participate in them. Rights are fundamentally normative social relations in which individuals are jointly involved.[93] Entitlements as rights at work establish "roles and relations and voices," as well as "positions from which and audiences to which [we] may speak."[94] They provide us with a language that is colored by boundaries of difference. At any given moment, with respect to given programs, we are either included or excluded, special or not special, deserving or undeserving, privileged or not privileged. We are encouraged to conceive of ourselves and others in the essential terms of those oppositions instead of more contextualized, relational ones. This by no means implies that such categories are the only social positions that we can envision for ourselves or, for that matter, that entitlements' categorical schemes never change. But contests about boundaries tend to remain contests over boundaries, rather than fundamental reconsiderations of the ways in which the social landscape is being mapped and divided. When institutions make classifications for us, as Mary Douglas has observed, "we seem to lose some independence that we might conceivably have otherwise had."[95]

Selective entitlements are particularly notable for inviting social and political behavior based upon intercitizen comparisons and analogical

[92] Joseph William Singer, *Entitlement: The Paradoxes of Property* (New Haven, CT: Yale University Press, 2000), p. 13, and more generally pp. 1–15. See also Laura S. Underkuffler-Freund, "Property: A Special Right," *Notre Dame Law Review* 71 (1996): 1044–6.

[93] *Operative Rights* (Albany: State University of New York Press, 1993), p. 5.

[94] James Boyd White, *Heracles' Bow: Essays on the Rhetoric and Poetics of Law* (Madison: University of Wisconsin Press, 1985), p. 98.

[95] *How Institutions Think* (Syracuse, NY: Syracuse University Press, 1986), p. 91. Douglas goes on to make the important point that "[t]he high triumph of institutional thinking is to make the institutions completely invisible."

thinking.[96] Citizens outside the boundaries of benefit categories who judge themselves to be close to possessing the requisite attributes of membership may try seek inclusion among the deserving by persuading the state to broaden its eligibility criteria.[97] Citizens too far from the boundaries to envision belonging to existing categories either become resigned to their status or may adopt other strategies for attaining benefits. One such strategy is to suggest the creation of *new* categories of desert and reward, either by drawing some sort of analogy with extant rationales or by suggesting fresh possibilities.[98] Yet another strategy is for excluded citizens to attempt inclusion in extant categories through fraudulent claims of membership, a strategy for attaining benefits that plagued the implementation of all of the early American entitlement programs chronicled in this book.

Any of these behaviors may lead to social and political conflict as feelings of relative deprivation are created and acted upon,[99] for as Runciman observed,

if people have no reason to expect or hope for more than they can achieve, they will be less discontented with that they have, or even grateful to hold on to it. But if, on the other hand, they have been led to see as a possible goal the relative prosperity of some more fortunate community with which they can directly compare themselves, then they will remain discontented with their lot until they have succeeded in catching up.[100]

[96] In the terms employed by sociologists and social psychologists, entitlements create social "reference groups" and associated reference group behavior. See Robert K. Merton, *Social Theory and Social Structure* (New York: Free Press, 1968, enlarged ed.), pp. 279–334 (with Alice K. Rossi) and 335–440; W. G. Runciman, *Relative Deprivation and Social Justice: A Study of Attitudes to Social Inequality in Twentieth-Century England* (Berkeley: University of California Press, 1966); and Ted Robert Gurr, *Why Men Rebel* (Princeton, NJ: Princeton University Press, 1970).

[97] This was precisely the strategy adopted by Army and Navy veterans originally excluded from benefits under the Pension Act of 1818, as we shall soon see in Chapter 3.

[98] As Chapters 4 and 5 detail, both of these options succeeded in spurring the establishment of land entitlements for various groups of Americans.

[99] Gurr defined relative deprivation as the perception of a discrepancy between social actors' "value expectations and their value capabilities. Value expectations are the goods and conditions of life to which people believe they are rightfully entitled. Value capabilities are the goods and conditions they think they are capable of getting and keeping." *Why Men Rebel*, p. 24. Runciman more generally observed that "[t]he related notions of 'relative deprivation' and 'reference group' both derive from a familiar truism: that people's attitudes, aspirations and grievances largely depend on the frame of reference within they are conceived." *Relative Deprivation and Social Justice*, p. 9.

[100] *Relative Deprivation and Social Justice*, p. 9. Obviously, an assessment of whether entitlement policies work to generate *excessive* expectations or dysfunctional attitudes of

Whether or not they attempt to improve their own situations, people drawing negative conclusions from reference group comparisons may come to resent and protest the redistributive obligations that particular benefit programs impose, especially if they perceive the moral worthiness of program beneficiaries to be relatively low and/or the cost of their benefits prohibitively high.[101] This could be seen in recent debates over welfare that led to the demise of AFDC as a national-level entitlement. As Hugh Heclo rightly has suggested, though, the complex relationship between entitlements and the state of the U.S. economy has never been unidimensional. Describing the poverty politics of the early 1990s, he notes that in economic good times,

it is politically easier to feel generous, and poverty may seem a more incongruous condition demanding attention. But the poor can also appear more aberrant, and fewer people may identify with their situation. In economic hard times more people may feel their economic situation precarious, and political opportunities for more encompassing antipoverty coalitions grow. But antipoverty efforts also become harder to pay for, and the scramble for survival may do more to divide than to unite people.[102]

Heclo might well have been writing about the entitlement politics of the early nineteenth century.

entitlement in individual citizens is beyond the scope of this work. However, psychiatrists have begun to analyze what has been described as "the sense of being special and entitled to special privileges." See Rafael Moses and Rena Moses-Hrushovski, "Reflections on the Sense of Entitlement," *Psychoanalytic Study of the Child* 45 (1990): 61–78, cited phrase p. 61; and *Attitudes of Entitlement: Theoretical and Clinical Issues*, ed. Vamik D. Volkan and Terry C. Rodgers (Charlottesville: University of Virginia Press, 1988). I am aware of only one empirical study that attempts to differentiate between and measure the expectancies ("subjectively *attainable* outcomes") and entitlements ("subjectively *deserved* outcomes") raised by certain features of advanced industrial welfare states: Ephraim Yuchtman-Yaar, "Expectancies, Entitlements, and Subjective Welfare," in *Evaluating the Welfare State: Social and Political Perspectives*, ed. Shimon E. Spiro and Ephraim Yuchtman-Yaar (New York: Academic Press, 1983), pp. 89–108.

[101] Recent work on relative deprivation suggests that beliefs about social justice mediate between people's assessments of situations and their reactions, and that people are more likely to acknowledge feelings of injustice at the collective or group level. See Tom R. Tyler, Robert J. Boeckmann, Heather J. Smith, and Yuen J. Huo, *Social Justice in a Diverse Society* (Boulder, CO: Westview Press, 1997), pp. 3–74.

[102] "Poverty Politics," in Sheldon H. Danziger, Gary D. Sandefur, and Daniel H. Weinberg, eds., *Confronting Poverty: Prescriptions for Change* (New York: Russell Sage Foundation, 1994), p. 398.

Entitlements and American Political Development

One of the most important advantages of recognizing entitlements as a discrete policy device is that it enables us to develop broader understandings of the causes and consequences of entitlement programs. To begin with, the ability to identify entitlements as policies creating statutory rights tied to reasons allows us to search for their historic origins in ways precluded by contemporary notions about social policy and welfare states. As Theda Skocpol so thoroughly revealed in her study of Civil War military pensions, the standard vision of the United States as a "welfare laggard" is seriously inadequate.[103] Yet, Skocpol herself disregarded the existence of earlier Federal entitlements that were not only the policy equivalents of the Civil War pensions she analyzed, but also in many crucial ways their direct ancestors.[104] As the case studies in the chapters that follow demonstrate, the policy strategy of selective entitlement, and entitlements as a legal form, have been key features of the American state since the period of the nation's founding. Early U.S. military pensions and land benefits cannot be ignored if we are to understand the dual dynamics of American social provision and state building. They established legal entitlement as one of the most powerful standard operating procedures of the American state even as the state itself was created, transforming conventional understandings about representation, confounding contemporary ideas about federalism, and rejecting egalitarian notions of the social rights of citizenship long before they would be articulated by nineteenth- and twentieth-century champions of the universal welfare state.

Thinking about entitlements as a policy device also allows us to reach beyond the understandings of the state that are yielded when we consider only the legislation most obviously classified as social policy. While that analytic classification is useful in some regards, it tends to blind us to the

---

[103] *Protecting Soldiers and Mothers.*

[104] Skocpol does devote a paragraph (p. 105) in *Protecting Mothers and Soldiers* to pensions for Revolutionary warriors and their survivors but then dismisses them as minimal in scope compared with the pensions granted to Union veterans of the Civil War. She thus overlooks the widest import of her assertion that the Civil War pension system was "an unabashed system of national public care" for the "deserving core of a special generation" (p. 151). Had Skocpol recognized that the Civil War pension system did not represent a new way of doing business, but rather the perfection of an ingrained state practice of selective legal entitlement, the social policy discontinuities of the early twentieth century that she and other scholars chronicle would have appeared all the more pronounced and important.

fact that individual public policies may simultaneously work toward multiple state purposes, leading to diverse (and sometimes contradictory) social and political outcomes. The Revolutionary veterans' pensions assayed in Chapters 2 and 3, for example, have long been classified and overlooked as mere "military" policies, yet they played vital roles in state organization and social provision that have only recently begun to be thoroughly documented.[105] Similarly, the preemption rights and land grants established for select categories of American veterans and civilians chronicled in Chapters 4 and 5 have long been relegated to studies of "land policy," yet they were also critical to the paths of development taken by the American state and its system of social provision.

A broad understanding of entitlements as a policy device is also useful in that it facilitates comparisons with other policy devices or strategies that states rely upon to achieve public purposes. As noted earlier in this chapter, an important policy alternative is that of the collective public good, whether provided directly by a given nation or indirectly by means of grants in aid to subnational units of government. The United States' first entitlements were enacted and expanded during the same period in which the Federal Government established a national postal network[106] and embarked upon a variety of public works projects or "internal improvements." Common schools also were created then, though due more to the efforts of state and local governments than to Federal sponsorship. Although an analysis of these collective goods is well beyond the scope of this book, their existence points to the importance of thinking about why state actors choose particular policy strategies to achieve their goals in particular situations when other strategies may be available. That the Federal Government turned to entitlement programs for some policy purposes but not for others in the early years of the Republic begs the question of why entitlements were utilized at all, especially given the dysfunctional consequences that often resulted from their enactment.

A final way in which viewing entitlements as a policy device is beneficial is that it facilitates the kinds of historically informed, cross-case and cross-national comparisons that are at the heart of studies of state development. One of the most frequently pursued questions in the literature on social policy is, of course, that of why the United States did not

---

[105] Laura S. Jensen, "The Early American Origins of Entitlements," *Studies in American Political Development* 10(2) (Fall 1996): 360–404; Resch, *Suffering Soldiers*.
[106] John, *Spreading the News*.

develop the comprehensive or universal welfare state that other nations did. This is essentially a way of asking why the United States has so far pursued a course of far more categorical or *selective* entitlement than other countries have. The exigencies of documenting the details of America's original entitlement programs have precluded a comparative approach in this book. However, learning how and with what effects the original entitlements of other nation-states contemporaneously partitioned (or did not partition) their respective populations into subsets of deserving and undeserving citizens would almost certainly shed more light on the ways in which the first U.S. entitlements shaped the American polity. Scholars would also do well to consider the changes in conceptions of entitlement that are currently taking place in the United States and abroad, comparing the recent legal disentitlement of poor American citizens with the reform initiatives that seem to be transforming the social rights of citizenship of European welfare states into more negotiated, tenuous, selectively granted benefits.[107]

The chapters that follow explain why the U.S. Government came to rely upon highly selective, programmatic entitlement in the first century of its existence instead of other modes of governance that might have been devised for achieving state and societal goals. As we shall see, the civic and social consequences of enacting selective entitlements tended to hinder those policies' evolution into more comprehensive, universal-type benefits. While their categories of desert and reward often expanded under pressure, they usually were not fundamentally transformed. The continued existence of differential categories of national care, and thereby differential categories of political incorporation and citizenship, in turn stratified and divided Americans into groups who understood their place in the polity differently.

Whether the tenants of distant eras or of the new millennium, people occupy multiple social positions, experience different histories, and struggle in a variety of social spaces and institutional settings.[108] As a consequence, their understandings as citizens are derived from a wide range of influences beyond the ways in which entitlements organize the nation that they inhabit. Entitlements are nonetheless powerful forces in structuring their efforts to make sense of social and political relations. It

---

[107] Cox, "Consequences of Welfare Reform," p. 13; Jytte Klausen, "Social Rights Advocacy and State Building: T. H. Marshall in the Hands of Social Reformers," *World Politics* 47 (January 1995): 244–67.

[108] McCann, *Rights at Work*, p. 283.

is more than time to move beyond the concepts and stances that have blinded us to the ways in which entitlements have figured in the constitution of the American nation and American citizenship. As Schattschneider observed, "What happens in politics *depends upon the way in which people are divided.*"[109] If we are to understand the development of the American state completely, we will need to investigate its entire historical trajectory and learn as much about its entitlements' constitutive grip as we do about their costs.

[109] E. E. Schattschneider, *The Semisovereign People: A Realist's View of Democracy in America* (1960) (Chicago: Holt, Rinehart and Winston, Inc., 1983), p. 60; italics in the original.

2

Pensions for Revolutionary Patriots

> I view the scheme as Altogether unjust and unconstitutional in its nature and full of dangerous consequences. 'tis an unhappy dilemma to which we seem to be reduced – provide for your Officers in terms dictated to you or lose all the valuable Soldiers among them – establish a Pension for Officers make them a seperate Body to be provided for by the honest Yeomanry and others of their Fellow Citizens many thousands of whom have equal claims upon every ground.... [S]uch provision will be against the grain of the People....
>
> Henry Laurens, 1778[1]

The framing of the U.S. Constitution has come to figure so momentously in our imaginations that it has distorted our perceptions of historical continuity and change. Ratification is often depicted as if it created a tabula rasa, upon which was inscribed a fundamentally new legal regime involving wholly new institutions. Such a portrait consigns the legal and institutional ground from which the American state emerged to the shadows of a largely irrelevant past. Yet, the citizens of late-eighteenth- and early-nineteenth-century America only gradually reconceived the ways in which their laws and institutions should operate, through practice that took place over a period of time spanning the pre- and postconstitutional eras, in a context rich with public actors, political forces, popular influences, and shifts in legal and constitutional theory.[2] If a "state of

---

[1] "The President of Congress (Henry Laurens) to George Washington," 5 May 1778, in *Letters of Members of the Continental Congress*, ed. Edmund C. Burnett, vol. III [hereafter *LMCC*, III], (Washington, DC: Carnegie Institution of Washington, 1926), p. 221.

[2] Christine A. Desan, "The Constitutional Commitment to Legislative Adjudication in the Early American Tradition," *Harvard Law Review* 111 (1998): 1384–5.

courts and parties"[3] existed by the 1830s, it was not because Americans adopted novel, unauthoritative central institutions in 1789. Rather, it was because the institutions born of the U.S. Constitution seized public authority and used it, adapting both structurally and behaviorally as old ideas about governance encountered the new demands of nation building.

Institutional fluidity, not fixedness, marked the Government of 1789. Although we typically assume a fundamental constancy of institutional operations, allowing contemporary notions about the respective legislative and adjudicatory functions of Congress and the judiciary to be projected backward in time, the founding's separation of powers did not immediately render obsolete ingrained practices seemingly at odds with the new Constitution's formal map or consolidate the judiciary's authority over the interpretation of public law.[4] From the early colonial era until the 1860s, monetary claims brought against the government were believed to be fiscal questions that were properly the province of the legislative bodies that maintained control over the public purse, not legal questions for the courts.[5] So, too, were requests for relief from debts, taxes, poverty, and disaster. The ratification of the U.S. Constitution and Congress's subsequent creation of an independent judiciary did not alter Americans' historic practice of approaching their elected representatives with demands for public aid. Nor, importantly, did it put an end to the adjudication of citizens' claims as a *legislative* practice that involved congressional judgments about debt and legal obligation, a practice that linked representatives and their constituents directly and intimately over matters of right and remedy. The First U.S. Congress indeed moved swiftly in its opening session in 1789 to preserve its authority over the determination of claims. Congress maintained its dominance well into the nineteenth century, perpetuating a mode of political representation that encompassed the power to adjudicate the

---

[3] Stephen Skowronek's famous characterization of the early American state. *Building a New American State: The Expansion of National Administrative Capacities, 1877–1920* (Cambridge: Cambridge University Press, 1982), ch. 1.

[4] Desan, "Constitutional Commitment."

[5] Desan, "Constitutional Commitment;" Floyd D. Shinomura, "The History of Claims Against the United States: The Evolution from a Legislative Toward a Judicial Model of Payment," *Louisiana Law Review* 45 (1985): 625–700; see also Desan, "Remaking Constitutional Tradition at the Margin of the Empire: The Creation of Legislative Adjudication in Colonial New York," *Law and History Review* 16 (1998): 257–317.

cases of constituents and determine rights that could not be enforced in courts.[6]

The mechanism for conveying citizens' claims of need and right to Congress was the petition. Although we have all but overlooked the practice of petitioning in our rush to account for the rise of political parties and a mass electorate, the petition was a form of political speech that was vitally important during the early years of the United States' existence, both as an expression of the will of the people and as a device that structured politics and the processes of government.[7] The right of citizens to petition their assemblies had evolved during the colonial period into an affirmative right that mandated legislative attention to the claims of the governed in ways that no other mechanism of political participation could. Although enfranchised, property-owning, adult white males seem to have exercised that right most vigorously, people with little if any formal political power – disenfranchised white males, women, African Americans, and Native Americans – also made use of the petition process to articulate social, political, and economic concerns.[8] That the right to petition emerged from the First U.S. Congress as the capstone of the First Amendment was not surprising, given the vehement protests over that right's denial in the Stamp Act Declaration of 1765 and the Declaration of Independence, its assertion in postwar state constitutions, and its centrality in arguments over theories of representation that began before the Constitution was ratified and continued in the First Congress's debate over petition versus instruction. In theory and in practice, the right to petition embraced an unmediated, personal politics of reciprocal obligation. On the one side, citizens were expected to communicate their concerns and grievances and suggest remedies for them, even in

---

[6] Desan, "Constitutional Commitment," p. 1384; Shinomura, "History of Claims," p. 637.

[7] Gregory A. Mark, "The Vestigial Constitution: The History and Significance of the Right to Petition," *Fordham Law Review* 66 (1998): 2153–2231; Stephen A. Higginson, "A Short History of the Right to Petition Government for the Redress of Grievances," *Yale Law Journal* 96 (1986): 142–66; U.S. Congress, Staff, House of Representatives Committee on Energy and Commerce, 99th Cong., 2nd sess., "Petitions, Memorials and Other Documents Submitted for the Consideration of Congress: March 4, 1789 to December 14, 1795" (Washington, DC: GPO, 1986, Comm. Print 99-AA).

[8] Raymond C. Bailey, *Popular Influence Upon Public Policy: Petitioning in Eighteenth-Century Virginia* (Westport, CT: Greenwood Press, 1979); Alison G. Olson, "Eighteenth-Century Colonial Legislatures and Their Constituents," *Journal of American History* 79 (1992): 554–9; Mark, "Vestigial Constitution," pp. 2175–87.

the form of proposed legislation. On the other, legislators were obliged to be receptive and responsive.[9]

Implementing this mode of representation on a national scale presented serious political and institutional challenges. Even the relatively limited category of cases of individual citizens presenting basic monetary claims against the United States required Congress to find a way to strike a balance between two contending duties: the duty to provide fair consideration and payment to individuals with meritorious legal claims and the duty to maintain control over the allocation of limited public revenues among competing public needs.[10] The scope of its authority, coupled with a constituency of unprecedented size and diversity, meant that Congress had to extend this balancing act to render judgment upon a wide variety of other kinds of individual and group appeals for public assistance.[11] These included petitions for aid to victims of poverty, disaster, and other calamities, and for relief from debts and penalties for trade law violations. People also prayed for patronage for intellectual property, for special contracts and projects, for postal routes, and for land grants and other property rights.[12] Congress also was required to respond to petitions and memorials that presented constituents' views and demanded legislative action on national policy issues. Those issues often intertwined public and individual interests, such as the Native American presence and slavery. Whatever the situation, the nation's new legislature was expected

---

[9] Mark, "Vestigial Constitution," pp. 2154, 2191–212; Higginson, "Short History of the Right to Petition," p. 155; U.S. Congress, "Petitions, Memorials, and Other Documents," p. 6. Noble Cunningham observed over twenty years ago that the sheer number of petitions presented to Congress contradicted "arguments that the legislators in Washington were isolated from the people they governed and that the people themselves were indifferent to what the national government did." Far from demonstrating that the national government was "distant and unapproachable," the records of the petitioning process of the Jeffersonian era contained "strong indications of a feeling that government was responsive to its citizens." *The Process of Government under Jefferson* (Princeton, NJ: Princeton University Press, 1978), pp. 300, 303.

[10] Shinomura, "History of Claims," p. 626. As will become clear later, the question of what constituted a strictly "legal" claim for the repayment of a public "debt" was by no means a simple one.

[11] During the early national period, petitions usually conveyed formal requests or prayers pertaining to the satisfaction of a private claim. Petitions of a more public nature were also sent to Congress by groups of people sharing common interests, requesting favorable action by Congress on mutually desired goals or reacting for or against certain legislation. Memorials were similar to petitions in form and substance but often contained no overt prayer. U.S. Congress, "Petitions, Memorials, and Other Documents," p. 1.

[12] U.S. Congress, "Petitions, Memorials, and Other Documents."

to reach decisions that comported with contemporary notions of agency, duty, and legality. The operative question for Congress was not whether to do so but *how*.

This question was especially pressing because the first U.S. Congresses did not assemble with blank statute books in hand. Policy decisions made by the Continental and Confederation Congresses joined the legacy of legal and institutional practice to shape the politics and governance of the early Republic. The U.S. Congress's newly elected members, many of whom had held prominent military or political positions during the Revolution,[13] could not simply abandon the statutory commitments of their predecessors. Instead, they had to find ways to accommodate them within the new enterprise that was the Government of the United States. Many national-level policies established after 1776 simply continued in effect after 1789, or were ratified formally or otherwise reenacted by early U.S. Congresses.

These policies included a commitment to support military veterans who were disabled in the service of the new nation. Among the first national-level entitlements to be legislated on American soil, the pension program for disabled veterans that was established and refined by the Continental and Confederation Congresses was embraced immediately by the First U.S. Congress. By contrast, the program of *service*-based pensions enacted in 1778–80 for the officers of the Continental Army and their survivors was not so embraced, so that its promises lingered, unmet and unheeded, on the fringes of the congressional agenda. Disability and service pensions would follow critically different paths until the nation emerged from the War of 1812 to contemplate its consolidation and expansion, when together they would powerfully affect the development of the American state and Federal social policy.

Critical Precedents: Disability, Officers', and Widows' Pensions of the Revolutionary War Period

Despite its somewhat dubious authority and capacity, the Continental Congress first enacted "national"-level "invalid pension" legislation in 1776 in response to increasing numbers of individual requests for aid

---

[13] Jack N. Rakove, "The Structure of Politics at the Accession of George Washington," in *Beyond Confederation: Origins of the Constitution and American National Identity*, ed. Richard Beeman, Stephen Botein, and Edward C. Carter II (Chapel Hill: University of North Carolina Press, 1987), pp. 261–94, 276–7.

received from the wounded after the outbreak of hostilities with Britain.[14] Reflecting British and colonial practice, the pension legislation offered half pay for life or during the period of disability to every officer, soldier, or sailor who lost a limb or was otherwise rendered incapable of earning a livelihood in the service of the United States.[15] Amendments refined and broadened coverage until the Confederation Congress issued its final invalid pension resolutions on June 11, 1788, limiting benefits to the disabled veterans who applied for benefits no more than six months later.[16] Because the provision of the disability pensions by the states during the war and Confederation years had proven inadequate, the newly established United States Congress agreed to begin making Federal arrears payments in 1789, placing the administration of national pension laws under the supervision of the secretary of war, Major General Henry Knox. Knox recommended against extending the application cutoff date of December 11, 1788, but large numbers of disability claims and petitions for relief continued to pour in to Congress in spite of the statute of limitations. As a result, Congress repeatedly extended the deadline for the admission of Revolutionary veterans to the invalid-pension rolls between 1792 and 1828, voting in 1805 to extend disability benefits to veterans who had at any time after the Revolution become unable to endure manual labor as a consequence of wounds received during the war.[17]

---

[14] This paragraph and the one that follows draw upon William H. Glasson, *Federal Military Pensions in the United States*, ed. David Kinley (New York: Oxford University Press, 1918), pp. 19–97.

[15] The difference between officers and enlisted men was significant not only in terms of rates of pension compensation, but also as an important social distinction. This distinction would figure in later conflicts over the provision of service pensions for the nondisabled. See the later discussion.

[16] *Journals of the Continental Congress, 1774–1789*, vol. XXXIV (January 1788–March 1789), ed. Worthington Chauncey Ford (Washington, DC: GPO, 1904–) [hereafter *JCC* (XXXIV, 1778–9)], pp. 209–10.

[17] Congress also voted in 1813, 1814, and 1816 to establish limited benefits for the widows and orphans of deceased members of the Navy and soldiers of the War of 1812. Until about 1800, disability pension provisions were the same for members of the Navy as for those of the Army, but legislation enacted in 1799 and 1800 established a Navy disability pension fund from the sale of prizes taken by Navy vessels at sea. Glasson, *Federal Military Pensions*, pp. 19–23, 54–63, 100–1, 108–9; "An Act to increase the pensions of invalids in certain cases," *Annals of Congress*, 14th Cong., 1st sess. (Washington, DC: Gales and Seaton, 1834–) [hereafter *AC* (14/1)], p. 1851, April 24, 1816; Report of the House Committee on Pensions and Revolutionary Claims, March 18, 1816, *American State Papers, Class IX, Claims* [hereafter *ASP, Claims*], pp. 473–4. According to Glasson, the 1805 law allowed veterans to attribute the ills and disabilities of old age to wounds from which they had previously recovered, setting a precedent for a similar provision in the Civil

Congress's support for a program of invalid pensions was consistent with a long-standing consensus in the American polity that veterans disabled in the service of the state should be entitled to some form of public provision. As the Fourteenth Congress would explain in 1816, a "just regard to sound policy and the injunctions of humanity" dictated that the government had a special duty to provide invalids with the means to support themselves "plentifully and comfortably."[18] The concept of service pensions, by contrast – cash benefits for veterans not premised upon combat-induced disability but simply in recognition of service to the state – was extremely controversial. Service pensions had long been opposed by many Americans as antithetical to two of the central tenets of a widely shared ideology: antipathy toward a professional or "standing" army and a corresponding belief in the virtue of the citizen-soldier. Even George Washington, facing the command of the winter encampment at Valley Forge in the wake of numerous officer resignations, resisted the idea of service pensions when it were first broached in 1777 as an incentive that could hold his flagging troops together. Their cost might contribute such weight to the national debt "as to sink the Colonies under the load of it." Moreover, service pensions would "give great disgust to the people at large."[19]

Early American antagonism toward permanent standing armies derived from a combination of history, political theory, and practical

War pension system. An 1817 law similarly extended pensions to the widows and orphans of men not only dying in the Navy but also "*in consequence of* disease contracted or of casualties or injuries received" while in the Navy. It was repealed in 1824 due to too large a demand upon the Navy pension fund. *Federal Military Pensions*, pp. 62, 101 (emphasis added).

[18] "An Act to increase the pensions of invalids in certain cases," *AC* (14/1), p. 1851, Apr. 24, 1816; Report of the House Committee on Pensions and Revolutionary Claims, March 18, 1816, *ASP, Claims*, pp. 473–4. This legislation seems to have created the first U.S. COLA (cost of living adjustment). Congress voted to use some of the U.S. Treasury surplus to raise the rates of the benefits paid to most disabled veterans on the grounds that the cost of living had increased.

[19] "Remarks on Plan of Field Officers for Remodeling the Army," in *The Writings of George Washington*, ed. John C. Fitzpatrick (Washington, DC: GPO, 1931–), vol. 10, p. 125. See also Sidney Kaplan, "Pay, Pension, and Power: Economic Grievances of the Massachusetts Officers of the Revolution," *Boston Public Library Quarterly* 3 (1951): 22. Sensitive to politics of disability versus service, Continental Army officers tried to justify their pursuit of service pensions between 1778 and 1783 with the claim that the war had inflicted *financial injury* upon them (a claim that was highly contested). The U.S. Congress's eventual establishment of a pension program for nondisabled Revolutionary veterans in 1818 required the basic criterion of military service to be coupled with those of poverty and, implicitly, age. See the later discussion.

experience. More than a half-century of struggle between Parliament and Crown over the existence and control of English armed forces had left distrust of military power and hostility to professional armies deeply ingrained in the British political and constitutional thought transmitted to America. Educated colonists were well acquainted with both classical tracts and the radical Whig writings of late-seventeenth- and early-eighteenth-century England describing military power as the ultimate power in society and the uncontrollable enemy of liberty. Where "marching" armies took the field against real enemies or danger out of necessity, armies "standing" in times of peace threatened a tyrannical imposition of unlawful power.[20]

As long as relations between the colonists and the British troops stationed in the colonies remained essentially peaceful,[21] the antimilitary philosophy infusing the pamphlets and sermons of Revolutionary leaders could be dismissed, if uneasily. Public opinion about the British army's presence deteriorated from skepticism to open protest, however, when several thousand soldiers were dispatched to the colonies in 1763, and civil–military skirmishes became increasingly common. When five civilians were killed by British regulars in the streets of Boston in 1770, political theory and reality were finally, and spectacularly, merged. The slaughter of liberty's "guiltless children"[22] in the Boston Massacre "permanently embedded the prejudice against standing armies into the American

[20] Richard H. Kohn, *Eagle and Sword: The Federalists and the Creation of the Military Establishment in America, 1783–1802* (New York: Free Press, 1975), pp. 3–4; Kohn, "The Creation of the American Military Establishment, 1783–1802," in *The Military in America: From the Colonial Era to the Present*, ed. Peter Karsten (New York: Free Press, 1980); J. G. A. Pocock, *The Machiavellian Moment: Florentine Political Thought and the Atlantic Republican Tradition* (Princeton, NJ: Princeton University Press, 1975), pp. 411, 410–20, 424–8, 506–7; Bernard Bailyn, *The Ideological Origins of the American Revolution* (Cambridge, MA: Belknap Press of Harvard University Press, 1967), pp. 23–6, 61–3, 112–19; Lois F. Schwoerer, *"No Standing Armies!" The Anti-army Ideology in Seventeenth-Century England* (Baltimore: Johns Hopkins University Press, 1974), pp. 195–7; Lawrence Delbert Cress, "Radical Whiggery on the Role of the Military: Ideological Roots of the American Revolutionary Militia," *Journal of the History of Ideas* 40 (January 1979): 43–60, 54, and *Citizens in Arms: The Army and the Militia in American Society to the War of 1812* (Chapel Hill: University of North Carolina Press, 1982), pp. 34–41.

[21] See John Shy, *Toward Lexington: The Role of the British Army in the Coming of the American Revolution* (Princeton, NJ: Princeton University Press, 1965), pp. 393–8.

[22] "Rules and Orders regulating the Army of Observation," Rhode Island, June 1775, cited in Charles Royster, *A Revolutionary People at War: The Continental Army and American Character, 1775–1783* (Chapel Hill: University of North Carolina Press, 1979), p. 4.

political tradition."[23] By 1776, early American opposition to a standing army had become a potent ideological symbol expressing deep-seated cultural suspicion of governmental power – one that substantiated a charge of British tyranny and justified revolt and the founding of a new government.[24] As historian Richard Kohn notes, it was no accident that American independence was declared in language that repeatedly charged George III with militarism and decried the abuses of a regular army.[25] Language striken from the final version of the Declaration of Independence indeed indicates that the king's decision "to send over not only

---

[23] Kohn, *Eagle and Sword*, p. 6. See also Shy, *Toward Lexington*, p. 398. Before the Massacre, pondering the 1768 garrisoning of four British regiments in Boston, Samuel Adams cautiously had temporized that although it was "a very improbable supposition, that any people c[ould] long remain free, with a strong military power in the very heart of their country," it was understood even by children "that in a city, in the midst of civil society, especially in a time of peace, soldiers *of all ranks*, like all other men, are to be protected, *govern'd, restrain'd*, rewarded or punish'd by the LAW OF THE LAND." No such illusion remained after that "fatal fifth of March 1770," when, in the words of Joseph Warren, the streets of Boston were "stained with the blood of our brethren," American ears and eyes "wounded by the groans of the dying" and "tormented with the sight of the mangled bodies of the dead." The acquittal of most of the Massacre's military perpetrators was the last straw. Standing armies were "ever to be dreaded as the ready engines of tyranny and oppression." Article signed "Vindex," *Boston Gazette*, December 12, 1768 (emphasis in the original), annotated "S. Adams," Harbottle Dorr Collection of Annotated Massachusetts Newspapers 1765–1776, Massachusetts Historical Society; *The Danger of Standing Armies*, commemorative ovation delivered on Massacre Day, March 5, 1772, cited in Karsten, ed., *The Military in America*, pp. 18–23.

   For a milder explanation of the colonists' view of the standing army in 1770, see Cress, *Citizens in Arms*, pp. 40–6. Cress asserts that even in the New England colonies immediately after the Massacre, the core issue was not the existence of professional armies per se, but rather that of their control. Only after the Coercive Acts of 1774 would the colonists come to link the profession of arms with the destruction of the political and civil liberties of a free society.

[24] See *Pamphlets of the American Revolution 1750–1776*, ed. Bernard Bailyn (Cambridge, MA: Belknap Press of Harvard University Press, 1965), vol. I, pp. 71–5; Jack C. Lane, "Ideology and the American Military Experience: A Reexamination of Early American Attitudes Toward the Military," in *Soldiers and Civilians: The U.S. Army and the American People*, ed. Garry D. Ryan and Timothy K. Nenninger (Washington, DC: National Archives and Records Administration, 1987), pp. 15–26, 18; and Robert E. Shalhope, "The Ideological Origins of the Second Amendment," *The Journal of American History* 69 (1982): 599–614.

[25] Kohn, *Eagle and Sword*, p. 6; see also Schwoerer, *"No Standing Armies!"*, p. 197. The Declaration of Independence, an action of the Second Continental Congress, July 4, 1776, read: "He has kept among us, in Times of Peace, Standing Armies, without the consent of our Legislatures. He has affected to render the Military independent of and superior to the Civil Power. He has combined with others to subject us to a Jurisdiction foreign to our Constitution, and unacknowledged by our Laws; giving his Assent to their Acts of pretended Legislation: For quartering large Bodies of Armed Troops among us: For protecting them, by a mock Trial, from Punishment for any Murders

soldiers of our common blood, but Scotch and foreign mercenaries to invade and destroy," was a grievous and unpardonable offense.[26]

If it was clear to Americans at the outset of the war that a standing army was "always dangerous to the Liberties of the People" because professional soldiers were "apt to consider themselves as a Body distinct from the rest of the Citizens,"[27] it was equally clear that the only military force appropriate in the new republic was one comprised of citizen-soldiers contributing selflessly to the common defense as members of the polity. This, of course, was the militia: a free army of free men who, because of their stake in society and belief in liberty, would mobilize to protect home and family and to preserve self-government. They were the modern Cincinnati,[28] who would disinterestedly leave their ploughs to defeat the enemy in a single day and return to their farms, relinquishing the reins of power as soon as the crisis had passed.[29] Virtue would triumph not only in their demonstration of the sacrifice of individual interests for the public good – the essence of civic republicanism – but also, as importantly, in their rejection of the standing army's corrupt association with patronage, rank, and pensions. America's citizen-soldiers were neither derelicts nor mercenaries, but men who faced their invaders by an act of free choice in righteous anticipation of the only just reward: immortal glory both on earth and in heaven.[30]

which they should commit on the inhabitants of these States.... He has plundered our Seas, ravaged our Coasts, burnt our Towns, and destroyed the Lives of our People. He is, at this time, transporting large Armies of foreign Mercenaries to compleat the Works of Death, Desolation, and Tyranny, already begun with circumstances of Cruelty and Perfidy...."

[26] Cited in *The American Enlightenment: The Shaping of the American Experiment and a Free Society*, ed. Adrienne Koch (New York: George Braziller, Inc., 1965), p. 381.

[27] Samuel Adams to James Warren, Jan. 7, 1776, in *The Writings of Samuel Adams*, ed. Harry Alonzo Cushing (New York: G. Putnam's Sons, 1904–), vol. 3, p. 250; James Otis, *The Rights of the British Colonies Asserted and Proved* (Boston: 1764), in Bailyn, *Pamphlets*, p. 469.

[28] Here the term "Cincinnati" refers generally to the legendary Roman statesman Lucius Quinctius Cincinnatus, who is said to have resigned his authority as dictator of Rome after saving that city from an invading army in one day. It does not refer to the post-Revolutionary Society of the Cincinnati, named after Cincinnatus, which will be discussed later.

[29] In the 1770s and 1780s, "disinterestedness," or unselfish, unbiased behavior not influenced by considerations of private advantage or profit, was a concept at the heart of American conceptions of civic virtue. See Gordon S. Wood, "Interests and Disinterestedness in the Making of the Constitution," in *Beyond Confederation*, pp. 69–109.

[30] Royster, *Revolutionary People at War*, pp. 35–40; Pocock, *The Machiavellian Moment*, pp. 406, 507, 527–8; Bailyn, *Ideological Origins of the American Revolution*, pp. 83–4; Cress, *Citizens*

Arguments over the provision of other earthly rewards to veterans of the Revolution – that is, Federal service pensions – were thus an integral part of the American people's attempt to construct the meaning of citizenship in their new nation. In the major reconsideration of political relationships that separation from Britain necessitated, none was more critical than that of the individual to the state. By 1776, the colonists had rejected the idea of natural, perpetual subjectship to Great Britain in favor of a theory of volitional, contractual allegiance. That theory failed to specify which entity in America's governmental system allegiance was to be directed toward, and it was conflicted with respect to which people could actually acquire the status of citizen.[31] Americans nonetheless understood that the crux of the contract was some kind of commitment to the twin ideals of individual liberty and community security.[32] In the inchoate formulations that constituted civic identity and membership in

in Arms, pp. 54–6. Political rhetoric was bound up with the language of evangelical Christianity in strengthening the pre-Revolutionary call to war. As Charles Royster has explained, "[r]eligious and political appeals to the [citizen] soldier combined the forces of the two most powerful prevailing explanations by which revolutionaries understood events.... By the time the war came, the religious call to seek salvation had taken on a political concern for the welfare of America and liberty, [while] the effort to secure liberty had acquired the emotional urgency of a test of righteousness." The failure of an individual to serve as a citizen-soldier in the effort to preserve the nation against British corruption and enslavement was not only a failure of his politics, but a moral failing as well: to "shun the dangers of the field" was to "desert the banner of Christ." It was God's will that the Revolution should succeed; virtue not only required, but necessitated, sacrifice. As one colonial preacher told his congregation, "the Man, who was able in this Country to wield a Sword and did not endeavor to stain it with the Blood of the King's Soldiers and their Abettors, would be renounced by the Lord Jesus Xt at the Day of Judgement." *Revolutionary People at War*, pp. 18, and 16, 21, citing John Murray, *Nehemiah, Or the Struggle for Liberty never in vain*, 1779, and Ambrose Serle to the Earl of Dartmouth, March 20, 1777. For an extended discussion of the role of religion in American attitudes toward the war and the Continental Army, see pp. 13–23, 152–89.

[31] Rogers M. Smith, *Civic Ideals: Conflicting Visions of Citizenship in U.S. History* (New Haven, CT: Yale University Press, 1997).

[32] James H. Kettner, *The Development of American Citizenship, 1608–1870* (Chapel Hill: University of North Carolina Press, 1978), pp. 9–10, 173–209. Kettner explains that while the colonists were committed to certain well-understood principles concerning the *acquisition* of American citizenship – that it began with an act of individual choice and that there existed a right to choose – the *meaning* of the *status* "citizen" was not well developed. The unanswered question of whether allegiance to America meant membership in a state or a nation of states would become critical in post-Revolutionary decisions concerning naturalization and expatriation, court jurisdiction, the status of the inhabitants of the American territories, states' rights, and slavery – as would the question of precisely who counted as "the people" of the United States (pp. 208 – 9). See also Smith, *Civic Ideals*, and Linda K. Kerber, *No Constitutional Right to Be Ladies: Women and the Obligations of Citizenship* (New York: Hill and Wang, 1998).

the polity of the 1770s, the idea of government compensation for the service of citizen-soldiers lacked a theoretical foundation.

If theoretical justifications for service pensions were lacking at the outset of the Revolution, the war itself left many Americans even less inclined toward their establishment. The colonial *rage militaire* that had so resolutely inspired rhetoric and action in 1775 and early 1776 declined appreciably when neither the battle nor its American combatants lived up to the extraordinary expectations that preceded their engagement. The war turned out to be unexpectedly long and enormously costly, and it was punctuated by military reverses that delivered what Charles Royster has described as "sharp, unexpected blows to the [colonists'] assumption that declaring independence was the paramount step to its accomplishment."[33] By 1777, most of the initial recruits in the Continental Army, reluctantly established by Congress in 1775 to augment the militia in the war, either had been killed or captured or had otherwise left the service, and new enlistments were alarmingly insufficient. America's citizen-soldiers, earlier the figurative ideals of a chosen people, had become "soldiers when they chose to be" for pay and enlistment bonuses.[34] As some of the units of the Continental Army increasingly were composed of poor whites and African Americans – unmarried farmers' sons, laborers, servants, transients, apprentices, slaves, felons, and recent immigrants – losses at Brandywine and Germantown caused widespread dissatisfaction with its gentlemen officers, particularly the Continental generals. From the public's point of view, it had become difficult to reconcile reality with the myth that their citizen-soldiers' "natural" determination, innate virtue, and love of liberty would lead to an early and overwhelming victory. Public opinion sunk even lower as stories spread about soldiers' drunken and disorderly behavior, looting, assaults on fellow citizens, and mutinies, along with tales

[33] Royster, *Revolutionary People at War*, p. 107.

[34] John Whiteclay Chambers II, *To Raise an Army: The Draft Comes to Modern America* (New York: Free Press, 1987), p. 21. The Continental Congress's September 1776 promise of land to officers and soldiers who engaged to serve until the end of the war (or until discharged by Congress) is discussed in Chapter 3. Numerous slaves also chose to fight because military service sometimes, though certainly not always, could be exchanged for freedom. The Continental Congress actually adopted a plan to enlist slaves who would receive no pay or bounty, but would be emancipated if they served until the end of the war and returned their arms; it was scuttled by South Carolina and Georgia. The British command in America and the king's ministers in London rejected a similar plan that sought to enlist slaves to fight on the side of Britain. Benjamin Quarles, *The Negro in the American Revolution* (Chapel Hill: University of North Carolina Press, 1961), pp. 51–93.

of the vanity, indecisiveness, stupidity, laziness, and alcoholism of their commanders.[35]

From the alternative perspective of most military leaders, America's citizen-soldiers had proven deficient for an eminently practical reason: they were inadequate to the all too real task of winning the war. Washington believed that the militia had actually been more "hurtful" to the cause than "serviceable." To rely upon them for victory, he bluntly told the Continental Congress in 1776, would be to rest "upon a broken staff." Where the "Jealousies of a standing Army, and the Evils to be apprehended from one" were remote, the consequences of lacking one were "certain, and inevitable Ruin." The need for a stable, disciplined, professional army was paramount, and the key to its establishment was a well-compensated officer corps, for, in Washington's estimation, time had long passed beyond the point where men would serve in the Army out of "any other principles than those of Interest."[36] The increasingly frustrated commander in chief reiterated this position for more than a year, until the extreme conditions of Valley Forge pushed him to inform Congress in no uncertain terms that without "some better provision for binding the Officers by the tye of Interest to the Service," he would no longer be able to hold the Army together.[37] In January 1778, the Continental Congress's committee on Army affairs finally proposed the enactment of service pensions of half-pay for life for all officers serving in the Army until the end of the war, along with pensions for the widows of officers dying in combat and regulations rendering the officers' commissions salable.[38]

---

[35] Chambers, *To Raise an Army*, pp. 21–2; Mark Edward Lender, "The Social Structure of the New Jersey Brigade: The Continental Line as an American Standing Army," in Karsten, ed., *The Military in America*, pp. 27–44; Royster, *Revolutionary People at War*, pp. 58–189; Russell F. Weigley, *History of the United States Army*, enlarged ed. (Bloomington: Indiana University Press, 1984), pp. 29–73.

[36] "George Washington to the President of Congress," 24 September 1776, cited in *American Military Thought*, ed. Walter E. Millis (Indianapolis: Bobbs-Merrill Company, 1966), pp. 9–16, 12, 14, 10. Regarding the contemporary meaning of "interest," see Wood, "Interests and Disinterestedness."

[37] "George Washington to the President of Congress," 23 December 1777, in *Writings of George Washington*, vol. 10, p. 197. Washington continued: "I do not, myself, expect to derive the smallest benefit from any establishment that Congress may adopt, otherwise than as a Member of the Community at large in the the good which I am perswaded will result from the measure."

[38] *JCC* (X, 1778), pp. 18–20; Glasson, *Federal Military Pensions*, pp. 12, 24–5. The proposal was modeled upon British precedent.

According to some participants in the debate that ensued, the issue of establishing half-pay service pensions for the officers of the Revolution was "the most painfull and disagreable question that hath ever been agitated in Congress."[39] Advocates of half-pay like Thomas Burke of North Carolina argued that "without it there c[ould be] no discipline, and almost no army," because officers subjected to "necessary strictness and severity" simply threatened to resign the commissions that "afford[ed] them no prospects but of pain, danger, fatigue, and ruin to their private fortunes." It was also "unjust to sacrifise the time and property of the men whose lives [we]re every day exposed ... without any prospect of compensation, while so many who [we]re protected by their valor and exertions [we]re emassing princely fortunes." Unable to subsist on their pay, which was both in arrears and reduced in value from the depreciation of the currency, the officers had already expended much of their own property, and would be ruined financially if they remained in the service. The provision of life pensions for the military's leaders would not constitute the creation of a standing army. Although some might doubt the authority of a Congress "instituted only for the purpose of War" to commit the new nation to the long-term financial obligation that pensions represented, a pension enactment would surely be no more questionable than Congress's decision to borrow money that would have to be repaid, with interest, from revenues raised long after the war.[40]

To the outraged opposition, the proposal to selectively entitle Continental officers to pensions of half-pay for life was absolutely antithetical to republican ideals and nothing more than a blatant attempt at extortion. As James Lovell of Massachusetts scornfully phrased it, there was "really no argument for [half-pay] but a fear of all of our *best* officers leaving the army." Recalling that the Revolution "*was* in its beginning a *patriotic* war," Lovell urged that "equallity in America be considered," for European military service pensions had introduced into society "a set of haughty idle imperious Scandalizers of industrious Citizens and Farmers."[41] Henry Laurens of South Carolina, president of the Continental Congress, fumed that the demand for officers' pensions was "as

---

39 Roger Sherman, Samuel Huntington, and Oliver Wolcott to the Governor of Connecticut (Jonathan Trumbull), *LMCC*, III, pp. 255–6.

40 Thomas Burke to the Governor of North Carolina (Richard Caswell), April 9, 1778, *LMCC*, III, pp. 160–3, 162.

41 James Lovell to Samuel Adams, January 13, 1778, *LMCC*, III, pp. 31–3, 32 (emphasis in the original).

unjust as it [wa]s extraordinary." The Continental Army's officers had not been drafted, but rather had volunteered in knowing acceptance of the terms of their service. Moreover, the hardships they had endured were not unique to them, but could be attributed "to every Citizen in the Union and to thousands who [we]re not Officers with greater force and propriety": namely, the army's *soldiers* and the thousands of men who served in the militia. Rank did not imbue the Continental officers with a "superior merit" that allowed them to demand a "seperate maintenance from the honest earnings of their fellow Citizens," especially when many of them would leave the Army in possession of large estates, some of them having "accumulated immense fortunes by purloin and peculation under the Mask of patriotism." In Laurens's view, congressional compliance with the officers' demand for pensions would create a dangerous precedent, taxing the people without their consent, exposing them to future arbitrary demands, reducing their representatives to a state of subservience, and laying the foundations of both a standing army and an aristocracy.[42] Even after George Washington convinced a majority of Congress that the "salvation of the cause" depended upon the creation of half-pay pensions, Laurens warned that without justice as one of their pillars, "necessity m[ight] be submitted to ... but Republicans w[ould] at a proper time withdraw a Grant which sh[ould] appear to have been extorted."[43]

In the long run, Laurens's predictions were not far off the mark, for when the Continental Congress enacted a compromise measure on May 15, 1778, establishing service pensions of half pay for seven years for Army officers serving until the end of the war along with lump-sum grants of eighty dollars for noncommissioned officers and soldiers,[44] the conflict over Revolutionary entitlements had only begun. The seven-year measure was immediately deemed insufficient by the officers, who had expected greater public recognition of their professional contribution to independence and clamored for greater satisfaction. By January 1779, Washington had "reluctantly" begun to press Congress to extend the

---

[42] Henry Laurens to William Livingston, April 19, 1778, *LMCC*, III, pp. 175–8, 177.

[43] George Washington to the President of Congress (Henry Laurens), cited in Glasson, *Federal Military Pensions*, p. 27; Henry Laurens to George Washington, May 5, 1778, *LMCC*, III, pp. 219–21, 221.

[44] *JCC* (XI, 1778), pp. 502–3. The service pensions for officers could not exceed the half-pay of a colonel and were not to extend to men "hold[ing] any offices of profit under the United States, or any of them."

officers' pensions from their present term to half-pay for life (reasoning that few of them would survive longer than seven years) and to enact pensions for their widows. The necessity of assuaging the "discontents and distresses" of an army reduced to "little more than [a] skeleton" again won out. Widows' pensions were created in August 1780, and in October of that year – almost two and half years after the original half-pay legislation – a bitterly divided Congress finally gave in to the concept of open-ended, lifelong pension benefits.[45]

As the war dragged toward its conclusion, the Army's officers worried that their service pensions would never become a reality. With the financial position of the Confederation precarious, their back pay still outstanding, and the half-pay provision only grudgingly enacted, they had good reason to fear that Congress might renege on its promise. Their anxiety turned to anger when efforts to persuade the states to guarantee the payment of the half-pay pensions failed and congressional reconsideration of the half-pay issue merely revived all of the old arguments against it. In December 1782, an irate officer corps sent a memorial to Philadelphia from their encampment at Newburgh telling Congress in no uncertain terms that life pensions were "an honorable and just recompense" for their years of hard service. Just as members of the public should receive an annuity on money lent for the war effort, the officers reasoned, so should they receive an annuity for the use of their blood and their services. They would be willing to accept the commutation of their life pensions into equivalent lump-sum payments at the conclusion of the war, but they demanded an immediate advance on the pay due them and the soldiers, or "further experiments on their patience m[ight] have fatal effects." When legislative debate stalled and failed to produce results, the

---

45 Glasson, *Federal Military Pensions*, pp. 30–5; Edmund Cody Burnett, *The Continental Congress* (New York: Macmillan Company, 1941), pp. 391–3; Kaplan, "Pay, Power, and Pension," pp. 27–9; *JCC* (XVII, 1780), pp. 772–3, Aug. 24, 1780; *JCC* (XVIII, 1780), pp. 958–61, Oct. 21, 1780. The resolution enacted on August 24, 1780, constituted the first national pension law for widows and orphans in the United States. It granted half-pay for seven years to the widows of those officers who had died, or would thereafter die, in the service or to their orphaned children if there were no widow surviving. It also repealed the 1778 Pension Act's prohibition on pensions for veterans employed in state or national office. Burnett largely attributed the slow pace of congressional action on half-pay to its attention to other continental problems (particularly finances and foreign relations) and to a high turnover in its membership. Yet half-pay was also strongly and consistently opposed by certain northern states that produced significant numbers of enlistees. The New Jersey, Massachusetts, Connecticut, and Rhode Island delegations all voted against the grant of half-pay for life.

Newburgh Addresses of March 1783 made the officers' threat more explicit: if their terms were not met, the Army would refuse to disband. Had it not been for the charismatic dissuasion of George Washington coupled with timely news of peace, conflict over pension entitlements might well have produced the first American military coup d'etat.[46]

Although the initial importance of the half-pay pensions for state actors lay in their potential to keep the Continental Army together through the end of the war, reconstructions of the events at Newburgh show that the legislation entitling Revolutionary officers and their survivors to pensions for life was also essential to the efforts of nationalist leaders (later the nucleus of the Federalist Party) to strengthen central government authority in the new nation. Recognizing that a congressional commitment to pay the Army's claims would necessitate the adoption of an impost amendment to the Articles of Confederation giving Congress greater powers of taxation, some of the nationalists conspired to encourage the officers to propose commutation and to threaten Congress with military force. Commutation was particularly critical to centralization because of the enormous lump-sum expenditure it would entail. Although George Washington refused to countenance a military threat to civil authority, calling an official meeting of the officers' council to denounce the "insidious purposes" of those who would advocate turning the Army's swords against the government,[47] Congress hastily passed a Commutation Act on March 22, 1783, two days before news of the signing of the preliminary agreement for a general peace. It provided that in lieu of half-pay for life, the Continental officers would receive five years' full pay in money or securities bearing 6 percent interest per annum. Lacking the resources required to implement the act, Congress had to ask the states to consent to the laying of a new impost duty in order to meet the

---

[46] Henry Knox et al., "The address and petition of the officers of the Army of the United States," December 1782, printed in *JCC* (XXIV, 1783), pp. 291–3, as Paper No. 7 to accompany the "Address to the States, by the United States in Congress Assembled" on the subject of the national debt (see later); Kohn, *Eagle and Sword*, pp. 17–39.

[47] Kohn, *Eagle and Sword*, pp. 17–39. Washington spoke directly to the officers at Newburgh to assure them that a distracted Congress ultimately would fulfill its promises. Kohn writes that when Washington had to grope for his spectacles in order to read a letter from Joseph Jones as proof of Congress's good intentions, and mumbled "unaffectedly" that he had grown both gray and blind in the service of his country, the assemblage was stunned. "The tension, the imposing physical presence of the Commander-in-Chief, the speech, and finally an act that emotionally embodied the army's whole experience, combined all at once and shattered the officers' equanimity. Spontaneously they recoiled. Some openly wept." The conspiracy thereby disintegrated (p. 32).

Government's extraordinary financial obligations, which included approximately $5,000,000 for the commutation of half-pay plus $300,000 per year in interest. The states' response in the face of such an onerous fiscal burden was slow at best and, at worst, extremely hostile.[48]

Popular opposition to officers' service pensions raged to such a degree in New England that it produced, in the words of James Madison, "almost a general anarchy." Just as James Lovell had predicted in 1778, no one outside of Congress could understand the *necessity* of such a grant, but they could judge its justice and feel its *impropriety*.[49] The fact that over half of the Army's troops were furnished by the New England states[50] was almost certainly an issue. Though the controversy was fueled by a staggering postwar economic downturn, high taxes, and antinationalist sentiment, public outrage over the officers' pensions and their commutation focused squarely on their inequity and the Continental Congress's abandonment of republican principles. Northern newspapers were filled with vehement indictments of the Army's officers and their newly established, hereditary Society of the Cincinnati, whose very creation seemed to substantiate the charge that officers' pensions would create an American aristocracy living off the labors of others. The Massachusetts assembly replaced its representatives in Congress as a penalty for their acquiescence in the Commutation Act, and formally censured Congress in July 1783 for enacting a law "inconsistent with that equality which ought to subsist

---

[48] *JCC* (XXIV, 1783), pp. 207, 277–83, 286, Mar. 22 and Apr. 26, 1783; Kohn, *Eagle and Sword*, pp. 33–5; E. James Ferguson, *The Power of the Purse* (Chapel Hill: University of North Carolina Press, 1961), pp. 164–7, 220–1; Glasson, *Federal Military Pensions*, pp. 41–2; Janet A. Riesman, "Money, Credit, and Federalist Political Economy," in *Beyond Confederation*, pp. 128–61, 143. When a mutinous band of soldiers demanding overdue pay descended upon Congress in Philadelphia in June 1783, Pennsylvania authorities told Congress it should not look for help from the state until actual violence occurred. Congress retreated to reconvene in Princeton two days later, "insulted by the soldiery which it commanded, [and] unsupported by the citizenry in whose name it governed." Gary B. Nash, " '... and Distinguished Guests,' " *Princeton Alumni Weekly* 64(1) (September 24, 1963): 37, cited in James Sterling Young, *The Washington Community 1800–1828* (New York: Columbia University Press, 1966), p. 14.

[49] James Madison to Edmund Randolph, September 8, 1783, in *The Papers of James Madison*, ed. William T. Hutchinson and William M. E. Rachal (Chicago: University of Chicago Press, 1962–), vol. 7, pp. 307–8, 308; James Lovell to William Whipple, May 25, 1778, *LMCC*, III, pp. 261–2, 262 (emphasis in the original).

[50] According to congressional figures, 51.01 percent of the troops in the service of the United States came from New Hampshire, Massachusetts, Rhode Island, and Connecticut; Massachusetts and Connecticut together contributed over 43 percent. U.S. Senate, "Report of the Committee on Pensions," 212 S. doc. 33 (22/1), January 24, 1832.

among citizens of free and republican States" and "calculated to raise and exalt some citizens in wealth and grandeur, to the injury and oppression of others." Protest also flared in Connecticut, where opposition to half-pay had mushroomed since that colony's 1778 proposal to amend the Articles of Confederation specifically to prohibit postwar pensions. Town meetings and state conventions passed hostile resolutions denouncing commutation as "unjust, impolitic, oppressive to the people, subservient of the principles of a republican government, and exceedingly dangerous when drawn into precedent." Not only did half-pay represent a blatant capitulation to self-interest, but its establishment would also provide civil authorities with a corrupt tool – the economic dependency of a select group of citizens – with which to expand its political influence, undermining the very ideals and institutions that the Revolution had been fought for.[51]

The bitter controversy over the half-pay pensions and their commutation that filled public debate in 1783 evaporated by the spring of 1784. Explanations of its disappearance generally attest to a relaxation of social tensions as the prospect of peace became evident and the Continental Army "melted away" toward home.[52] According to Glasson, opposition to commutation subsided because citizens came to divorce their antagonism toward the Society of the Cincinnati from legitimate congressional action aimed at keeping the late Army together.[53] Charles Royster likewise has explained that as citizens gradually learned that commutation had been legally voted, opponents of half-pay "could not create the aura of united revolutionary indignation to which they were accustomed when denouncing the sycophantic agents of tyranny. Even Samuel Adams upheld Congress's right to grant pensions in order to obtain 'a disciplined

---

[51] "Massachusetts Legislature to Congress," *JCC* (XXV, 1783), July 11, 1783, pp. 607–9; Resolution of the Town of Farmington, August 4, 1783, *Connecticut Courant*, August 12, 1783, p. 2. See also Glasson, *Federal Military Pensions*, pp. 42–9; Royster, *Revolutionary People at War*, pp. 345–7; Sidney Kaplan, "Veteran Officers and Politics in Massachusetts, 1783–1787," *William and Mary Quarterly* 3rd. ser. 9 (1952): 34–41; Richard Buel, Jr., *Dear Liberty: Connecticut's Mobilization for the Revolutionary War* (Middletown, CT: Wesleyan University Press, 1980), pp. 304–11. The Massachusetts legislature's message actually went so far as to inform Congress "with great pain" that "the extraordinary grants and allowances which Congress have thought proper to make to their civil and military officers" had produced such effects in that Commonwealth that the dissolution of the union between the United States was threatened. Agitation was not limited to New England; George Washington reported violent opposition to the Society of the Cincinnati in Virginia.

[52] Ferguson, *Power of the Purse*, p. 171.

[53] Glasson, *Federal Military Pensions*, p. 47 (especially n. 3) and pp. 52–3 (especially n. 1).

Army.' "[54] Particularly when it became clear that the Continental officers would not achieve social distinction premised upon superior Revolutionary merit, concern over the pensions that were to symbolize that merit fell off sharply. The American people

> wanted the officers, like the privates, to return to civilian life inconspicuously, not only laying aside their military character for the safety of republicanism but also forgoing invidious claims to have done more for independence than civilians had done. Officers could share the celebration of national victory, just as Charleston and New York, but they should not presume to take it personally and claim a superior patriotism symbolized by a pension. . . . Americans did not want to forget the War of Independence; they wanted to believe that all of them had won it.[55]

The idea that citizens were the true defenders of liberty undoubtedly was supported by the fact that when the Army was formally disbanded by Congress in November 1783, those entitled to benefits were forced to return home without actually receiving anything toward their pensions or land bounties.[56] Commutation certificates drawing 6 percent interest were distributed in lieu of cash in early 1784, but because the Government lacked the funds to redeem them or even pay the interest due on them, the Revolutionary veterans' treatment by the state could be seen to be essentially no better than that accorded other citizens who had sought to create the new nation.

Veterans' Benefits and Early Nation Building

The issue of the Revolutionary service pensions remained unresolved for decades after the ratification of the U.S. Constitution and its creation of a federal system of government. Between 1784 and 1789, the Confederation government continued in default, forcing many Continental veterans to sell their commutation certificates on the open market for a return as low as twelve and a half cents on the dollar. By the time the

---

[54] *Revolutionary People at War*, p. 349, citing Samuel Adams to Noah Webster, April 30, 1784. Adams had echoed radical Whig writings against standing armies less than a decade earlier. Webster, by contrast, began his career as a political writer with a series of essays condemning the anticommutation movement in the *Connecticut Courant*. He justified the half-pay enactment as a reward for the officers' superior patriotism, but admitted that it was the distinction between the officers' reward of five years' full pay and the soldiers' one year's pay that was largely responsible for inciting and sustaining public outrage. See Glasson, *Federal Military Pensions*, p. 46, and Cress, *Citizens in Arms*, p. 73.

[55] Royster, *Revolutionary People at War*, pp. 349, 357–8.

[56] Land entitlements for officers and soldiers are discussed in Chapter 3.

newly established U.S. Government enacted a provision for the certificates' redemption in 1790,[57] many of them were in the hands of speculators, so that many veterans lost a large portion of the benefits that the Continental Congress had conferred upon them. Those who had parted with their certificates before 1790 complained that the Confederation's fiscal incapacity had caused them to suffer great injustice. They would petition Congress demanding satisfaction for decades. The Revolution's officers maintained that they had been cheated twice: first by the government, when it reneged upon its promise of life pensions, and then by the speculators who took advantage of them.[58] As Washington had argued upon the disbanding of the Army, half-pay for life was the "price of their blood and of [American] Independency." It was "therefore more than a common debt, it [wa]s a debt of honor," which could "never be considered as a Pension or gratuity, nor be cancelled until it [wa]s fairly discharged."[59]

Such arguments constituted powerful logic in the 1780s and 1790s, when the relationships between creditors and debtors were understood as social and moral bonds that were far stronger than mere legal obligation. Because such bonds depended ultimately upon personal faith and trust, defaulting debtors were viewed as more than unfortunate victims of bad times. They were moral failures, "violators of a code of trust and friendship who deserved to punished and imprisoned."[60] To citizens accustomed to this code of debtor–creditor relations, and to a mode of political representation predicated upon a legislative obligation to hear and resolve constituents' claims, the government's refusal to heed or satisfy the veterans' claims must have been little short of astonishing.

After 1783, however, the nation's legislators were involved in many larger issues of nation building, including western land policy, foreign relations, the location of a permanent seat for the Government, and the

---

[57] "An Act making provision for the debt of the United States," August 4, 1790, *AC* (1/2), pp. 2243–51. This legislation took effect in 1791.

[58] John Resch, *Suffering Soldiers: Revolutionary War Veterans, Moral Sentiment, and Political Culture in the Early Republic* (Amherst: University of Massachusetts Press, 2000), pp. 208–9.

[59] George Washington, "Circular Letter to the States" [copies sent to the thirteen state governors], June 8, 1783, in *The Writings of George Washington*, vol. 26, pp. 483–96, 492. Washington declared half-pay and commutation to be a "subject of public justice" (p. 493). The 1828 resolution of the issue of the devalued and/or lost commutation certificates is discussed later.

[60] Wood, "Interests and Disinterestedness," pp. 106–7.

revision of the Articles of Confederation. Military policies remained a vital concern, but to the dismay of the men petitioning for relief or for the resolution of pension and land claims, the question of what kind of military establishment was appropriate for the new Republic in peacetime had a much higher place on the congressional agenda than the problem of how to live up to past promises to veterans. The image of the citizen-soldier was resurgent in the minds of many Americans, who viewed the end of the war as a victory of popular rather than military virtue and continued to link any kind of militarism with the inevitable rise of corruption and tyranny. As Sarah Livingston Jay, John Jay's wife, put it as she toasted the official treaty of peace between Britain and the newly established United States of America, "May all our Citizens be Soldiers, and all our Soldiers Citizens!"[61]

Not surprisingly, the Continental Congress initially turned to the states and their militias for the nation's defense, formally resolving that standing armies in time of peace were "inconsistent with the principles of republican Governments, dangerous to the liberties of a free people, and generally converted into destructive engines for establishing despotism."[62] Despite the cultural resonance of the citizen-soldier ideal, though, it was becoming increasingly clear to most Americans, including members of Congress, that some sort of regular professional army was required to ensure internal order, overcome hostile Indians, prevent foreign encroachments, and establish the United States as a "respectable" member of the emerging international order. The dual military "system" of national and state forces that finally was confirmed by the U.S. Constitution and the Bill of Rights represented an ambiguous compromise between the citizen-soldier ideology, often associated with localistic, antistatist, anti-Federalist thinking, and the practical necessity driving the nationalistic, state-building Federalists. Because the Constitution failed to spell out a mechanism for enlistment or conscription,[63] the U.S. Government

---

[61] Royster, *Revolutionary People at War*, pp. 327–68; Kohn, *Eagle and Sword*, pp. 282–3; Sarah Livingston Jay, Paris [After 3 September 1783], cited in Linda K. Kerber, "May All Our Citizens Be Soldiers and All Our Soldiers Citizens: The Ambiguities of Female Citizenship in the New Nation," in *Women, Militarism, and War: Essays in History, Politics, and Social Theory*, ed. Jean Bethke Elshtain and Sheila Tobias (Savage, MD: Rowman & Littlefield, 1990), pp. 89–103, 89–90.

[62] Resolution of June 2, 1784, *JCC* (XXVII), pp. 518–24.

[63] Chambers, *To Raise an Army*, pp. 23–9; Kohn, *Eagle and Sword*, pp. 40–88; Cress, *Citizens in Arms*, pp. 75–109, 116–21; the Constitution of the United States, Article I, Sec. 8. Chambers argues that "an attempt to give the new central government such

was left to rely solely upon its fiscal powers to "raise and support Armies." As a consequence, military service was implicitly linked to compensation, rather than explicitly defined as a (male) obligation of citizenship, until the conscription legislation of the Civil War.[64]

In the early years of the Republic, compensation in the form of one-time enlistment bounties or wages paid to military personnel, or pensions provided to men *disabled* in the military, remained conceptually distinct from pensions granted merely as a consequence of service, particularly when such benefits were granted after the fact. Petitions from the Revolution's veterans nonetheless showered early U.S. Congresses. Some aging veterans pleaded for public assistance on the grounds of illness and infirmity, describing deprivation and mental anguish resulting from deepening poverty and inadequate disability pensions. Other individuals

authority would have been unprecedented and might well have led to popular rejection of the Constitution." Even the British Army did not draft, and although the Framers had said little about conscription in Philadelphia, Edmund Randolph of Virginia had warned his colleagues that "draughts stretch the strings of government too violently to be adopted." The Uniform Militia Act of May 8, 1792 [*AC* (2/1), pp. 1392–5] did require all "free able bodied white male citizen(s)" between the ages of eighteen and forty-five to arm themselves and enroll in local militia units that the national government could ostensibly have called up, but because implementation was left in the hands of state governments and the act did not provide for any effective means of presidential or congressional oversight, the measure was largely ineffectual. Not until the Civil War would the first national conscription law be enacted, to be denounced as "tyrannical, oppressive, and un-American, and as class legislation designed to draft the destitute and make it 'a rich man's war, but a poor man's fight.'" *To Raise an Army*, pp. 26, 41.

[64] The citizen-soldier ideology would continue to color the speech and actions of government leaders even after national-level military drafts were instituted. President Woodrow Wilson, for example, asserted that the World War I draft bill was "in no sense a conscription of the unwilling," but, rather a "selection from a nation which ha[d] volunteered in mass." Statement of May 18, 1917, in *The Papers of Woodrow Wilson*, ed. Arthur S. Link et al. (Princeton, NJ: Princeton University Press, 1966–), vol. 42, p. 181.

Kettner has observed that while certain general principles may have seemed clear after the Revolution – that citizenship should be consensual, uniform, without invidious gradations, and confer equal rights – "questions about the source, character, and effects of citizenship remained open well into the nineteenth century." *The Development of American Citizenship*, pp. 10, 213–333. These certainly included questions about the existence of *responsibilities* of citizenship, particularly military service. If the precise meaning of citizenship, in terms of responsibilities, was unclear for white property-owning yeoman farmers, it was even more ambiguous for women, free blacks, Native Americans, and even some young and/or propertyless males (Kerber, "May All Our Citizens Be Soldiers," pp. 97–8).

requested aid on the grounds that their wartime sacrifices had either caused them to be poor or impaired their ability to be self-sufficient.[65] Still others asked for remuneration as an expression of national honor and gratitude. Disgruntled Continental Army officers also argued that pensions were quasi-contractual obligations of the Government, and sent petitions demanding that Congress settle their equitable claims for benefits. All of these petitions, and the testimony sent to accompany them, revealed how veterans perceived their own worthiness and attested to their expectation that Congress would attend to their pleas.

Congress originally delegated the review of citizens' monetary claims to officials in the newly created, semi-independent Treasury Department. However, it retained final authority over their determination, even to the extent of denying federal court jurisdiction in situations where the United States was a defendant or respondent under the Judiciary Act of 1789. So deeply ingrained was the practice of legislative adjudication that the Supreme Court's challenge to congressional control over the resolution of claims in *Hayburn's Case*[66] and *Chisholm v. Georgia*[67] resulted in the immediate proposal and ratification of the Eleventh Amendment and Congress's creation of new procedures more firmly ensconcing its adjudicatory authority.[68] While some claims continued to be delegated to the Treasury Department and to other departments and nonjudicial bodies subject to final determination by Congress (to which appeals of the decisions of Treasury and other officials were brought), Congress

---

[65] Resch, *Suffering Soldiers*, pp. 85–6.

[66] 2 U.S. (2 Dall.) 409 (1792). Note that the issue in this case was specifically the administration of Federal disability pensions for veterans.

[67] 2 U.S. (2 Dall.) 419 (1793).

[68] Shinomura, "History of Claims," pp. 637–44; see also William M. Wiecek, "The Origin of the United States Court of Claims," *Administrative Law Review* 20 (1968): 387–93. As Shinomura notes, the Eleventh Amendment was introduced in Congress in 1793, adopted almost unanimously by the Third Congress in 1794, and apparently ratified by the requisite number of state legislatures by early 1795, though its passage was not officially certified until 1798. The amendment addressed the question of suits against the states but did not resolve the question, left open by the Court in *Hayburn's Case* and *Chisholm v. Georgia*, of whether the Constitution vested the authority to determine claims in the judiciary or Congress. A new judicial model of claims determination rooted in a new theory of the separation of powers was emerging, but it stood at odds with long-standing practice, the First Amendment's right of petition, and Article I Section 9's injunction that money be drawn from the U.S. Treasury only "in Consequence of Appropriations made by Law" (that is, as the result of an exercise of congressional authority).

instituted mechanisms for handling claims internally. The House established a standing Committee of Claims in November 1794, whose function it was

to take into consideration all such petitions and matters or things touching claims or demands on the United States, as sh[ould] be presented, or sh[ould] or m[ight] come into question, and be referred to them by the House, and to report their opinion thereupon, together with such propositions for relief therein, as to them sh[ould] seem expedient.[69]

The creation of this committee reflected the belief that it was "the peculiar province of the Representatives, immediately chosen by the people, to superintend the contributions and distributions of all public moneys."[70] As time passed and the volume of claims presented to Congress increased, the House expanded its machinery for the administration of justice, establishing standing committees charged with particular categories of claims, including a Committee on Public Lands in 1805, a Committee on Pensions and Revolutionary Claims in 1813, and a Committee on Private Land Claims in 1816. Doubtless aware of their vital role in the House, where the norms of specialization and deference were becoming well established,[71] the Senate established its first standing committees in 1816, starting with a Committee of Claims and a Committee on Public Lands.[72]

Congress initially attempted to act on all of the petitions and claims it was presented with, typically by referring them to select committees or to the standing committees appropriate to their consideration. However, the petitions and claims of the Revolution's many veterans were not easily settled. Numerous and diverse, they continued to pour in to Congress in

---

[69] *H. Journal*, Third Cong., 2nd sess. (Washington, DC: Gales & Seaton, 1826), p. 229.

[70] Rep. William Giles, *Annals of Congress*, 3rd Cong., 1st sess., 1794, cited in Joseph Cooper, *The Origins of the Standing Committees and the Development of the Modern House* (Houston: Rice University Press, 1970), p. 35.

[71] Cooper states that by the late 1820s, these norms were treated as simple axioms. Standing committees were seen as units that "took a general or impartial view, possessed intimate knowledge of their subject areas, and proceeded in a deliberate manner with concern for consistency, precision, and past experience.... [I]t became common for members to refer to the standing committees as 'tribunals,' i.e., to analogize committee decision making and judicial decision making." As one member of the Twentieth Congress put it, the House's ability to get through its agenda depended upon the "wisdom, justice and impartiality" of its committees. *Origins of the Standing Committees*, pp. 52–5, cited phrases on pp. 55, 53.

[72] Elaine K. Swift, *The Making of an American Senate: Reconstitutive Change in Congress, 1787–1841* (Ann Arbor: University of Michigan Press, 1996), pp. 132–3.

the early decades of the nineteenth century, even as a second war for independence was fought and won. Veterans' petitions and claims containing need-based arguments often received the response that "Congress cannot undertake the support of paupers merely because they may have been at some point engaged in the public service."[73] The Committee of Claims gradually became more sensitive to the legalistic, rights-based argument that was beginning to be articulated by the Revolution's officers. However, the House repeatedly ignored its committee's findings to maintain that no unfulfilled contractual obligation existed between the Government and the officers, because they had freely accepted (and even advocated) the commutation of their pensions into lump-sum payments in 1783. Moreover, Congress had settled the Revolution's outstanding public debts in 1790.[74]

Thus it was that in late 1817, President James Monroe, himself a former Revolutionary officer, proposed a solution to the problem of veterans' demands in the form of a new program of service pensions for surviving officers and soldiers of the Continental Army. The condition of the nation, Monroe told the newly assembled Fifteenth Congress in his first annual message, was exceptional. Never before had Americans had so much to congratulate themselves upon. The "abundant fruits of the earth" had filled the nation with plenty; an "extensive and profitable commerce" had "greatly augmented our revenue"; public credit had "attained an extraordinary elevation"; and defense preparations were "advancing, under a well digested system, with all the despatch which so important a work w[ould] admit." Moreover, the nation's "free Government, founded on the interest and affections of the people," had "gained, and [was] daily gaining strength," and "local jealousies" were "rapidly yielding to more generous, enlarged, and enlightened view of national policy."[75] "Never," as Monroe had proclaimed in his inaugural address nine months earlier, "[ha]d a government commence[d] under auspices so favorable, nor ever was success so complete."[76] In Monroe's view, it was the service of the officers and soldiers of the Revolutionary Army that had "so eminently

---

[73] Committee of Claims to John Montgomery of Ohio, petitioner, 1816, cited in Resch, *Suffering Soldiers*, p. 87.

[74] Laura S. Jensen, "The Early American Origins of Entitlements," *Studies in American Political Development* 10 (1996): 360–404, 393–5; Resch, *Suffering Soldiers*, pp. 87–8. The officers' "legal" claim and its resolution is discussed further later on.

[75] *AC* (15/1), p. 12, Dec. 2, 1817.

[76] "Inaugural Address of James Monroe, President of the United States," March 4, 1817, *American State Papers, Class I, Foreign Relations*, vol. 4, ed. Walter Lowrie and Walter S.

contributed" to the laying of the nation's foundation, yet some of those remaining veterans were "reduced to indigence, and even to real distress." It would "do honor to their country to provide for them," for such "very meritorious citizens" had "a claim on the gratitude of their country." The president urged Congress to enact a pension program immediately, before the opportunity to aid the Continental Army veterans was forever lost, arguing that so much time had already passed "that the number to be benefitted by any provision which m[ight] be made, w[ould] not be great."[77] The Revolution had, after all, ended some three and a half decades earlier.

The House of Representatives was swift to act favorably, and unanimously, upon Monroe's recommendation. The select committee to which his proposal concerning the "surviving Revolutionary patriots" had been referred, all but one of whose members had served as Revolutionary officers like the president, reported back with a bill in a mere ten days. It proposed that "every commissioned and non-commissioned officer, musician, or soldier" who had "served in the revolutionary war" before the September 1783 treaty of peace with Great Britain, *and* who was "reduced to indigence," or "by age, sickness, or other cause rendered incapable to procure subsistence by manual labor," should become entitled to receive half of the monthly pay allowed to his grade for the remainder of his life from the U.S. Government.[78] The bill was essentially universal in its plan to entitle virtually all poor, aged Revolutionary veterans to Federal assistance. Potentially, it would provide a life pension "to every superannuated man who ever carried a musket against the British."[79]

Most of the House's deliberation revolved around the scope of the pension bill rather than the idea of creating a new pension program, which appeared to be an almost forgone conclusion as the nation's Revolutionary patriots were eulogized by their representatives. The introduction of the pension bill alone was hailed as "gratifying evidence of the re-connexion of public feeling with the principles of the Revolution."

Franklin (Washington, DC: Gales and Seaton, 1834) [hereafter *ASP, Foreign Relations*], pp. 126–9, 129.

[77] *AC* (15/1), p. 19, Dec. 2, 1817.

[78] H.R. 8, "A Bill to provide for certain surviving officers and soldiers of the revolutionary army," *Bills and Resolutions of the House of Representatives and the Senate* (Washington, DC: Library of Congress, 1964), (15/1), 1817–18; *AC* (15/1), p. 446, Dec. 12, 1817. The bill contained the caveat that no pension given to a commissioned officer would exceed the half-pay of a lieutenant-colonel.

[79] Resch, *Suffering Soldiers*, p. 101.

House members generally agreed that the war's "heroes of liberty, from whose fortitude and valor the present blessings of our country have, in a great measure, resulted, [we]re really entitled to the gratitude and consideration of the Government."[80] Though a few members felt that pensions should be given only to those who had served for a significant length of time, most maintained that a more "liberal spirit should prevail." Some even argued for the establishment of pensions for all Revolutionary veterans based upon service only, rather than service coupled with indigence. As George Strother of Virginia vehemently declared, "all who contributed to build up our magnificent political fabric" should be "embraced in the wide circle of gratitude."[81] The bill passed without division in the House on December 24, 1817, having been amended to provide a pension of $8 per month to every soldier and $20 per month to every officer who had served in the Revolutionary War in any of the regiments or navies raised by either Congress or the states, provided that they were "reduced to indigence and incapable of procuring subsistence."[82]

Public support for the inclusive House bill was broad and bipartisan, and its passage was celebrated widely. Newspaper editorials emphasized that it was more than time to support the nation's aging soldiers, whose exertions had secured the United States' existence. The *Federal Republican and Baltimore Telegraph* framed the issue rhetorically, asking, "If a patriot when dead deserves a marble monument at the expense of his country, how much more does he deserve during life?" However festive, the "paltry panegyrics" of Fourth of July remembrances were hardly sufficient to express the nation's gratitude to the "poor, emaciated, hoary veterans" who had braved death in the battlefield. This was the moment for the nation to demonstrate some "timely benevolence," so that history would attest that the country had "not entirely lost [its] sense of justice, honor and humanity."[83]

---

[80] *AC* (15/1), pp. 497 and 510, Dec. 22, 24, 1817, remarks of George Strother of Virginia and Richard Johnson of Kentucky, respectively.

[81] *AC* (15/1), pp. 491–9, 498–9, Dec. 19, 22, 24, 1817 (emphasis added). Strother was reacting against Representative William Henry Harrison's proposal to limit pensions to Continental Army veterans who had served for at least three years or until the end of the war, reviving the historic divide between regulars and the militia.

[82] H.R. 8, SEN 15A-C1, Records of the U.S. Senate, Bills and Amendments, First Session, National Archives, Washington, DC.

[83] *Federal Republican and Baltimore Telegraph*, 30 December 1817 and 6 February 1818; *Boston Columbian Centinel*, 20 December 1817; and *Philadelphia Aurora*, 27 December 1817, all cited in Resch, *Suffering Soldiers*, pp. 101, 102, 106.

The urge to grant national-level pensions to Revolutionary veterans in 1817–18 was emblematic of an age in which Americans anxiously struggled to reconcile the liberal and republican values of their Revolutionary heritage and to devise ways to shore up civic virtue against the erosion of rapid societal change. As early as 1789, historian David Ramsay had felt compelled to conclude his pioneering account of the Revolution and the founding of constitutional government with the exhortation that his fellow citizens should "cherish and reward" those men who had left their private concerns to work in the public interest, so as to "rescue citizens and rulers of republics, from the common and too often merited charge of ingratitude."[84] From the 1780s to the eve of the War of 1812, the expansion and commercialization of society had elicited patterns of behavior seemingly at odds with an American ideology of "disinterestedness" emphasizing the subordination of individual preferences to the public good.[85] By the beginning of the second war for independence, many had begun to doubt the viability of the American experiment as citizens succumbed to opportunities for self-interested behavior, scrambling for material prosperity in a developing capitalist market economy. America's second, decisive victory over British power, however, fostered a resurgence of national self-confidence that allayed fears that the United States could not survive as a virtuous commercial republic[86] and brought about an awakening of historical consciousness.[87] Presidential and congressional

---

[84] *History of the American Revolution* (Philadelphia, 1789), II, p. 355, cited in Fred Somkin, *Unquiet Eagle: Memory and Desire in the Idea of American Freedom, 1815–1860* (Ithaca: NY: Cornell University Press, 1967), p. 137

[85] See Wood, "Interests and Disinterestedness," and Jean M. Yarbrough, *American Virtues: Thomas Jefferson on the Character of a Free People* (Lawrence: University Press of Kansas, 1998), pp. 105, 143–4, 146.

[86] Jean V. Matthews, *Toward a New Society: American Thought and Culture, 1800–1830* (Boston: Twayne Publishers, 1991), pp. 5–6; see also Somkin, *Unquiet Eagle*, pp. 11–54.

[87] Congress initiated the systematic publication of its records (beyond the two chambers' journals) in 1817, and in 1818 authorized the printing of 1,000 copies of the journal of the Constitutional Convention of 1787, which previously had been held secret. Congress also, in the last weeks of the Madison administration in early 1817, authorized the president to commission four paintings from John Trumbull commemorating the most important events of the Revolution. Pauline Maier, *American Scripture: Making the Declaration of Independence* (New York: Alfred A. Knopf, 1997), pp. 175–8; Noble E. Cunningham, Jr., *The Presidency of James Monroe* (Lawrence: University Press of Kansas, 1996), pp. 186–7.
      Maier asserts that the awakening of this historical consciousness began after 1815 and the Treaty of Ghent, emphasizing John Adams's January 1817 observation that his countrymen lacked any "disposition to celebrate or remember, or even Curiosity to enquire into the Characters, Actions, or Events of the Revolution." Resch, by contrast, locates a

reconsideration of the fate of America's surviving Revolutionary patriots was almost natural in a society where an outpouring of paintings, historical tracts, public monuments, and literary works like Parson Weems's best-selling biography of George Washington revived the potent symbolism of the founding and "held up Revolutionary heroes as models of selflessness and public spirit."[88] What better than a program of pensions for the nation's original patriots to constitute tangible evidence of a special, enlightened, effectively governed people, especially given an extraordinary U.S. Treasury surplus?[89]

The pension proposal also was put forth at a time when the idea of public aid for the poor had become deeply ingrained in American culture, although opponents of public assistance worried that it fostered the attitude that relief was a right among the poor. Many encouraged a shift in social provision away from local aid toward more "efficient" institutional arrangements at the county and state levels of government, and some public and private welfare institutions had begun to appeal to the U.S. Government for support. Scarcely more than a year after the new Revolutionary pension program was proposed, for example, Congress granted the Connecticut Asylum for the Deaf and Dumb, a private institution, 23,000 acres of public land that it would sell for approximately $300,000.[90] The Revolutionary pension plan was nonetheless novel in its proposal to require the national government to provide *individual-level*

---

new historical consciousness in the early years of the nineteenth century, noting a rise of interest in the heroes of the Revolution, the publication of revisionist histories portraying the Continental Army as a republican institution, and the publication of sentimental stories about aged Revolutionary veterans. According to Resch, the "image of the suffering soldier" became so powerful by 1818 that it both transformed American political culture and justified the enactment of a new pension program. Although this analysis maintains that there were powerful political and institutional imperatives driving the passage of the pension bill in addition to moral sentiment, Resch must be credited for being the first scholar since Glasson to emphasize the importance of Revolutionary War pensions as national-level entitlements. Adams to John Trumbull, 1 January 1817, cited in Maier, *American Scripture*, p. 175; Resch, *Suffering Soldiers*, pp. 71–85. See also Resch, "Federal Welfare for Revolutionary War Veterans," *Social Service Review* 56 (1982): 171–95; and "Politics and Public Culture: The Revolutionary War Pension Act of 1818," *Journal of the Early Republic* 8 (1988): 139–58.

[88] Matthews, *Toward a New Society*, p. 21.

[89] As Rogers Smith has observed, "political elites must find ways to persuade the people they aspire to govern that they are a 'people' if effective governance is to be achieved." *Civic Ideals*, p. 9.

[90] Walter Trattner, *From Poor Law to Welfare State: A History of Social Welfare in America*, 3rd ed. (New York: Free Press, 1984), pp. 53–63.

monetary benefits derived from the redistribution of national tax revenues. Such a scheme was inherently more conflictual than giveaways of "public" lands, variously acquired from Native Americans and/or other nations, to institutions and individual citizens.[91]

The arguments made by Senate pension advocates in early 1818 effectively amplified those put forward in the House. Referring to the surplus, Senator Robert Goldsborough of Maryland reasoned that because the nation was "opulent, powerful, and prosperous," it had both the ability and the obligation to uphold the principles of justice and gratitude by remunerating those few remaining "worthy and indigent men" who, "by their services and sufferings, ha[d] rendered themselves most dear to our recollections." Goldsborough admitted that none of the Revolutionary veterans had "any strict claim in law" to government benefits, but he insisted that a case could be made to authorize the country to reward men "justly entitled to [its] grateful remembrance." Moreover, they should be entitled to receive Federal pension benefits without having to undergo the humiliation of a degrading means test, which would attach the stigma of pauperism to service pensions, transforming the nation's intended benevolence into "polluted bounty." Goldsborough urged his congressional colleagues to admit that beyond the "high and solemn duty" incumbent upon them to compensate the veterans, there were also motives of "national feeling and national character" at issue that they could not disregard. Would they allow the history of the United States to "add another instance for those with whom the 'ingratitude of Republics' is a maxim?"[92]

Rhetoric about justice and gratitude aside, the version of the pension bill that had emerged from the Senate Committee on Military Affairs differed significantly from the House version in that it restricted pension

---

[91] Early American land entitlements are discussed in Chapters 4 and 5.

[92] Remarks of Robert Goldsborough of Maryland, *AC* (15/1), pp. 191–8, Feb. 12, 1818. Goldsborough addressed his colleagues by pointedly asking the president of the Senate, "Shall it be said, sir, that the brave officers and soldiers of the Revolution were abandoned by us in their advanced age and infirmities, to the precarious offerings of public charity; to the protection of the almshouse, and such receptacles of human wretchedness, whilst the Treasury of the country is ample to relieve them? . . . Shall the veterans of the Army of Independence, whose wants and infirmities arise from having devoted the best portion of their lives to the service of their country, now languish in penury, neglected by that country? Feeling as I do upon this occasion, sir, I exult in the opportunity which is this day presented me, of doing honor to my country by doing justice to her brave defenders; and I do not now appeal to the cold and calculating policy of the politician, but to the generous hearts that are near me. . . ." (p. 197).

eligibility to veterans of Continental forces – and among them, only to those men who had served for a minimum of three years or until the end of the Revolution. There was little doubt that many veterans who had fought in the war were aged, poverty-stricken, and in need of assistance. The issue, however, was whether the nation should provide pensions to all veterans or economize and extend them only to those veterans who, in Congress's opinion, had served the longest and suffered the most. Thus, in advocating passage of the Senate bill, Goldsborough maintained that it was not his purpose "to detract from the merits of any." It was just that, if there was "any one definite class of men *more* meritorious than another . . . who, by their services and sufferings, ha[d] rendered themselves *most* dear to our recollections, and *most* worthy of our gratitude, they were the officers and soldiers of the Revolutionary Army." In Goldsborough's opinion, there was simply "no comparison between the sufferings of these men" and the men of the militia, who typically had served close to home, where they were "plentifully fed and comfortably lodged at night," and able during the day to attend to family and domestic concerns while they were not busy defending their neighborhoods. The Continental Army, by contrast, had traveled widely, and fought and bled for the nation at large. "It was for the country they encountered all their hardships, and it is from the national Treasury [that] they ought to be reimbursed."[93]

Many supported the Senate's exclusionary version of the pension bill. To a small group of senators, however, the pension proposal was "an entire departure from any principle heretofore established in th[e] country."[94] Although they knew that their position was decidedly in the minority, Nathaniel Macon of North Carolina, a former Continental Army officer, and William Smith of South Carolina vehemently condemned all of their colleagues' justifications for the pension scheme in logic echoing the anticommutation protest of 1783. Their objections demonstrated deep concern over Congress's turn toward programmatic entitlement, particularly selective programmatic entitlement, as a policy device. They recognized that societal divisions and inequities would inevitably result from the Government's creation of arbitrary legal boundaries separating deserving and undeserving citizens. The redistributive obligations imposed by the proposed legislation were ominous not simply because they would require the payment of taxes. More importantly, Smith and Macon could not understand how the distribution of national revenues to a select group of

---

93 *AC* (15/1), pp. 191, 196, Feb. 12, 1818 (emphasis added).
94 Remarks of Nathaniel Macon of North Carolina, *AC* (15/1), p. 158, Jan. 29, 1818.

citizens could be justified, especially when some of the men who were to be excluded from receiving benefits seemed essentially similar to those who were to become entitled. As Representative Strother had suggested in the House debate, the bill's intent to bar some veterans of the Revolution from receiving pensions was incomprehensible and unprincipled if veteran status was to be the formal basis of deservingness.[95] So, too, was its lack of attention to the nation's nonmilitary poor if poverty was the criterion motivating congressional generosity. Rufus King's amendment attempting to revive the Continental Congress's original promise of pension benefits to Army officers alone was simply "language not known to our Constitution . . . repugnant to the principles of our Government, and at war with good sense and public justice." How, Smith asked, could the "benevolence, sympathy, and gratitude" supposedly prompting the pension bill "draw a line between the officer and the soldier, when both ha[d] served their country, and both [we]re indigent"? And how, for that matter, could the members of Congress "believe the public mind [wa]s prepared to pay a tax to maintain a pension system, because it [wa]s said that those officers cannot submit to any industrious pursuits for a living"? There existed "thousands of poor" who were unable to work and who demanded Congress's attention "in an equal degree." Was Congress prepared to put all of the nation's poor citizens on the pension list? Smith declared himself "opposed to both the bill and [King's] amendment in any form in which they could be presented," because "no particular merit could be ascribed to any particular portion of the people of the United States, for services rendered during the Revolutionary war, in exclusion to any other portion who espoused that cause." Given the indispensable efforts and sacrifices of the militia and of other men, widows, and orphans north and south, the notion that the country was "exclusively" indebted to the Continental Army was patently false.[96]

---

[95] Questioning Harrison's proposal to exclude the militia, Strother had asked: "Why shall this invidious distinction be drawn in our legislative provisions?" He went on to declare the length of time of a veteran's Army service a "criterion of merit equally fallacious and unjust." *AC* (15/1), p. 498, Dec. 22, 1817.

[96] Remarks of William Smith of South Carolina, *AC* (15/1), pp. 140–7, Jan. 29, 1818. Macon extrapolated: "If the pensions are to be given, because the army deserved well of the country, and some of them are now poor," he asked, "would it not follow that if any members of the Congress . . . were now alive and poor, that they too, for the same cause, ought to have a pension?" It was, he thought, "difficult to give a reason for one, which would not apply as forcibly to the other" (same date, pp. 153–7). Senator James Barbour of Virginia also argued at length about the "impossibility" of providing for *all* veterans

Smith and Macon found their colleagues' arguments eliding benevolence and justice similarly specious. Their understanding of justice in both theoretical and legal terms made the notion of a "debt" of gratitude preposterous.[97] Macon pointed out that "if justice required that the bill should pass, neither the condition of the Treasury nor the [small] number [of veterans] to be provided for" – policy-analytic "facts" repeatedly offered in support of the bill – "ought to be taken into consideration."[98] Macon also, like Smith, found justice completely lacking in the legislation's intent to benefit the Army at the expense of other citizens of arguably equal merit. To "tax th[o]se people to give a pension to any, because they were in the regular army," seemed like "taxing the bones of the brave and the ashes of distress." At the end of the war, the officers had received five years' full pay, and both officers and soldiers had obtained land from the United States. Even if the Continental troops had been paid in certificates that had depreciated, so had the currency depreciated, which was "a national calamity, from which no one was exempt."[99] In addition to the commuted pay and land grants received by

and the "impracticability of discriminating between the different classes provided for," and thus moved an indefinite postponement of the bill (p. 140, same date, exact remarks not recorded). Supported only by his own vote and those of Smith and Macon, the motion to postpone failed in a vote of 30 to 3 (p. 200, Feb. 13, 1818).

These arguments about the illegitimacy of the pension proposal may have been partially animated by what Howard Gillman has termed the "master principle" of legality in nineteenth-century America: namely, the principle that legislation was valid only if it promoted the general welfare as opposed to the special interests of particular groups and classes. Much more research would need to be done on national-level legislative behavior to demonstrate that this was the case, however, especially given Congress's central role in determining legality (*not* the federal courts') in matters involving claims against the U.S. Treasury during the late eighteenth and nineteenth centuries. Gillman, *The Constitution Besieged: The Rise and Demise of Lochner Era Police Powers Jurisprudence* (Durham, NC: Duke University Press, 1993).

97 The remarks of Representative John Forsyth of Georgia during the House consideration of the pension bill illuminated this perspective. Although Forsyth generally favored the passage of pension legislation, he felt compelled to protest the assertions of other House members that needy veterans had "claims upon the justice of the country for pecuniary assistance." In his opinion, both the financial and moral obligations of the nation had been satisfied through commuted half-pay and the fact that the veterans had long been "the peculiar objects of the patronage of the Government, and of the people's love." Forsyth was disposed to "vote for the bill without scanning too curiously the motives of his conduct," for it was "enough for him to know, that there were men, the recollection of whose services always inspired the most grateful emotions," but he nonetheless stated: "We owe the Revolutionary officers no debt." *AC* (15/1), p. 506, Dec. 23, 1817.

98 Remarks of Nathaniel Macon of North Carolina, *AC* (15/1), p. 159, Jan. 29, 1818.

99 *AC* (15/1), pp. 155–6; see also the remarks of Smith, pp. 141–2, 148.

the troops, "there ha[d] not been an office of honor or profit in the gift of the United States, or any individual State, which ha[d] not been filled by a Continental officer, if he asked for it." Moreover, the government had given to "every officer and soldier who ha[d] applied, a pension for life, if he had been wounded or disabled in the public service." Smith dismissed concern over a possible reproach of "ingratitude" by European nations by asking, "what is it that they have not said to reproach us"? America did not suffer by comparison with Europe in its treatment of its veterans. It was the pensioner who complained of ingratitude, and not the farmer and mechanic who paid the tax.[100]

Finally, Smith and Macon expressed fear about the pension legislation's impact as a policy precedent. Clearly, if Congress could circumvent constitutional limits upon its authority to choose *one* subset of citizens, identify them as uniquely deserving, and endow them with rights to public benefits, it could do the same for others. Smith took exception to Congress's intended use of the spending power to create programmatic benefits by noting that one of America's primary reasons for shaking off the British government was precisely "to get rid of pensions and placemen, and the power of their Parliament." Of "what avail is the Constitution," Smith asked, "if [legislative] precedent is to govern? Once establish a precedent, and you have no control over Congress but the discretion of its members; and, like the British Parliament, it will soon become omnipotent." Opponents of the current pension bill might be told that the country could never have another Revolutionary War, but, as Macon charged, it did "not require the gift of prophecy to foretel that thirty or forty years hence, as much may be said in favor of the army engaged in the second war for independence, as we have now heard about the first."[101]

Despite the objections voiced by Smith and Macon as well as by Virginian James Barbour, an amended Revolutionary veterans' pension

---

[100] *AC* (15/1), pp. 147–8.

[101] *AC* (15/1), pp. 148–9 (Smith), 157 (Macon). Macon said he regretted that he could not vote for the service pension legislation recommended to Congress by Monroe, a "Revolutionary character," but noted that his regret would have been much greater "if all the preceding Presidents had not also been Revolutionary characters," and he did not recollect that any of them had made a similar recommendation, including George Washington, who was "as much attached to the Army as any man in the nation" (p. 159). Note that Congress had enacted a cost of living adjustment for disabled veterans in 1816 and extended benefits to widows and orphans of deceased members of the Navy and War of 1812 soldiers in 1813, 1814, and 1816. Veterans of the War of 1812 were already beginning to lobby for benefits when the Act of 1818 was passed, but service pensions were not established for them by Congress until 1871.

bill was passed by a large majority of the Senate.[102] The final compromise version that became law on March 18, 1818, limited benefits to former Continentals, omitting men who had served in the militia, but shortened the period of service required for eligibility. It provided that all men who had served in the nation's Army or Navy until the end of the Revolutionary War, or for a term of at least nine months at any period during that war, who were still resident citizens of the United States, and who were or thereafter would become, by reason of their "reduced circumstances in life, ... in need of assistance from [their] country for support," would be entitled to receive a pension equal to $20 per month for life for officers and $8 per month for life for noncommissioned officers, musicians, mariners, marines, or soldiers. Benefits were contingent upon a veteran's making a declaration of need to a district judge of the United States or before any judge or court of record of the state, county, or territory in which he resided. Judges were required to certify and transmit the record of the veteran's testimony and the proceedings thereon to the secretary of war, who was delegated final authority in the determination of pension claims. No one would be entitled to the provisions of the act until he had relinquished his claim to any disability pension or pension allowed him by the United States in private legislation, but Federal benefits otherwise would commence to be payed from the date of the applicant's declaration of need.[103]

The Fifteenth Congress had achieved what Senator Goldsborough had called its "great object." Yet it remained to be seen whether all of its members would come to judge, as Goldsborough had predicted, that they had "discharged a great duty" or that "every heart w[ould] bear testimony to the truth of that sublime and heartfelt precept – that it is better to give than to receive." In the eyes of Senator Smith, Congress had invoked "the curse of a nation."[104]

---

[102] The vote on February 26, 1818, was 23 to 8. The eight recorded nays came from Senators Smith, Macon, Barbour, Dickerson (New Jersey), Morrow (Ohio), Taylor (Indiana), and Lacock and Roberts (Pennsylvania).

[103] "An Act to provide for certain persons engaged in the land and naval service of the United States, in the Revolutionary war," approved March 18, 1818, *AC* (15/1), pp. 2518–19. The law used the word "entitled," along with male pronouns, to refer to its patriot beneficiaries. Its gender exclusivity is discussed later. See also Resch, "Federal Welfare for Revolutionary War Veterans," for a demographic analysis of the 1818 pension program's claimants and their households.

[104] *AC* (15/1): Goldsborough, p. 199, Feb. 12, 1818; Smith, p. 150, Jan. 29, 1818.

3

Revolutionary Policies

Here is one fact not to be controverted: if you can give a pension to one man you can give it to another, without regard to his character.... This will be the beginning of a military pension system that posterity may regret.

Senator William Smith, 1818[1]

The disability pensions established by the First U.S. Congress and the service pensions for indigent veterans of the Continental Army and Navy established by the Fifteenth Congress were the first Federal entitlements to cash income assistance. For eligible veterans, they created positive, substantive, programmatic rights to individual-level public benefits. Men who had served in the Army or Navy but did not qualify did not, of course, acquire such rights. Nor did veterans of militia service or many other citizens of the United States.

The enactment of the Pension Act of 1818, with its fusion of the service pension concept and the concept of public assistance for the aged poor, was an extremely significant act of Federal domestic policymaking. Most obviously, it established the precedent from which an enormous system of American military service-related benefits directly evolved. Less than a month after the act's passage, a resolution was introduced in the House of Representatives urging supplementary legislation for "rewarding such meritorious officers and soldiers of the Revolution (as well of the militia as the regular army) as [were] not ... embraced within the provisions of the act [just] passed," because many "were illy paid; and many, though not reduced in their circumstances, ha[d] strong claims on the justice and

[1] *Annals of Congress*, 15th Cong., 1st sess. (Washington, DC: Gales and Seaton, 1834–) [hereafter *AC* (15/1)], p. 149, Jan. 29, 1818.

gratitude of their country."[2] Although it took until 1832 for pensions to be established for most Revolutionary veterans without the qualification of indigence, and until 1836 for the passage of general legislation providing pensions for the widows of Revolutionary officers and soldiers, Congress had resolutely set forth upon the path to establishing benefits for those citizens serving in, or related to those serving in, the nation's military forces of the future.[3]

Even more importantly, these benefits foreshadowed the future of American social policy by establishing the *programmatic entitlement of groups of citizens* as the device that eventually would be relied upon to address a wide variety of policy problems and goals. As Senators Smith and Macon and their colleagues clearly understood as the Fifteenth Congress "qualified" certain veterans for public benefits, entitlements operate by creating legal categories based upon the possession of chosen – not intrinsic – criteria of deservingness. In its final form, the 1818 Pension Act attributed desert to a select group of individuals who could demonstrate nine months' service in the Continental Army or Navy (or service until the end of the war), old age, financial need, and U.S. citizenship

[2] Resolution of Representative John Holmes of Massachusetts, *AC* (15/1), p. 1698, Apr. 9, 1818. Holmes's introduction of the resolution provides insight into the House's legislative strategy with respect to the March pension bill. After "it was so severely opposed and criticised" in the Senate and returned to the House with amendments, "its friends feared to propose any alterations, lest, on a disagreement between the two Houses, the bill should be lost. It was however expected, that from applications under the act, cases would be developed which would require a supplementary act." Holmes was not sanguine that the legislation would pass during the remainder of that session of Congress, but hoped progress would occur in the next, when he promised to show the House "that many not included in the late act [we]re entitled to their country's consideration."

[3] The fact that Revolutionary pensions were consistently mentioned in contemporary newspapers as well as in the circular letters sent by the members of the Fifteenth Congress to their constituents attests to their rank, along with internal improvements, the public debt, the reduction of the Army, the Seminole War, the Bank of the United States, and slavery and the admission of Missouri, as one of the most important national issues of 1817–19. Five of the seven known circulars written at the end of the Fifteenth Congress's first session announced the enactment of the Revolutionary service pensions. This suggests the inadequacy of James Sterling Young's description of a "government at a distance and out of sight," headed by a president with a domestic policy record "barren of any evidence of presidential leadership," whose governance during the "era of good feelings" generated "not one memorable policy controversy at Washington that aroused significant citizen interest outside the capital." *Circular Letters of Congressmen to Their Constituents 1789–1829*, ed. Noble E. Cunningham, Jr. (Chapel Hill: University of North Carolina Press, 1978, 3 vols.), vol. 3, pp. 1015–45; Young, *The Washington Community 1800–1828* (New York: Columbia University Press, 1966), pp. 160, 186–7. See also Cunningham, *The Process of Government under Jefferson* (Princeton, NJ: Princeton University Press, 1978), p. 300, n. 28.

and residency. As the debate in both the House and the Senate amply demonstrated, however, many other criteria or combinations of criteria were within the realm of the possible for constructing the virtuous patriot in law. Many believed that service in the militia should count if military service was to become a basis for entitlement, for it was the militia who had fought for the nation's independence at Lexington and Concord before the Continental Army existed and who had comprised the troops that had provided essential military forces in the South. Other citizens "engaged in other spheres, and employed in other occupations," had also been as essential and indispensable to victory as the Army. This was why Senator Smith and some of his colleagues remained unalterably opposed as a matter of principle to the selective entitlement of a "particular portion" or category of U.S. citizens of "particular merit" or desert, no matter how such a category was defined.[4] To allow that kind of discretionary action would be to encourage the growth of arbitrary power within the Federal Government.

We can only wonder whether the objections of Senators Smith, Macon, and Barbour would have been as intense if the Senate version of the pension bill had been as inclusive as the House's.[5] The House bill would have entitled almost all aged, poor, and/or infirm veterans who had fought for the United States in the Revolution to pensions, including members of the militia, effectively according equal merit to all. Avoiding rates overtly tied to the contentious half-pay principle, the House version of the bill dissociated itself from the Army officer corps' taint of self-interest and elitism. By setting its pension rates equal to those paid to disabled veterans, the House bill also effectively transformed indigence or the inability to be self-supporting into a service-related disability, validating the arguments of petitioning veterans who claimed that their poverty and infirmities stemmed at least in part from military service.[6]

In enacting the 1818 Pension Law, most of the members of the Fifteenth Congress seem to have separated specific arguments about the new pension program's selectivity from general arguments over the wisdom of statutory entitlement per se. Adopting a *programmatic* approach to assuaging the problems and discontents of many of the nation's

---

[4] *AC* (15/1), pp. 142–7, Jan. 29, 1818.

[5] John Resch has also made this observation. *Suffering Soldiers: Revolutionary War Veterans, Moral Sentiment, and Political Culture in the Early Republic* (Amherst: University of Massachusetts Press, 2000), pp. 111–12.

[6] Resch, *Suffering Soldiers*, pp. 105–6.

15 Cong.
16th. 3 L

March 26 agreed to

[155]

IN SENATE

OF

THE UNITED STATES,

MARCH 24, 1818.

The Committee on Pensions, to whom was referred the petition of Alexander Levie,

REPORT:

That your committee have examined the case of the petitioner. He states that he is poor, and prays to be placed on the pension list, in consequence of his services as a soldier in the revolutionary war, and also asks for the arrearages of pay, which he says is due him. The committee are of opinion that the act of Congress passed at their present session, entitled " An act to provide for certain persons engaged in the land and naval service of the United States in the revolutionary war," will, upon proper proof, give the relief asked for by the petitioner, so far as regards pension; and that the existing laws provide for the payment of arrearages of pay due the soldiers of the revolutionary war. The following resolution is, therefore, submitted:

Resolved, That the petitioner have leave to withdraw his petition.

X except cases barred by the Statute of limitations

FIGURE 3.1. An 1818 report of the Senate Committee on Pensions, informing Alexander Levie that he should withdraw his petition for aid and apply for a veterans' pension under the program established days earlier by the Pension Act of March 18, 1818. Courtesy of the National Archives and Records Administration, Records of the U.S. Senate.

surviving patriots evidently appeared more fair and efficient to a majority of Congress than adjudicating the claims of veterans on a case-by-case basis, which was what Congress had been doing since the end of the Revolution in response to the petitions and memorials of aggrieved individuals and groups[7] (Figure 3.1). The debate over the 1818 pension

---

[7] Immediately after the 1818 Pension Act was enacted, individuals approaching Congress for aid were told to withdraw their petitions and seek relief by applying to the pension program. See, for example, Congress's response to the petition of Alexander Levie (Figure 3.1).

bill manifested the tension inherent in America's original constitutional regime, in which certain rights were simultaneously binding upon the government and dependent upon the government's balancing of public and private ends.[8] Admitting the veterans' lack of a "strictly legal" claim, pension advocates framed their arguments in terms of a "debt of gratitude." They then proposed that an act of beneficence would be just and in the national interest if legislation extending the bounty and generosity of the nation to its veterans could be enacted yet appropriately constrained. Hence the entitlement program that finally was established only for certain poor, surviving veterans of the Revolution. In one fell swoop, the Pension Act of 1818 categorically compromised between guarding the public purse and satisfying citizens' individual needs and interests. In enacting it, Congress moved away from legislative adjudication toward a more modern programmatic mode of legislative behavior, and worked to transform contemporary understandings about representation and distributive justice.

It is important to note that the Federal disaster relief of the early national period was remarkably similar to pension and land entitlements in the broad conception of legislative authority that it embraced.[9] It also became markedly categorical between 1794 and 1822, shifting dramatically away from appropriations responding to individual aid requests toward relief measures aimed at *classes of victims* of particular disasters. As was the case with military service pensions, conflicts ensued over the constitutionality of supplying Federal disaster aid. However, worries over the limits of Congress's authority and fears about setting policy precedents were trumped by the desire of congressional majorities to attend to the plights of certain groups of citizens. Once the decision to grant assistance was made, Congress's task became that of crafting appropriate categories of desert for disaster victims, predicated upon legislative determinations of their innocence and fault.[10]

---

[8] Christine A. Desan, "The Constitutional Commitment to Legislative Adjudication in the Early American Tradition," *Harvard Law Review* 111 (1998): 1382, 1383.

[9] This paragraph draws upon the work of Michele Landis. "Let Me Next Time Be 'Tried by Fire': Disaster Relief and the Origins of the American Welfare State 1789–1874," 92 *Northwestern University Law Review* (1998): 967–1034. See also Landis, "Fate, Responsibility, and 'Natural' Disaster Relief: Narrating the American Welfare State," *Law & Society Review* 22 (1999): 257–318, 265–70.

[10] Landis argues that late-eighteenth-century disaster relief measures were the first Federal entitlements. Because disaster-related appropriations were made by Congress only sporadically, in response to petitions for relief after particular disasters, I do not consider

Whether the pension program enacted in 1818 would continue to be considered good national policy remained to be seen. Members of the Fifteenth Congress clearly understood that even as the state establishes formal administrative categories identifying those who deserve to receive public benefits, they also create de facto categories of "others" defined either implicitly or explicitly as not deserving and excluded from the state's consideration. Senator Goldsborough's remarks were particularly telling in this regard when he tried to rationalize the exclusionary details of the Senate version of the 1818 pension bill by professing that there were relative *degrees* of deservingness rather than a hard boundary dividing citizens who were deserving and those who were not. When the compromise bill became law and was implemented, it necessarily created an outgroup of undeserving Americans, because it contained language that qualified some, but not all, citizens for government benefits. Those other, excluded citizens ranged from men who had served in the Continental Army and Navy for less than nine months, to members of the militia, to, at the extreme end of the spectrum, colonial women. Since the daughters of the Republic were barred from formal military service, they could not be considered Revolutionary veterans of any kind.[11]

them to have been entitlements or the product of an "organized, sustained" public benefit "program." Landis nonetheless has revealed a critically important line of early Federal social provision, one that casts additional doubt on both the conventional "big bang" account of New Deal social policymaking and more recent scholarship situating the origins of the American welfare state in the Civil War pension system. "Let Me Next Time Be 'Tried by Fire' "; "Fate, Responsibility, and 'Natural' Disaster Relief."

[11] A few women actually did engage in combat in the Army, but only by disguising themselves as men. The most famous of them was Deborah Sampson, who is believed to have enlisted in the Fourth Massachusetts Regiment in April 1781 under the alias Robert Shurtleff and fought at White Plains, Tarrytown, and Yorktown. Sampson survived both sword and bullet wounds, and her gender was discovered only when, succumbing to a fever after the battle of Yorktown, she was taken to a hospital. She was honorably discharged; in 1784 married Benjamin Gannett, with whom she had three children; and died in 1827. Sampson Gannett was granted a pension from the Commonwealth of Massachusetts in 1792. In 1837, ten years after her death, the Twenty-fifth Congress granted her *husband* a pension as a Revolutionary soldier's *widower.* Julia Ward Stickley, "The Records of Deborah Sampson Gannett, Woman Soldier of the Revolution," *Prologue* 4 (Winter 1972): 233–41. [For a different, and more critical, account of Sampson Gannett's history, see Vera O. Laska, *"Remember the Ladies:" Outstanding Women of the American Revolution* (Commonwealth of Massachusetts: Bicentennial Commission, 1976), pp. 61–94.]

The language of the Massachusetts resolution granting Deborah Sampson Gannett's pension is remarkable in that it constructed her deservingness as a military veteran in

This was despite the fact that they, too, had survived the conflict and considered themselves patriotic. The efforts of many American women were critical to the war for independence, their ostensibly noncombative role, "natural" weakness, and essentially invisible status under common law notwithstanding. Among other things, they provided indispensable physical support to the Army by cooking, cleaning, sewing, and nursing. They also kept family farms and businesses in operation while men were away from home, sustained colonial boycotts of British goods, raised funds for the war effort, and protected children and property against squatters and marauding soldiers. At least some of these women believed that their contributions to the Revolution were as worthy of recognition as those made by the war's official (male) patriots.[12] Petitioning the "Honnorabell" Continental Congress in 1786 in an effort to recover the loss of interest payments on money that she had loaned the State of New

a manner simply not applicable to men: ". . . said Deborah exhibited an extraordinary instance of female heroism by discharging the duties of a faithful gallant Soldier, *and at the same time preserving the virtue & chastity of her Sex unsuspected & unblemished*, & was discharged from the service with a fair & honorable character." Paul Revere's letter in support of Sampson Gannett's 1805 petition asking Congress for a pension employed a similar logic: "We commonly form our Idea of the person whom we hear spoken off, whom we have never seen, according as their Actions are described. When I heard her spoken off as a Soldier, I formed the Idea of a tall, Masculine female, who had a small share of understanding, without education, & one, of the meanest of her Sex. – When I saw and discoursed with [her] I was agreeably surprised to find a small, effeminate, and converseable Woman, whose education entitled her to a better situation in life. . . . I think her case much more deserving than hundreds to whom Congress have been generous." Resolve of the General Court of Massachusetts, January 20, 1792, Archives Division, Commonwealth of Massachusetts (emphasis added), and Paul Revere to William Eustis, Member of Congress, February 20, 1804, Massachusetts Historical Society, photostatic copies in Stickley, "Records of Deborah Sampson Gannett," pp. 240 and 236, respectively. Insights into the complex role of women as what Jean Bethke Elshtain calls "the collective 'other' to the male warrior" include Elshtain, *Women and War* (New York: Basic Books, 1987), cited phrase, pp. 3–4; and *Women, Militarism, and War: Essays in History, Politics, and Social Theory*, ed. Elshtain Tobias and Sheila Tobias (especially Chapter 4, by Linda K. Kerber, "May All Our Citizens Be Soldiers").

[12] Abigail Adams wrote: "Patriotism in the female Sex is the most disinterested of all virtues. Excluded from honours and from offices, we cannot attach ourselves to the State of Government from having held a place of Eminence. Even in freest countrys our property is subject to the controul and disposal of our partners, to whom the Laws have given a sovereign Authority. Deprived of a voice in Legislation, obliged to submit to those Laws which are imposed upon us, is it not sufficient to make us indifferent to the publick Welfare? Yet all History and every age exhibit Instances of patriotic virtue in the female Sex; which considering our situation equals the most Heroick." Abigail Adams to John Adams, June 17, 1782, cited in Linda K. Kerber, *Women of the Republic: Intellect and Ideology in Revolutionary America* (Chapel Hill: University of North Carolina Press, 1980), p. 35.

Jersey during the Revolution, Rachel Wells, a self-described "Sitisen" and widow "far advanced in years," put it this way:

> I have Don as much to Carrey on the Warr as maney that Sett now at ye healm of government . . . ye poor Sogers has got Sum Crumbs That fall from their masters tabel. . . . Why Not Rachel Wells have a Littel intrust?

> if She did not fight She threw in all her mite which bought ye Sogers food & Clothing & Let Them have Blankets & Since that She has bin obliged to Lay upon Straw & glad of that. . . .[13]

Similar claims and requests for relief inundated the nation's legislators during the Revolution and afterward, but, as Linda Kerber has documented, the litany of women's petitions fell on unresponsive ears, leaving the daughters of the Republic to beg or turn to the states for assistance.[14] Even when fifty-three years after the war Congress programmatically granted pensions to women, it was only by virtue of their relationships with men deemed deserving by the state. Those who were not widows of Revolutionary officers or soldiers, no matter what their situation, were not citizens who qualified to be placed among the nation's entitled.[15]

---

[13] Rachel Wells, Petition to Congress, May 18, 1776, cited in *Women's America: Refocusing the Past*, ed. Linda K. Kerber and Jane Sherron De Hart (New York: Oxford University Press, 3rd ed., 1991), p. 87.

[14] Burdened with war debts, the states' legislatures only occasionally granted pensions to women, and then on a case-by-case rather than a programmatic basis. Kerber, *Women of the Republic*, pp. 92–3. See also Gregory A. Mark, "The Vestigial Constitution: The History and Significance of the Right to Petition," *Fordham Law Review* 66 (1998): 2183–5, 2227. Congress's record of granting private pensions to women was similarly spotty. In 1816, the House Committee on Pensions and Revolutionary Claims decided that to reject the pension request of Elizabeth Hamilton, Alexander Hamilton's widow, "would not comport with that honourable sense of justice and magnanimous policy which ought ever to distinguish the legislative proceeds of a virtuous and enlightened nation." Yet Congress previously had denied Elizabeth Hamilton's claim, and it typically denied women's petitions for aid. In 1820, for example, the Senate Pension Committee rejected Margaret Clark's request for a pension as the widow of Continental Army Major John Clark, stating that "it would be inexpedient to establish such a precedent as the granting of the prayer of the petitioner would go to establish under the Act of 18th March 1818." Claim of the Widow of Colonel Alexander Hamilton for Commutation, February 24, 1816, and January 11, 1810, *American State Papers, Class IX, Claims* [hereafter *ASP, Claims*], pp. 467, 370; Petition of Margaret Clark, SEN 16A-G10, and Senate Committee on Pensions report on the Petition of Margaret Clark, 3 March 1820, SEN 16A-D10, Records of the U.S. Senate, Record Group 46, National Archives, Washington, DC.

[15] It should be noted that Congress's new acknowledgment of the needs of American women during the Progressive era (the Sheppard–Towner Act) did not come in the form of national-level entitlements accruing to individual women, but rather as a short-lived

The Logic of Expansion

Male citizens who had seen combat in the war, who were closer to the legal boundary defining deserving Revolutionary veterans and who were not precluded from consideration by gender, could and did struggle to be included within the group of men entitled to Federal pensions benefits after the 1818 Pension Act was passed. Some continued to petition Congress for private aid bills, drawing analogies between their situations and the situations of men receiving programmatic Federal assistance on account of disability or service. Maine resident Robert Newsom, for example, asked Congress for a pension after a large timber fell on his left leg while he was working in the Portsmouth Navy Yard. The accident had resulted in the leg's amputation, leaving Newsom unable to support his wife and four children. Newsom was "aware that (as he was not an entered Seaman at the time of his misfortune) he [wa]s not *legally* entitled to a pension." Having served for twelve to thirteen years in the various New Hampshire revenue cutters, however, he hoped that "his long & faithful services w[ould] be considered by Congress."[16]

Other men endeavored to persuade a majority of Congress to broaden the pension program's eligibility criteria, typically by asserting that their characteristics and circumstances were not meaningfully different from those of the men chosen to receive benefits. One such man, Phinehas Cole of New Hampshire, petitioned Congress after his application for a pension under the law of 1818 was rejected by the War Department. (Figures 3.2, 3.3) Cole had seen more than nine months' service during the Revolution, but because some of that time was spent fighting in state forces instead of the Continental Army, he did not qualify for benefits. He told the members of the House and Senate that

[i]f the liberality of the Country is intended, as a reward to those who found its battles, and sacrifised their property to secure its liberty, why surely then, no one has a stronger claim to its liberality than your petitioner. He envies no one his good fortune, but he deems it a hard case, to see his companions in arms enjoying the country's bounty, while he, whose claim is as strong as any

Federal *grant-in-aid program* providing funding to *subnational government agencies*. Even when some women were finally deemed entitled to individual-level aid in the Social Security Act of 1935, the programmatic definition of their deservingness still derived from the presence or absence of a worthy man in their lives.

[16] Petition of Robert Newsom, 24 February 1820, SEN 16A-G10, Records of the U.S. Senate, Record Group 46, National Archives, Washington, DC.

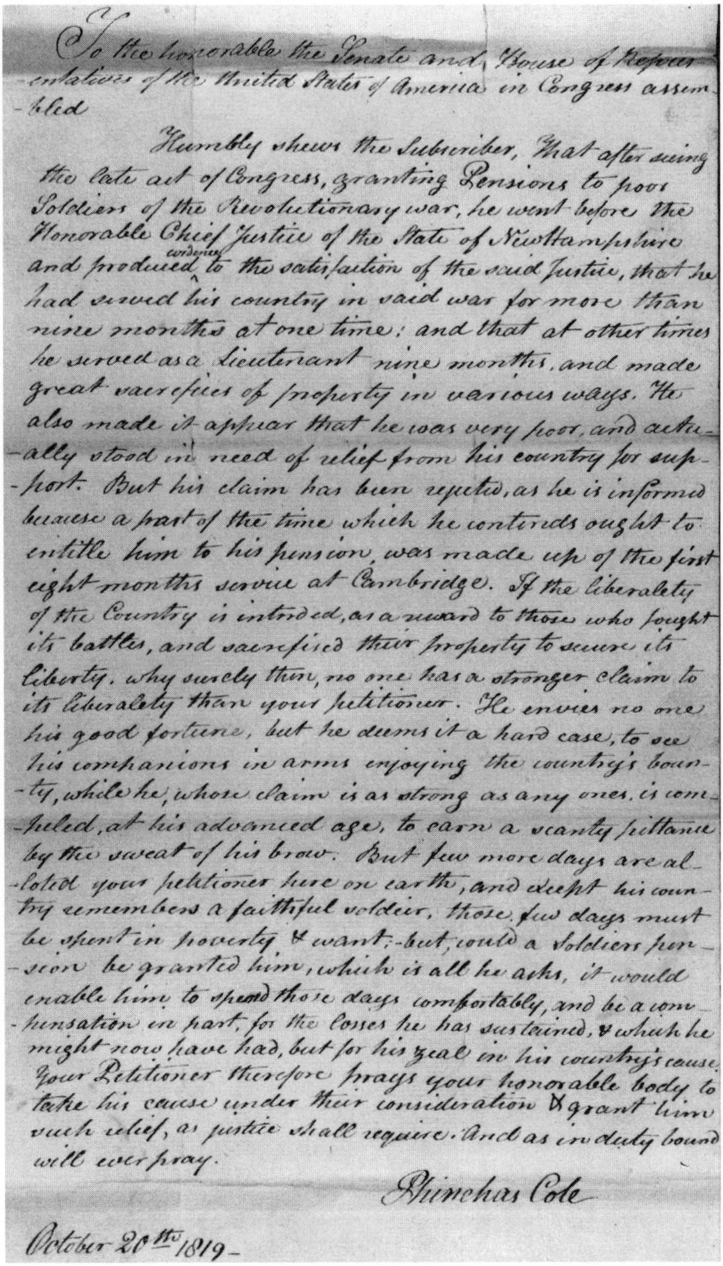

To the honorable the Senate and House of Representatives of the United States of America in Congress assembled

Humbly shews the Subscriber, That after seeing the late act of Congress, granting Pensions to poor Soldiers of the Revolutionary war, he went before the Honorable Chief Justice of the State of New Hampshire and produced to the satisfaction of the said Justice, that he had served his country in said war for more than nine months at one time; and that at other times he served as a Lieutenant nine months, and made great sacrifices of property in various ways. He also made it appear that he was very poor, and actually stood in need of relief from his country for support. But his claim has been rejected, as he is informed because a part of the time which he contends ought to entitle him to his pension, was made up of the first eight months service at Cambridge. If the liberality of the Country is intended, as a reward to those who fought its battles, and sacrificed their property to secure its liberty. why surely then, no one has a stronger claim to its liberality than your petitioner. He envies no one his good fortune, but he deems it a hard case, to see his companions in arms enjoying the country's bounty, while he, whose claim is as strong as any ones, is compelled, at his advanced age, to earn a scanty pittance by the sweat of his brow. But few more days are allotted your petitioner here on earth, and except his country remembers a faithful soldier, those few days must be spent in poverty & want;—but, could a Soldiers pension be granted him, which is all he asks, it would enable him to spend those days comfortably, and be a compensation in part, for the losses he has sustained, & which he might now have had, but for his zeal in his country's cause. Your Petitioner therefore prays your honorable body to take his cause under their consideration & grant him such relief, as justice shall require. And as in duty bound will ever pray.

Phinehas Cole

October 20th 1819—

FIGURE 3.2. The Petition of Phinehas Cole, October 20, 1819. After Cole's application for a pension under the Pension Act of 1818 was rejected by the War Department, he petitioned Congress for assistance, suggesting that the act's eligibility criteria were flawed. Courtesy of the National Archives and Records Administration, Records of the U.S. Senate.

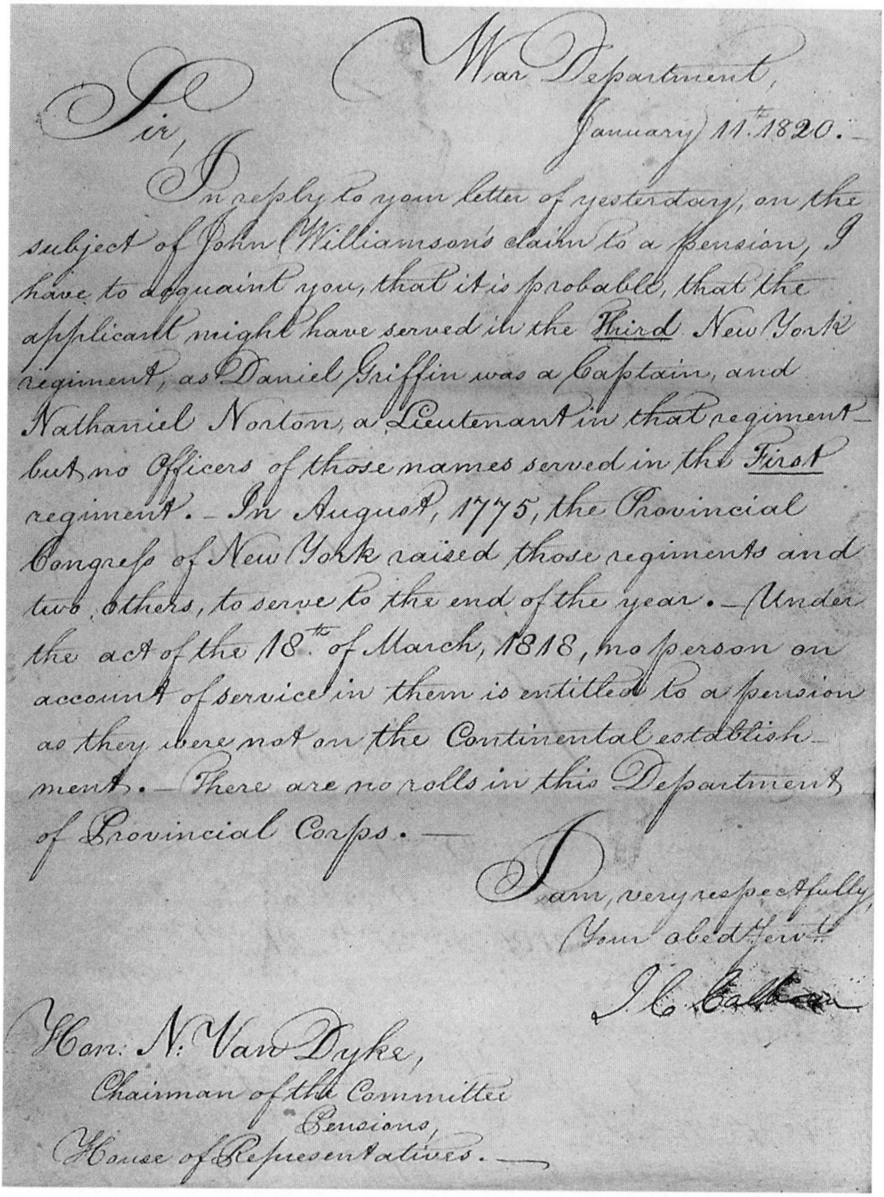
War Department,
January 11th 1820.—

Sir,

In reply to your letter of yesterday, on the subject of John Williamson's claim to a pension, I have to acquaint you, that it is probable, that the applicant might have served in the Third New York regiment, as Daniel Griffin was a Captain, and Nathaniel Norton, a Lieutenant in that regiment—but no Officers of those names served in the First regiment.— In August, 1775, the Provincial Congress of New York raised those regiments and two others, to serve to the end of the year.— Under the act of the 18th of March, 1818, no person on account of service in them is entitled to a pension as they were not on the Continental establishment.— There are no rolls in this Department of Provincial Corps.—

I am, very respectfully,
Your obedt Servt.
J. C. Calhoun

Hon: N: Van Dyke,
Chairman of the Committee
Pensions,
House of Representatives.—

FIGURE 3.3. Letter of Secretary of War John C. Calhoun to Senator Nicholas Van Dyke, Chair of the Committee on Pensions, January 11, 1820, reminding Van Dyke that service in state-level forces did not qualify veterans for pensions under the Pension Act of 1818. Eligibility was conferred only by service in the Continental Army or Navy. Courtesy of the National Archives and Records Administration, Records of the U.S. Senate.

ones, is compeled, at his advanced age, to earn a scanty pittance by the sweat of his brow.[17]

Comparisons like these routinely were made by veterans who were not entitled to benefits by the 1818 Pension Act. One group of such men informed Congress that the pension program's category of desert "was Perfectly agreeable, to Every officer and soldier of that description." But a Congress that respected the people would not omit other men who had fought to secure the nation's independence. "[N]o sirs," they wrote, "we hope Better things of you." Begging to be included under the terms of the Pension Act, they told their representatives that "if the sum given was to[o] much, set the compensation less but let all share in the Pension."[18]

Still other men attempted inclusion in the 1818 pension law's categories of desert and reward more directly, through fraudulent claims of membership. Whatever the approach taken, pressures for new pension benefits and program expansion strained the abilities of Congress, officials in the War, Treasury, and Justice Departments, and field agents charged with pension administration. They led to additional legislation, administrative regulation, and, inevitably, the expansion of fiscal and bureaucratic capacities at the center of what had been designed to be a federally organized, decentralized state.[19] In addition to establishing a legacy of categorical social benefits, the selective entitlements enacted for certain survivors of the Revolution played a direct role in the development

[17] Petition of Phinehas Cole, 20 October 1819, SEN 16A-G10, Records of the U.S. Senate, Record Group 46, National Archives, Washington, DC. Pension Bureau officials were steadfast in maintaining that only service in the Continental Army entitled veterans to pensions under the Pension Act of 1818. As Secretary of War John Calhoun put it, "There are no rolls in this Department of Provincial Corps." Letter of J. C. Calhoun to N. Van Dyke, Chairman of the House Committee on Pensions, 11 January 1820, SEN 16A-D10, NARA. See Figures 3.2 and 3.3.

[18] Petition of Ebenezer Cousens and others, praying Compensation for Services during the Revolutionary War, 18 December 1820, Records of the U.S. Senate, Record Group 46, National Archives, Washington, DC.

[19] Congress originally had attempted to involve the federal courts in the determination of veterans' disability claims under the invalid pension legislation of March 1792, but as Congress had retained final decision-making authority, the courts refused to participate. See *Hayburn's Case*, 2 U.S. (2 Dall.) 409 (1792); Floyd D. Shinomura, "The History of Claims Against the United States: The Evolution from a Legislative Toward a Judicial Model of Payment," *Louisiana Law Review* 45 (1985): 639–40; Maeva Marcus and Emily Field Van Tassel, "Judges and Legislators in the New Federal System, 1789–1800," in *Judges and Legislators: Toward Institutional Comity* ed. Robert A. Katzmann (Washington, DC: Brookings Institution 1988), pp. 36–40.

of a Federal "machine" whose actors and activities were a presence in local communities.[20]

As William Glasson wrote in a classic understatement, President Monroe and those members of Congress who had declared that there were few remaining survivors of the Revolutionary Army "must have been surprised" at the scramble for veterans' benefits under the Pension Act of 1818.[21] General Joseph Bloomfield of New Jersey, chairman of the House Committee on Revolutionary Pensions, originally had introduced the pension bill in the House with the calculation that the cost of *full-*pay pensions would rapidly decrease from an initial $34,376 per year, spurring an immediate amendment to increase the amount that the *half-*pay measure would deliver. Senator Goldsborough had estimated (despite an admitted lack of evidence with which "to ascertain, with exactness," the number of surviving Continentals) that some 200 officers and 1,687 privates still lived, who would generate an expenditure of no more than $115,480 in the first year the pension program was implemented and less than one-tenth of that figure after ten years.[22] Six months after the Pension Act was enacted, the War Department was so inundated with applications for pensions that it could not act upon them as fast as they came in. In December 1819, Secretary of War John Calhoun reported to Congress that he had received some 28,555 claims and had issued 16,270 pension certificates. Calhoun stated that, notwithstanding the continued vigilance of his department, it appeared probable that "impositions or mistakes" had occurred to a "considerable extent." Pension expenditures under the Pension Act of March 18, 1818, came to $104,901 for the remainder of 1818, then ballooned to an alarming $1,811,329 in 1819, a year of national economic panic. Added to the cost of disability pensions and the annuities and grants established for Revolutionary veterans and survivors through private legislation, the Government spent $2,281,115 on pension expenditures in 1819, or approximately 10.6 percent of the Federal budget.[23] The total cost of the 1818 Pension Act was projected

[20] See Matthew A. Crenson, *The Federal Machine: Beginnings of Bureaucracy in Jacksonian America* (Baltimore: Johns Hopkins University Press, 1975); Resch, *Suffering Soldiers,* pp. 123–5.

[21] William H. Glasson, *Federal Military Pensions in the United States,* ed. David Kinley (New York: Oxford University Press, 1918), p. 68.

[22] *AC* (15/1), pp. 491–2, Dec. 19, 1817, and p. 196, Feb. 12, 1818. If there was an error in his reckoning, Goldsborough said, it unquestionably was by "making the estimate too large."

[23] *Niles' Weekly Register,* Sept. 19, 1818, pp. 63–4; John C. Calhoun to Joseph Bloomfield, Chairman, House Committee on Revolutionary Pensions, Dec. 22, 1819, *ASP, Claims,*

to reach more than $75 million, a figure exceeding the cost of fighting the Revolutionary War.[24]

For a government staggering from financial reverses, the expense of the pension program enacted in 1818 was alone a serious concern, and matters were exacerbated by reports of benefits paid to applicants not truly in need of government assistance. Stories and negative commentary about extraordinary numbers of claims, incredible expenditures, and associated fraud were printed and reprinted in newspapers around the country from mid-1818 through late 1819,[25] when the Sixteenth Congress assembled and immediately took up the subject.[26] But with

pp. 682–3, 683; Calhoun to James Noble, Chairman, Senate Committee on Pensions, Feb. 8, 1823, *ASP, Claims*, p. 885; "Statements showing amount of revolutionary pensions paid annually from 4th March, 1789, to 31st December, 1838," 342 S. doc. 307, p. 16. Military pension expenditures as a percentage of all U.S. Government expenditures were calculated from figures in Davis Rich Dewey, *Financial History of the United States* (New York: Longmans, Green, and Co., 1915, 5th ed.), p. 169. In 1821, the War Department employed some twenty clerks to handle correspondence, record keeping, and pension claims. Leonard D. White, *The Jeffersonians: A Study in Administrative History 1801–1829* (New York: Macmillan Company, 1951), p. 234.

[24] Resch, *Suffering Soldiers*, p. 143. Resch details the pension program's explosive growth, associated frauds, and Government attempts to regain control over the program via bureaucratic growth and administrative rulemaking on pp. 124–34.

[25] For a luminous account of the communications revolution and the national community that resulted from Congress's establishment of the U.S. postal system, see Richard R. John, *Spreading the News: The American Postal System from Franklin to Morse* (Cambridge, MA: Harvard University Press, 1995).

[26] See, e.g., *Middlesex Gazette* (Middletown, Connecticut), July 16, 1818, p. 3, citing an article in the *National Intelligencer* regarding claims so numerous that they might reach 50,000, subjecting the Government to an expenditure of $5,000,000 per year; and *Niles' Weekly Register*, Dec. 12, 1818, and Oct. 16, 1819. Middletown, the site of Connecticut's 1783 anticommutation convention, held a town meeting regarding national pension fraud on December 6, 1819, where it was resolved that "whereas great impositions ha[d] been practiced by persons … who not only [we]re not needy, but who [we]re in fact in affluent circumstances … and consequently many in the community less able to bear the burthens of government [we]re compelled to pay heavy taxes to support their more opulent neighbors," the town selectmen should take measures to ascertain who was improperly placed on the pension list and report their names to a member of the Connecticut delegation in Congress. *Middlesex Gazette*, Dec. 9, 1819, p. 3. That same issue of the *Middlesex Gazette* also reprinted a Nov. 1, 1819, letter to the editor of the *Pittsfield* [Massachusetts] *Sun* from Representative Henry Shaw, member of Congress from the Berkshire district, asking Massachusetts selectmen to report the names of fraudulent claimants to him so that he might transmit them to the secretary of war. "As we venerate the deserving and *destitute* Soldier of the Revolution," Shaw said, "we should frown upon the attempts of *fraud* and *perjury* to cover him with contempt, by sharing this bounty. The Law was not designed as a *reward* for services – the Treasury would be inadequate" (p. 3). Shaw's letter was also printed in the Washington, DC, *Daily National Intelligencer* of Dec. 9, 1819, p. 2. It should be noted that in its second session, the Fifteenth Congress had

the pension program already in operation (and widely understood to be saving the nation from the sin of ingratitude), and with much larger problems occupying Congress's attention (including the admission of Missouri to the union and the extension of slavery), the issue was no longer that of the propriety of programmatic entitlement per se. Instead, Congress focused its attention upon the more technical questions of precisely *who* the U.S. Government should entitle and *how* it should do so. Finding it neither expedient nor in comportment with "the honor and dignity of the American nation" to repeal the Pension Act,[27] the House Committee on Revolutionary Pensions asked Secretary of War Calhoun to determine whether the act could be amended to better effect its purpose. Calhoun had been concerned over the potential for fraud that the pension law posed ever since its enactment because Congress had not specifically defined what it meant by veterans in "reduced circumstances." Yet, he was unable to suggest any amendment other than the requirement of absolute indigence that might render the administration of the act free from "a latitude of construction."[28] After a protracted and heated debate that revived arguments about the 1818 Pension Act's inegalitarian treatment of officers and soldiers, its exclusion of the militia, and the limits of the Government's obligation to its veterans, a divided Sixteenth Congress enacted remedial legislation suspending the payment of pensions promised under the act until program beneficiaries appeared before a court of record to produce proof of their poverty and swear under oath that they had neither disposed of property nor

raised the issue of amending the Pension Act but did not. The House was described in a March 1819 issue of the *Daily National Intelligencer* as "of the opinion . . . that something ought to be done in regard to that law, though it is found difficult to determine what that something is." Cited in the *Middlesex Gazette*, Mar. 30, 1819, p. 3. As Glasson pointed out, the Pension Act also had its defenders. An editorial in the *New York Evening Post* of Dec. 15, 1819, for example, maintained that the complaints about the act that had found their way into the nation's newspapers "were engendered by a few disorganizers in Connecticut, from the worst of motives." The writer trusted that Congress, "in its wisdom and philanthropy," would "let the subject pass undisturbed." Cited in Glasson, *Federal Military Pensions*, p. 69.

[27] *AC* (16/1), pp. 851–2, Jan. 4, 1820.

[28] John C. Calhoun to Joseph Bloomfield, Chairman, House Committee on Revolutionary Pensions, Dec. 22, 1819; John C. Calhoun to Heman Allen, May 11, 1818, in *The Papers of John Calhoun*, ed. Robert L. Meriwether and W. Edwin Hemphill et al. (Columbia: University of South Carolina Press, 1959–), vol. 2, p. 288; see also pp. li–lii. Calhoun specifically mentioned the difficulty of preventing mistakes or abuse given the vagueness of the legislation and the War Department's dependence upon many local actors for the verification of service record and financial need.

hidden assets in order to qualify for benefits.[29] The secretary of war was empowered to remove from the pension list those veterans who, in his opinion, were able to support themselves, with the caveat that any man stricken from the rolls who had relinquished a disability pension in order to receive the benefits of the act of 1818 would have his disability benefits restored.[30]

As the solvency of the national government continued to deteriorate, requiring Secretary of the Treasury William Crawford to report that additional loans would be required to meet projected budget deficits, the Sixteenth Congress persevered in its efforts to find means of reducing Federal expenditures.[31] Representative Thomas Cobb of Georgia suggested that the Revolutionary pensions constituted a potential area for retrenchment, for by lowering the compensation rate of privates from $8 to $5 per month, an annual savings of more than $300,000 could be achieved. Cobb's acknowledgment that he was "walking on ticklish ground" in making such a proposal was accurate, for the idea was rejected by his colleagues almost immediately, though in a close vote.[32] By the time the Seventeenth Congress assembled in December 1820, a majority of the House had abandoned the idea of further cuts in pension expenditures. Instead, they hoped to revive the original provisions of the 1818 Pension Act by granting the secretary of war the authority to restore veterans stricken since 1820 to the pension rolls – an authority that the U.S. attorney general had decided the secretary of war did not possess. A bill for that purpose carried in the House by a vote of 128 to 23 but was postponed by the Senate until it was passed in the next session in early 1823.[33] The new statute empowered the secretary of war to reinstate any veteran stricken from the 1818 pension list who could prove that he was "in such indigent circumstances as to be unable to support himself

---

[29] Cf. Medicaid.

[30] Act of May 1, 1820, *AC* (16/1), pp. 2582–3. For a discussion of the legal arguments raised in the pension amendment debate, see later.

[31] Annual Report on the State of the Treasury, Dec. 1, 1820, presented to Congress Dec. 4, 1820, *AC* (16/2), pp. 487–99. Congressional action in May 1820 had authorized a loan of $3,000,000; the proposed additional $5,000,000 loan was authorized in an act of March 3, 1821 [*AC* (16/2), pp. 1807–8].

[32] *AC* (16/2), pp. 730, 822. The resolution introduced by Cobb on Jan. 11, 1821, defeated in a 59 to 53 vote, proposed to reduce officers' pensions in addition to the soldiers' (p. 822). None of the specifics of the debate on the resolution were recorded, other than that it met with "great objection."

[33] *AC* (17/1), pp. 1372 and 409, Mar. 26 and Apr. 22, 1822, respectively; Act of Mar. 1, 1823, *AC* (17/2), pp. 1409–10.

without the assistance of his country, and that he ha[d] not disposed of, or transferred, his property, or any portion thereof, with a view to obtain a pension." As of September 4, 1822, the Pension Act of 1820 had resulted in some 2,328 claimants being rejected or dropped from the pension list, and another 4,221 had either failed to exhibit required schedules of property or died, leaving 12,331 men on the pension list compared with 16,270 in December 1819.[34]

One veteran dropped from the rolls was Elias Stevens of southern Killingworth (now Clinton), Connecticut, whose story suggests how selective entitlement programs encourage preferences, create expectations, and establish understandings. Stevens had served as a soldier in the Connecticut regiment for three years until his honorable discharge from the Army in October 1783. He applied for a pension only a month after the Pension Act of 1818 passed, was placed on the pension list by the order of Secretary Calhoun, and began receiving a pension of $8 per month. When the Sixteenth Congress suspended the benefits of the Act pending proof of poverty, the fifty-five-year-old Stevens traveled to the Middlesex County Court in Haddam, Connecticut, to present his declaration of need and an inventory of his assets. He swore that lameness and rheumatism limited his ability to pursue his occupation as a blacksmith, while feeble constitutions rendered his wife and daughter unable to work. His thirteen-year-old son, Jedidiah, had the ability to provide roughly half of his keep, but his elder son, Nathaniel, who was apprenticed to a tailor in New Haven, required his father to provide him with clothing. Stevens apparently believed that his situation qualified him to receive a pension, to the extent that he was willing to testify about his personal circumstances before judges and local witnesses. Yet, the schedule of property that he presented to the court on June 14, 1820, suggested that he was a man of means: the owner of a dwelling house and barn, two-thirds of an "old" house and barn, over seventy acres of land, farm animals and equipment, home furnishings, and a variety of personal items.[35] Less than a month after his court appearance, Stevens was informed by the War Department that his name had been stricken from the pension list on account of his property. The words "not entitled" were

---

[34] *AC* (17/2), p. 1409; Calhoun to James Noble.

[35] The houses and one of the barns still stand in Clinton, Connecticut. The "old" house and barn referred to in the inventory are undoubtedly those of the Stevens homestead, located across from the historic Red Schoolhouse on Cow Hill Road. Elias Stevens's dwelling, enlarged significantly by Jedidiah Stevens after his father's death and owned by the author of this book from 1984 to 1997, sits on the adjacent property to the north.

inscribed on the cover of his pension file, where they remain to this day[36] (Figures 3.4–3.7).

Elias Stevens's efforts to retain his pension in the face of congressional struggles to curb the Revolutionary pension program illustrate the pressures for expansion and contraction that occur along the sociopolitical boundaries that entitlements create. Beset by fiscal stress and accusations of fraud and abuse, the state actors charged with the guardianship of the public purse had to grapple with the dual sense of national honor and purpose that had inspired them to create the pension legislation in the first place, while a cacophony of protest and the anguished cries of disenfranchised claimants resonated discordantly in the background. An economic upturn, coupled with a requisite fine-tuning of pension eligibility criteria, afforded a brief respite in which most of the members of the Seventeenth Congress could believe that they had achieved the proper balance in dividing the deserving and undeserving. Because many military veterans not entitled to benefits under the 1818 law were actively and ever more stridently petitioning Congress for inclusion in the pension program, however, that interval was brief.

Powerful arguments could be made in favor of expanding the pension program's coverage. Its overt exclusion of certain Revolutionary veterans from the nation's beneficence, whether members of the militia or regulars who had served for less than nine months, had sat uneasily with many members of the public and Congress since the passage of the 1818 law. Such an exclusion, it was argued, was inappropriate in a democratic society. So, too, was the original pension law's two-tier system of benefits, which in paying former officers and soldiers pensions of $20 and $8 per month, respectively, effectively rendered the wartime services of the officers more valuable than those of the soldiers and embedded old class lines in public policy. Sentimental appeals for the nation's gratitude, invoking the image of old, suffering soldiers, were also quite persuasive, especially because they deflected debate "from the divisive issues of class and privilege to the unifying ideals of national honor, patriotism, and America's mission."[37]

There were, of course, alternative perspectives among the people and their representatives. Some people believed that officers had contributed more to the war effort than soldiers, ranked the services of Continental forces over those of the militia, and/or believed length of service to be a

[36] See Figures 3.4–3.7.
[37] Resch, *Suffering Soldiers*, p. 138.

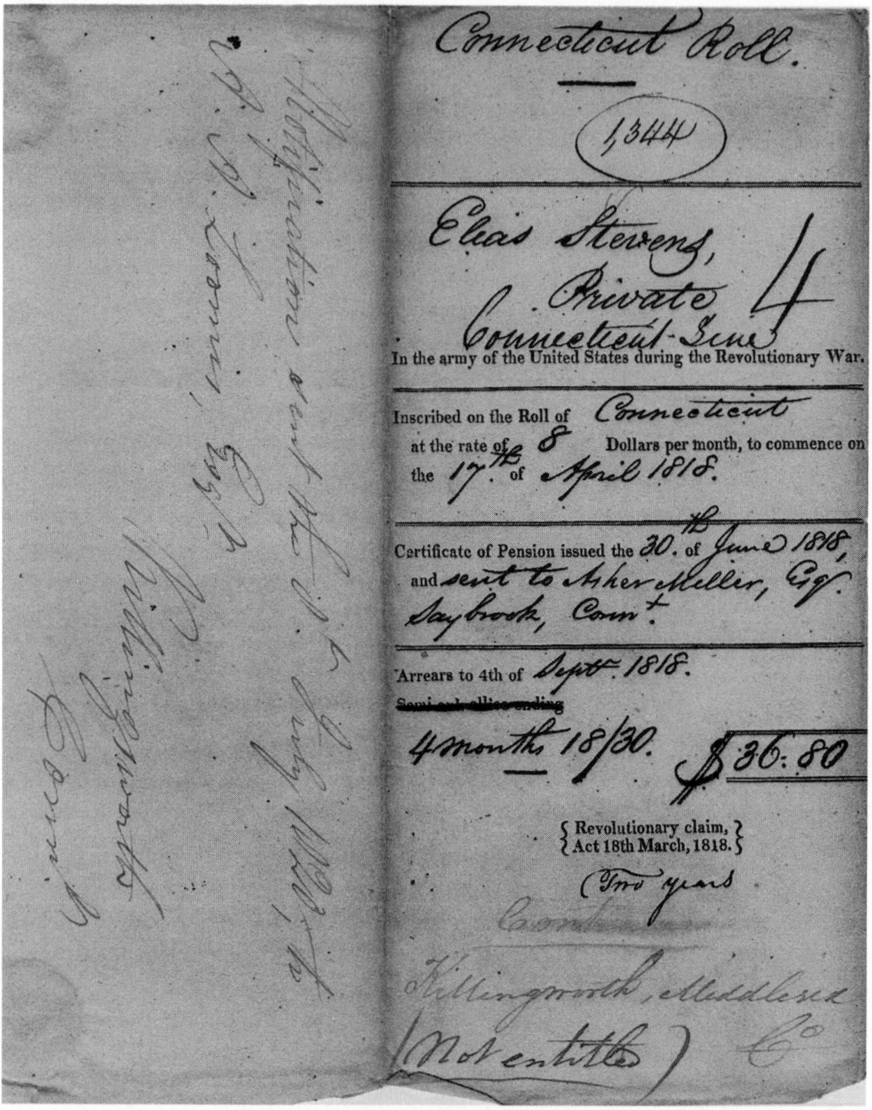
Connecticut Roll.

1,344

Elias Stevens, 4
Private
Connecticut Line

In the army of the United States during the Revolutionary War.

Inscribed on the Roll of Connecticut
at the rate of 8 Dollars per month, to commence on
the 17th of April 1818.

Certificate of Pension issued the 30th of June 1818,
and sent to Asher Miller, Esq.
Saybrook, Connt.

Arrears to 4th of Septr. 1818.
~~Semi-annual allowance ending~~
4 months 18/30. $36:80

Revolutionary claim,
Act 18th March, 1818.

(Two years

Killingworth, Middlesex Co

(Not entitled)

FIGURE 3.4. The cover of the pension file of Revolutionary soldier Elias Stevens of southern Killingworth (now Clinton), Connecticut. Stevens was granted a pension in April 1818, but it was withdrawn in 1820 when a new means test was imposed upon recipients. The words "not entitled" were written on the cover of his file. Courtesy of the National Archives and Records Administration, Records of the Veterans Administration.

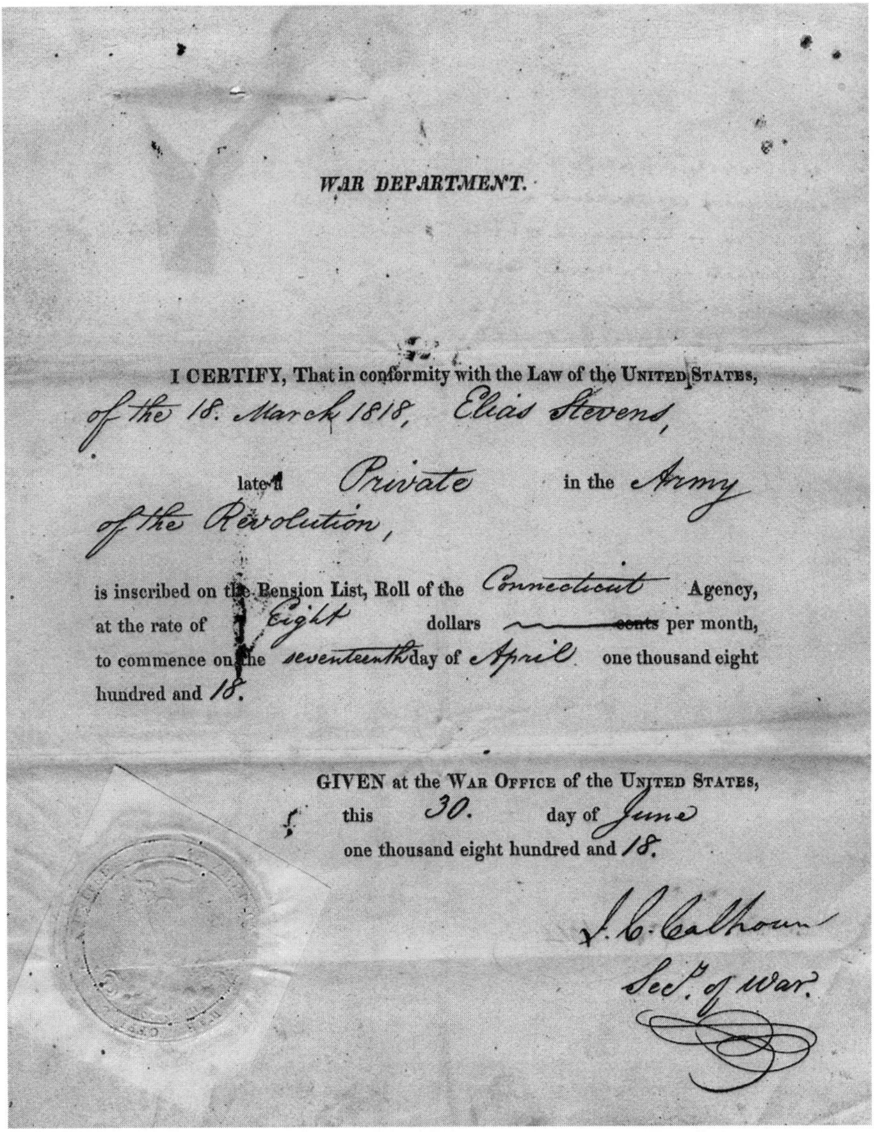

WAR DEPARTMENT.

I CERTIFY, That in conformity with the Law of the UNITED STATES, of the 18. March 1818, Elias Stevens, late a Private in the Army of the Revolution, is inscribed on the Pension List, Roll of the Connecticut Agency, at the rate of Eight dollars cents per month, to commence on the seventeenth day of April one thousand eight hundred and 18.

GIVEN at the WAR OFFICE of the UNITED STATES, this 30. day of June one thousand eight hundred and 18.

J. C. Calhoun
Sec'y. of War.

FIGURE 3.5. The certificate signed by Secretary of War John C. Calhoun that placed Elias Stevens on the nation's pension list in April 1818. Courtesy of the National Archives and Records Administration, Records of the Veterans Administration.

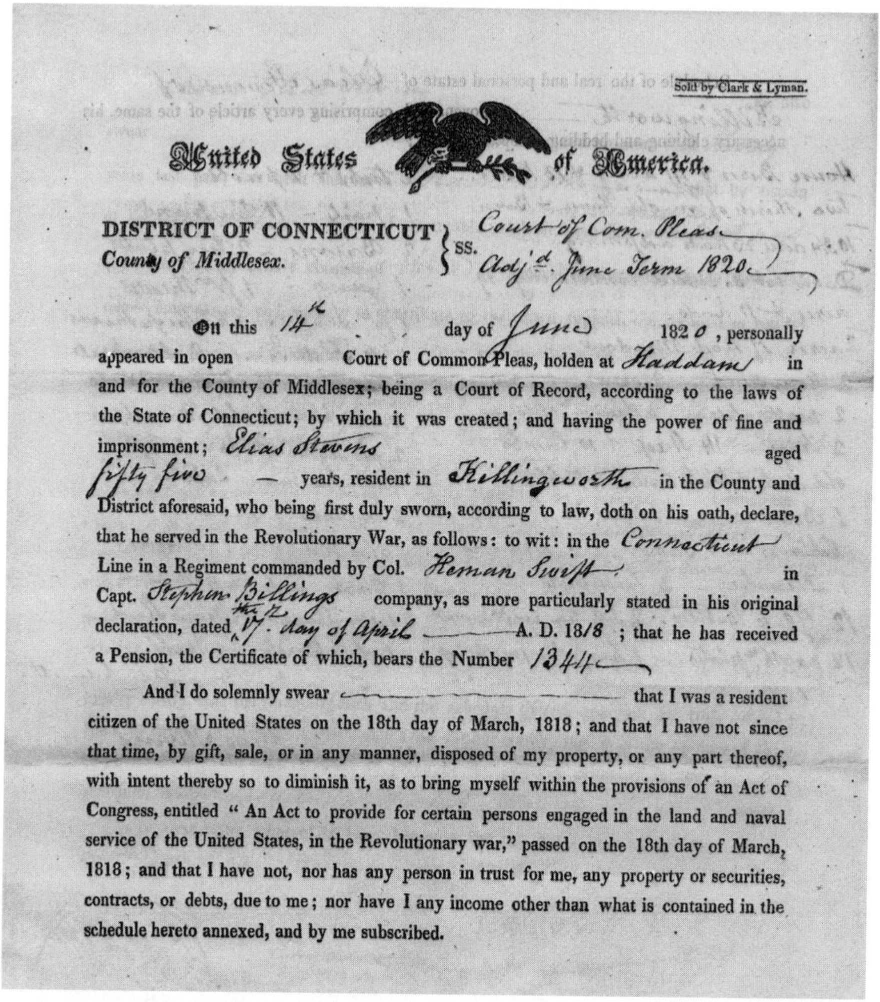

Sold by Clark & Lyman.

United States of **America.**

DISTRICT OF CONNECTICUT ⎱ ss. *Court of Com. Pleas.*
County of Middlesex. ⎰   *Adj'd June Term 1820.*

On this *14th* day of *June* 182*0*, personally appeared in open   Court of Common Pleas, holden at *Haddam* in and for the County of Middlesex; being a Court of Record, according to the laws of the State of Connecticut; by which it was created; and having the power of fine and imprisonment; *Elias Stevens* aged *fifty five* — years, resident in *Killingworth* in the County and District aforesaid, who being first duly sworn, according to law, doth on his oath, declare, that he served in the Revolutionary War, as follows: to wit: in the *Connecticut* Line in a Regiment commanded by Col. *Heman Swift* in Capt. *Stephen Billings* company, as more particularly stated in his original declaration, dated *17th day of April* A. D. 18*18*; that he has received a Pension, the Certificate of which, bears the Number *1344*

And I do solemnly swear that I was a resident citizen of the United States on the 18th day of March, 1818; and that I have not since that time, by gift, sale, or in any manner, disposed of my property, or any part thereof, with intent thereby so to diminish it, as to bring myself within the provisions of an Act of Congress, entitled " An Act to provide for certain persons engaged in the land and naval service of the United States, in the Revolutionary war," passed on the 18th day of March, 1818; and that I have not, nor has any person in trust for me, any property or securities, contracts, or debts, due to me; nor have I any income other than what is contained in the schedule hereto annexed, and by me subscribed.

FIGURE 3.6. Remedial legislation enacted in 1820 required all veterans receiving pensions under the Pension Act of 1818 to demonstrate their financial need before a court of record. These pages document Elias Stevens's visit to the Middlesex County (Connecticut) District Court on June 14, 1820. The schedule of property that Stevens presented to the court was held by the War Department to be grounds for removing him from the pension list. Courtesy of the National Archives and Records Administration, Records of the Veterans Administration.

Schedule of the real and personal estate of *Elias Stevens* of *Killingworth* abovenamed, comprising every article of the same, his necessary clothing and bedding excepted: to wit:

House Barn & 41 acres & 13 Roods.
Stand &c
two thirds of an old House & Barn
10.3/4 acres 23 Rood adjoining. —
Davis lot so called containing 19.
acres & 11 Roods —
2 acres of Nod Meadow
2 Horse Kind — 2 oxen — 1 Cow —
2 two Y'r olds — 3 three yr olds —
2 Hogs — 14 Sheep & 10 lambs
old desk & Book Case — 3 tables —
1 Beaureau — 1 Chest — 15 old
Chairs — 1 Table — 2 Stands
1 Decanter — 2 Tumblers —
12 Glass Bottles — 2 Setts tea Cups & Saucers
12 earthen plates — 1 Tea pot — 1 milk Cup
1 Earthen platter — 1 pitcher — Canister
pepper Box — Vinegar Cruet — Salt Cellar
1 Cream pot — 1 pot — 2 dish Kettles
1 tea Kittle — 1 Frying pan
1 pr and Irons — 2 old cases axes
Slice & tongs — 1 Grid Iron
1 Brass Kittle — 3 Candle sticks
1 Lamp — 1 Crow Barr —
1 Chape & saw — 2 Hows 4 augers
1 draw shave — 1 hand Saw
5 pitch forks

2 tubs & 2 pails
1 pail — 11 tin pans
2 Basons — 2 tin plates
1 Gunn — 1 pr shears
1 pr Snuffers — 1 pr Sheep Shears
1 pr Flatt Irons — 2 old wheels
1 old Reel 12 old Flour Barrels
4 old things 6 old Barrels —
2 old Scythe Sticks — 1 Scythe
1 old womans Saddle —
2 mens ___ do ___
1 old Waggon & Harness
1 Cart — 1 ox yoke —
1 ox Sled — 1 Stone Sled
1 old Bridle 1 Bible
1 Psalm Book — Blacksmith
Shop & part Sett of Tools —
3 old Silver Tea Spoons
1 Sett Knives & Forks —
1 Steel How — 1 pr Small
Steelyards —

I am indebted to various
persons in the Just Sum
of $705.50

Elias Stevens

FIGURE 3.6. (*Continued*).

I, the said *Elias Stevens* , do also

swear   that my occupation is, and for more than *thirty*

years last past, has been that of a *Blacksmith* ; that by reason

of *Lameness & Rheumatism* I am unable to labour more than *one fourth part*
                                   in my occupation

the year, that my family consists of *three* persons who steadily reside with me;

whose names, ages, and capacity to contribute to their own support, are, as near as can be

ascertained by me, as follows, to wit: *Lucilla Stevens*

                         my wife aged *53 ys* ; ability equal to *half*

her support. *Being weakly & her Constitution impaired & not*
able to endure labour without essential injury to her health
Jedidiah C Stevens a son, aged *13* ; ability *no more* his support.
than equal to one half his Support — Louisa Stevens a
Daughter aged 19 years who has a feeble Constitution & whose
ability is not equal to her Support. I have also a Son an
apprentice to the Tailors trade named Nathaniel aged 16 —
residing in New Haven whom I am Bound to furnish
with Cloathing

~~who   wholly unable to contribute   support~~

                                          14
                    SWORN to and declared on the *14* day

of *June*   182*0* before *Court of Common pleas for Middlesex County*

                              [signature]   Clerk of said Court.

―――――――――

I, *[signature]* Clerk of *the Court of Common Pleas* , do

hereby certify, that the foregoing oath and the schedule thereto annexed, are truly copied

from the record of the said Court: and I do further certify, that it is the opinion of the

said Court, that the ~~total~~ amount in value of the property exhibited in the aforesaid

schedule, is *Two Thousand Two Hundred* dollars and

IN TESTIMONY whereof, I have hereunto set my hand, and affixed the seal of

the said Court, on this *14* day of *June* 182*0*

                              [signature] Clerk of said Court

~~Clerk of the Court for the~~

FIGURE 3.6. (*Continued*).

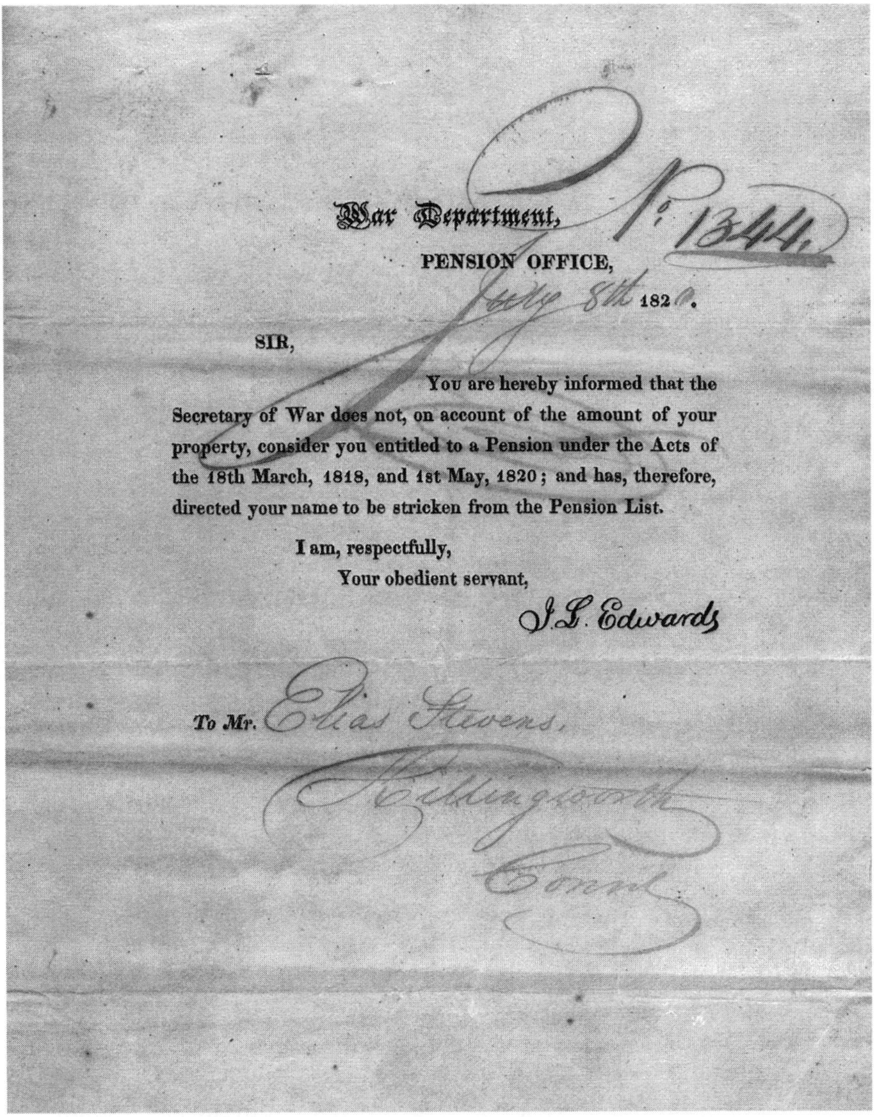

No. 1344.

War Department,

PENSION OFFICE,

July 8th 1820.

SIR,

You are hereby informed that the Secretary of War does not, on account of the amount of your property, consider you entitled to a Pension under the Acts of the 18th March, 1818, and 1st May, 1820; and has, therefore, directed your name to be stricken from the Pension List.

I am, respectfully,

Your obedient servant,

J. L. Edwards

To Mr. Elias Stevens,

Killingworth

Conn.

FIGURE 3.7. The letter from the War Department of July 8, 1820, informing Elias Stevens that he was not entitled to a pension because his assets were too great. Courtesy of the National Archives and Records Administration, Records of the Veterans Administration.

vitally important distinction. Still others understood all pensions, except those granted to veterans physically disabled in combat, to violate the ideology of the citizen-soldier. But the idea that the nation owed a debt of gratitude to all of the men who had served in the Revolution was gaining strength. Americans were uncomfortably aware of the classical charge that republics were ungrateful to their benefactors – part of a larger argument that popular rule meant control by the mean-spirited, while magnanimous virtues could emanate only from an aristocracy. By the time the Marquis de Lafayette returned to the United States in 1824 at the invitation of President Monroe after an absence of forty years to travel as "the Nation's Guest" into every corner of the Union, Americans would be primed and ready to welcome his reappearance "as a heaven-sent opportunity for such a clear-cut display of national gratitude as would vindicate republican government from [that] ancient aspersion."[38]

If any group of military veterans believed that the American Republic was guilty of the sin of ingratitude, it was the officers of the Continental Army who had parted with their commutation certificates before Congress acted to settle the nation's debts in 1790. The language of the petitions and memorials that they sent to Congress over the years attested to a significant evolution of the terms of the debate over national-level entitlements and to changing beliefs about the nature of those benefits. Early on, their communications (and related congressional deliberation) had framed the officers' desert in terms of national gratitude and benevolence. As early as 1808–9, however, the disgruntled officers began to assert a more legalistic conception of entitlement based upon rights claims. Like future Americans who would deny Congress's ability to reform the Social Security pension program on the basis of property rights established by payroll "contributions," the Continental officers argued that their claims rested upon "such a very different ground from all other public creditors" that the justice of the country simply had to be aroused. They believed themselves to be "legally and equitably entitled" to benefits, because the Government's inability to fund fully its 1783 promise and commutation of half-pay had constituted an unfulfilled contractual obligation on the part of the nation. Some officers even went so far as to assert that Congress's *discussion* of their claims in a previous session had "disclosed a tacit recognition of obligations" on the part of the nation.

---

[38] Fred Somkin, *Unquiet Eagle: Memory and Desire in the Idea of American Freedom, 1815–1860* (Ithaca, NY: Cornell University Press, 1967), p. 137.

Although not all veteran officers were "equally urged by necessitous circumstances to present themselves as objects of the public generosity," the situation compelled them "to advance a demand upon the public equity and honor"[39] (Figure 3.8).

Thus it was that the Revolutionary officers, represented by attorney William Jackson, approached Congress in December 1818 to demand, "on the footing of right," that the government execute its original contract with the men who had brought about the nation's independence. Their argument was a forceful one, given Congress's established role in the adjudication of claims against the Treasury and the sanctity of the principles of contract in the legal thinking of the day, and it succeeded in splitting the issue of veterans' benefits into two distinct strains. While many Revolutionary veterans, particularly members of the militia, were left to argue for inclusion in the pension program on the basis of financial need, meritorious service, and legislative precedent, the officers were able to use the language of rights to press for an equitable settlement of their "legal" claims.[40]

[39] "Petition of a number of the surviving Officers in the Pennsylvania Line of the Army of the United States," 7 December 1808; "Petition of the late officers in the Virginia Continental line of the revolutionary army," 10 January 1809; and "Memorial of sundry surviving officers of the late revolutionary army, residing within the State of Maryland," 13 January 1809, Records of the U.S. House of Representatives, Record Group 233, National Archives, Washington, DC.

In 1810, the House committee to which petitions from the surviving Revolutionary officers were referred reported that, in its opinion, "the contract entered into by Congress with the officers of the late revolutionary army, for giving them half-pay for life, ha[d] not been substantially complied with by the Government." "Half-Pay for Life in Lieu of Five Years' Full Pay," January 31, 1810, *ASP, Claims*, pp. 372–3, 373. This seems to be the first congressional reference to pensions as contractual obligations conferring property rights upon the veterans; a member of the Senate later referred to the 1810 utterance as the first of its kind [*Register of Debates in Congress, 1825–1837* (the continuation of the *Annals of Congress*), hereafter *RD* (20/1), p. 128, Jan. 24, 1828.] But note Ferguson's description of the centralizing strategy of Financier Robert Morris and the nationalists in 1782–3, in which the public debt (composed mostly at that point of loan certificates) was portrayed as creating both a moral obligation and an implied contract between Congress and public creditors. *The Power of the Purse* (Chapel Hill: University of North Carolina Press, 1961), pp. 143, 147.

[40] The pension-as-contract argument appeared full-blown in December 1818, nine months after service pensions for aged, poor Revolutionary veterans were legislated, in a "memorial and statement" presented to Congress by attorney Jackson. As "Solicitor on behalf of the Officers of the Revolutionary Army of the U.S.," Jackson submitted congressional records, financial and actuarial calculations, and George Washington's "price of their blood" quote as proof of the officers' claim. A former Revolutionary officer himself, Jackson served as secretary general of the Society of the Cincinnati from around 1800 to 1828. Retained by the Pennsylvania Society with the

To the Honorable the Senate and House of Representatives of the United States, in Congress assembled.

The Memorial of the Surviving Officers of the late Revolutionary Army and Navy of the State of New-York,

Respectfully Sheweth,

THAT, prompted by a sense of their Country's wrongs, they entered the service without regard to personal or pecunairy considerations; and were impelled by the same motives, strengthened by the subsequent provisions of Congress, for their compensation, to persevere through the hardships and vicissitudes of a long and arduous war, to the final establishment of the Independence of the United States.

The annals of the Revolution, and the Records of Congress, afford the most ample and unequivocal testimonies of their services and privations; and that, ultimately, under circumstances the most humiliating and embarrassing, they retired patiently to their homes and avocations, confidently relying on the justice of their country, for the speedy and complete performance of its engagements—among which they beg leave to claim your first attention to that of *Half Pay, for Life.* A reference to the Journals of Congress of twenty-second March, one thousand seven hundred and eighty-three, will shew that such provision appearing invidious to many of the citizens, it was determined by the officers to make a sacrifice to public opinion; and to that end, as well with a view to some capital for their respective occupations or pursuits, Memorials were presented to Congress, proposing a *Commutation* thereof, which they were induced to do, under a full persuasion of receiving the MONEY, as expressed in the resolution; or Certificates, which would have been rendered equal to it, by the immediate establishment of Public Credit. The disappointment of these expectations, through the long procrastination of the Funding Act, so necessary to realize them, and the consequent distress of many of our old Revolutionary Companions, are too well known to need any further illustration, than that the proposed object was defeated, and many of them absolutely compelled to part with the evidences of that debt, for little more than the amount of a *single year's half pay.* Had it been possible to have received an actual payment in specie, at that important crisis, it would obviously have proved more beneficial than any subsequent arrangement.

Your Memorialists beg leave further to state, That, by the mode adopted for funding the public debt, they are convinced, a considerable saving has accrued to the United States, and a corresponding loss to the Revolutionary Officers: two-thirds only of the principal of the public debt, having been by the Act of Congress of August, 1790, funded at an immediate interest of six per cent, and the remaining one third, forming a deferred stock, without interest for ten years. The interest thereon having been funded at three per cent.

That your Memorialists therefore further conceive they have the most just and equitable claim on their country, for the difference of the interest of six per cent, on their final settlement certificates for pay for the years one thousand seven hundred and eighty-two and one thousand seven hundred and eighty-three, and on the commutation certificates, from first January, one thousand seven hundred and eighty-four to first January, one thousand seven hundred and ninety-one, which as before stated, was funded at three per cent.

That your Memorialists beg leave further to state, That in their opinion, they have likewise a just and equitable claim on the United States, for ten years interest, upon one third of the principal of their respective final settlement and commutation notes which constituted the six per cent deferred stock.

FIGURE 3.8. A memorial from the surviving Continental Army and Navy officers from New York, c. 1808–9, arguing that Revolutionary officers had a "just and equitable claim" to pension benefits, with interest, dating back to the Continental Congress's promises of 1783. Courtesy of the National Archives and Records Administration, Records of the U.S. House of Representatives.

Under this view of the subject, added to the losses sustained by them, and the consequent saving to the public, by the mode of funding the army debt, your Memorialists respectfully conceive, that they have an equitable claim, and urged by a sense of duty to themselves and families, as well as by the considerations abovementioned, are emboldened to appeal to the justice and magnanimity of your Honorable Body, for a remuneration.

Should it be said that the claim has lain dormant, they would beg leave to observe, that representations of a similar nature were submitted to Congress, by the officers of several states, after the resources of the country were brought into operation, and they are ignorant that any final measures were adopted in regard to such applications.

Your memorialists will not intrude longer, with reiterations on a subject so well understood, but pray that Congress will be pleased to take it into consideration, and decide thereon as their justice and wisdom shall direct.

And your memorialists, as in duty bound, will ever pray, &c.

FIGURE 3.8. (*Continued*).

107

The Sixteenth Congress considered the aggrieved officers' claims as it debated how to amend the pension law to prevent fraud and abuse. In that debate, members invoked the usual distinction between "debts of gratitude" and "debts of justice" – that is, between benevolence and legal obligation – but with a new twist. They asserted that Congress's *enactment of the 1818 law*, rather than the Revolutionary veterans' military service, had given those veterans vested legal rights to pension benefits. That this was still a tenuous argument in early 1820 is evidenced by the mix of appeals to morality and legality in speeches defending the pension program. Representative Clifton Clagett of New Hampshire, for example, asked whether Congress could, "consistent with moral principles, withhold the [Act of 1818's] stipulated relief," stating that

> whether you consider this law as founded on a debt due by contract, or mere gratitude to the Revolutionary soldier, he has a vested right in his pension for life; and you are bound, morally bound, to perform your engagement. . . . It has been contended that the soldier's right to his pension, under the law, is not vested, . . . [but] what remains to make this a vested or perfect right? Was not the act of the Government as perfect and as solemn as it was possible to make it? Was it not founded upon a good and valuable consideration? And has not the soldier accepted it? Yes, sir, all this clearly appears. What more, then, could have been done by either party to perfect this right? I know of nothing.[41]

Some of Clagett's colleagues thought differently. Relying on an early vision of the right–privilege distinction that would so powerfully affect twentieth-century entitlements, they countered that the pensions granted by the Fifteenth Congress "could not be deemed a vested right." As

promise of being paid 4 percent of whatever Congress might give to each officer, he persisted for years in urging the other state societies to join in lobbying the Federal Government. When the South Carolina Society engaged Jackson as their agent in August 1818, they provided him with a memorial they had written to Congress "demanding as a right rather than soliciting as a favor a proper attention to their just and honorable demands." Alexander Garden, vice-president of the South Carolina Society, observed that the memorial "certainly appear[ed] in a far greater degree the language of remonstrance rather than petition": in his opinion, the form "more likely to ensure success." *AC* (15/2), pp. 350–9, Dec. 7, 1818 (see also pp. 347–50 for the House committee's positive reaction to the assertion of legal rights in the memorial); Minor Myers, Jr., *Liberty without Anarchy: A History of the Society of the Cincinnati* (Charlottesville: University Press of Virginia, 1983), pp. 216–18; Garden to Jackson, 6 August 1818 and 4 August 1818, The William Jackson Papers, Manuscripts and Archives, Yale University Library.

[41] *AC* (16/1), p. 1714, Apr. 2, 1820.

Senator James Barbour phrased it, the 1818 Pension Act "was one of gratuitous bounty, and not of justice.... [B]eing an act of charity, [the pension program of 1818] continued at the option of the Government."[42]

The existence of such radically different congressional perceptions of the 1818 pension program helps to explain why veterans like Elias Stevens might have believed themselves to be entitled to pensions when the Government declared their behavior fraudulent. Arguments over the true nature of veterans' pensions continued to inflame congressional debate as pressures for the expansion of the pension program and a response to the aggrieved officers' demands mounted in the 1820s. Initially, bills introduced for the purposed of "adjust[ing]" and "settl[ing]" the officers' claims failed to pass.[43] However, the Revolution's officers finally received "payment" on their debt of justice in May 1828, when a sharply divided Twentieth Congress granted *full* pay for life to *both* the surviving officers entitled to half pay for life by the resolution of 1780 *and* the noncommissioned officers and soldiers entitled to $80 in 1778, *without* the requirement that they demonstrate poverty. The conceptual divorcement of these new benefits from previously created veterans' pensions was so complete that the 1828 statute vested their administration directly in the Treasury Department rather than with the secretary of war.[44]

[42] *AC* (16/1), p. 1653, Mar. 18, 1820. Note that members of Congress advocating an expansion of the 1818 pension program began to invoke the legal argument that pensions could be considered contractual obligations when the program came under attack in 1819. See, e.g., the debate over amending the pension program to ensure against fraud, remarks of Josiah Cushman of Massachusetts, *AC* (16/1), pp. 1707–9, Dec. 15, 1819. Arguments framing pension benefits as contractual obligations peppered debates about both the aggrieved officers' situation and program expansion throughout the 1820s.

[43] See, e.g., the failure of a bill in the first session of the Sixteenth Congress, *AC* (16/1), pp. 1845–6, Apr. 14, 1820; and debate in the Nineteenth Congress, second session, when a bill to benefit the officers variously was criticized and stalled for its failure to include soldiers, widows and orphans, and members of the militia. Notably, arguments were made for the inclusion of the *heirs* of *deceased* officers, upon whom the purported legal rights of original claimants should have devolved. *RD* (19/2), pp. 602–34, 636–7, 654–69, 672–714, 717–32, 777–8, Jan. 3–22, 1827.

[44] "An Act for the relief of certain surviving Officers and Soldiers of the Army of Revolution," May 15, 1828, *RD* (20/1), Appendix, p. xv. The act provided officers with full pay retroactive to March 1826, less any pension monies received since then; any other pensions they received would also cease payment with the receipt of the new benefits. Noncommissioned officers, musicians, and privates were also entitled to received full pay from March 1826 unless they were already on the Federal pension list, which disqualified

Revolutionary Pensions and Sectional Politics

Although the passage of this law might be said to have legitimized the rightful claims of some of the Revolution's officers and soldiers, the fractious debate leading to its enactment included staunch rejections of those rights. Where advocates like Daniel Webster contended that the officers would surely be entitled to relief in a court of equity, opponents including John Tyler and William Smith ridiculed the notion of an unfulfilled legal "contract" with a party who not only had agreed to commutation, but also had requested it.[45] The final votes in both the House and Senate demonstrated the extent to which the pension issue had become divisive, and not just with respect to differing interpretations of moral or legal principle. Congress was not split along party lines, for as one member noted in the Senate, the "zeal and ability" displayed by each party in support of the 1828 bill had been so great that after its passage, it would be difficult to determine which party would be awarded credit for having procured it.[46] Rather, the pension issue had developed into a geographic contest of wills, which increasingly pitted proponents from the Northeast and the Middle Atlantic states against naysayers from the South. Though hotly denied, accusations of regional self-interest were made on both sides of the question, because the distribution of pensions appeared to benefit

them from the benefits of the 1828 Pension Act. The phrase "debt of justice" is drawn from President John Quincy Adams's December 4, 1827, message to Congress, in which he recommended consideration of "the debt, rather of justice than of gratitude, to the surviving warriors of the Revolutionary War," a subject "of deep interest to the whole Union." *RD* (20/1), p. 2785.

While the language of legal entitlement seems to have worked very powerfully toward passage of the Pension Act of 1828, it should be noted that the legislation was enacted a mere two and a half years after the Marquis de Lafayette's year-long tour of the United States, in which the aged major general of the Continental Army was hailed and feted by tens of thousands of Americans. According to Fred Somkin, "the affecting nature of his pilgrimages to Revolutionary battlefields, the poignancy of his reunions with aged comrades, and the spectacular series of entertainments arranged for him captured the imagination of the entire country.... [A]s the year-long Lafayette festival proceeded to hold up for reverent consideration every facet of the General's life and character it became ever clearer that in praising Lafayette a generation of Americans were explaining themselves to one another and to the world." *Unquiet Eagle,* pp. 132–5.

[45] *RD* (20/1), pp. 703–9, 228–34, and 187–96, Apr. 25, Feb. 1, and Jan. 29, 1828, remarks of Webster, Tyler, and Smith, respectively. Webster had also argued the merits of the officers' legal claims from a lawyer's perspective in the previous Congress as a member of the House. *RD* (19/2), pp. 685–90, Jan. 12, 1827.

[46] Remark of Senator Thomas Cobb of Georgia, *RD* (20/1), p. 215, Jan. 30, 1828.

disproportionately veterans in one area of the country at the expense of the others.[47]

The extent to which regional conflicts over pensions reflected larger sectional cleavages that had developed over Federal fiscal policy became clear in the congressional debate following President Andrew Jackson's 1829 proposal that national benefits be further extended to every Revolutionary soldier "unable to maintain himself in comfort."[48] Revolutionary entitlements had become implicated in struggles for control of the political economy as well as in battles over its virtue. Before the War of 1812, import duties had been the widely accepted tax mode of choice, supplying almost all of the nation's revenues, with little complaint among elites or the mass public, but the end of the wars for independence had removed military expenditures as one of their main justifications. The South might have expected a leveling or reduction of tariffs in conjunction with other postwar tax reform measures, especially after financial recovery from the panic of 1819 (which had hit some areas of the South particularly hard)

[47] See Table 3.1. It is somewhat difficult to assess whether congressional charges of distributional inequity contained any merit. As Table 3.1 shows, the number of pensioners in each state clearly bore some relationship to that state's number of Army enlistees and population. Moreover, new states were created between 1783 and 1820, and veterans were highly mobile during that period. Resch estimates that approximately 10,000 pension recipients moved during the thirty years following the Revolution, of whom some 4,000 relocated to another state within their region and 6,000 relocated to another region of the country. *Suffering Soldiers*, Appendix B, Tables 16 and 17, p. 218.

Congressional votes on service pension issues generally demonstrated regional divisions from 1818 on, although arguments for and against benefits were justified otherwise. Before 1829, allusions to those divisions were few and outright accusations of sectional partisanship rare, though some were registered. In January 1827, for example, House member James Clarke of Kentucky, while intending "no offensive reflections" and "insinuating no reproach," asked how it had happened that out of all of the Representatives from New England, New York, and New Jersey, only four had voted to recommit a much-debated pension bill. "Could it be," he asked, "because it is there these great disbursements are to be made?" Peleg Sprague of Maine replied to Clarke's "inference" of "interested motives" by questioning whether those in the West had voted in favor of recommitment because "the disbursements were not to be made among themselves." He too then disclaimed, "as cheerfully and sincerely" as had the gentleman from Kentucky, "any intention to impute interested motives." *RD* (19/2), pp. 708–9. Despite such interchanges, the circular letters written by members from Virginia, North Carolina, and Kentucky between 1827 and 1829 all cited the unequal treatment of different classes of veterans as the main problem with the 1828 Pension Act. Cunningham, ed., *Circular Letters of Congressmen to Their Constituents 1789–1829*, vol. 3, pp. 1351, 1373, 1374, 1428, 1437, and 1550.

[48] "Message of the President to Both Houses of Congress," Dec. 8, 1829, *RD* (21/1), Appendix, p. 14.

TABLE 3.1. The Geography of Pension Distribution, February 1820, Under the Act of 1818

State/Territory	Army Enlistees	Pension Recipients	1790 Population	1820 Population
New Hampshire	12,496	1,142	142,000	244,000
Massachusetts (including Maine)	67,907	4,338	476,000	821,000
Rhode Island	5,908	249	69,000	83,000
Connecticut	31,939	1,373	238,000	275,000
New York	17,781	3,196	340,000	1,373,000
New Jersey	10,726	467	184,000	278,000
Pennsylvania	25,723	1,090	434,000	1,049,000
Delaware	2,387	41	59,000	73,000
Maryland	13,912	575	320,000	407,000
Virginia	26,678	693	692,000	938,000
North Carolina	7,263	212	394,000	639,000
South Carolina	6,417	130	249,000	503,000
Georgia	2,679	46	83,000	341,000
Vermont		1,296	85,000	236,000
Alabama		5		128,000
Mississippi		6		75,000
Louisiana		1		153,000
Missouri		6		67,000
Illinois		4		244,000
Indiana		96		147,000
Tennessee		214	36,000	423,000
Kentucky		474	74,000	564,000
Ohio		647		581,000

Compiled from data in H.doc., 16th Cong., 1st sess., No. 77, 7 February 1820; *The Statistical History of the United States from Colonial Times to the Present* (New York: Basic Books, 1976), pp. 24–37.

and Treasury surpluses in 1822–3. Instead, however, the notion of tariffs as "protection" for young native industries developed, so that a congressional alliance of middle Atlantic and western states, with help from a divided New England, enacted the Tariff of 1824. After the passage of the so-called Tariff of Abominations of 1828 increased import duties again, a bitter South complained that it was "no longer an equal beneficiary of the national government's activities."[49] Senator Robert Hayne, part

[49] Dall W. Forsythe, *Taxation and Political Change in the Young Nation 1781–1833* (New York: Columbia University Press, 1977), pp. 62–86, cited phrase on p. 82; F. W. Taussig, *The Tariff History of the United States* (New York: G. P. Putnam's Sons, 1923, 7th

of the militant South Carolina delegation in the Twenty-first Congress, emphatically denounced the "specious pretext of paying a debt of national gratitude to the soldiers of the Revolution" as nothing more than an "ingeniously contrived," degenerate "scheme" for the distribution of public money: part of a great system "calculated and intended to create and perpetuate a permanent charge upon the treasury." How had it happened, he asked his fellow congressmen, that such a "spirit of gratitude for Revolutionary services should have slumbered for fifty years?" That it had never previously been discovered that the men who were to be embraced by the most recent pension bill were "entitled to the bounty of their country?" That "*without a single petition* praying for such an addition to the pension system,

we should be seized with such a sudden and inveterate fit of gratitude to the old soldiers, that we seemed determined to seize them by force, and, taking no denial, to insist on their receiving our bounty, whether they will or no? Sir, the reason is obvious. The period for the final extinction of the public debt is at hand. Colonization has not yet been sanctioned; internal improvement advances too slowly; the distribution of the revenue meets with but small favor; the existence of a surplus must, by some means or other, be prevented; and this must be accomplished without any reduction of duties. The friends of the [American] system have therefore gone forth upon the highways, and "all are bidden to the feast."[50]

Hayne presented a detailed analysis of the trajectory of American pension legislation beginning in pre-Revolutionary times, when "a deep, settled, and salutary prejudice against pensions [had] almost universally prevailed." In Hayne's view, the expansion of the pension system beyond the principle of disability ("a wise and safe principle, limited in its extent, and almost incapable of abuse") had been an unjust and unprincipled enterprise that had established benefits for a "large class of persons whose services were in no respect more valuable than those of the great body of the people." That policy history convinced him that Congress was about to "commence a new system" that would not and could not stop short until it extended beyond military benefits to civil pensions, precluding any reduction in the "enormous amount of indirect taxation with which the people of the United States [we]re ... burthened, and under the weight

ed.), pp. 68–108; Edward Stanwood, *American Tariff Controversies in the Nineteenth Century* (Boston: Houghton Mifflin and Co., 1904), pp. 200–90; Dewey, *Financial History*, pp. 161–81. The Tariff of 1828 was enacted days after the 1828 Pension Act granting further relief of the Revolutionary officers and soldiers.
[50] *RD* (21/1), pp. 400–1, Apr. 29, 1830, emphasis added.

of which the whole South [wa]s fast sinking into ruin." Southerners had "never complained" about their unequal tax burden when the pension system had been confined "to the proper objects of national bounty," but when it degenerated into a "mere scheme for the distribution of the public money," Hayne argued, they had a "right to complain of the gross inequality of the system."[51]

The pension system continued to be linked explicitly with the tariff by the South – and thereby, at least implicitly, to an increase of Federal power at the expense of states' rights – after Jackson's proposal to entitle all needy Revolutionary veterans to pension benefits was revived in both chambers of the Twenty-second Congress in 1831–2. In the House, Charles Johnston of Virginia termed the measure a mere prop to "large schemes of prodigal expenditure of money," intended to prevent the reduction of taxes oppressing the southern people. As his Virginian colleague Thomas Bouldin had asserted, only the deluded could deny that for every $1 people south of the Potomac paid to pension poor soldiers, they paid $2 to rich manufacturers. Warren Davis of South Carolina, calling "a spade a spade," accused the wild, extravagant, "mammoth bill" of "establishing an indiscriminate, wholesale pension system, extending it beyond all former, beyond all describable limits, and beyond all calculable cost," requiring national revenue both "unequally and unjustly levied, and unequally, unjustly, and partially disbursed." Despite such opposition from the South, however, the pension bill passed in the House by a vote of 126 to 48.[52] Advocates pointed to the justice of its new inclusivity, noting

[51] *RD* (21/1), pp. 396–403, Apr. 29, 1830. Forsyth has observed that despite the South's contention that pensions and the tariff were linked, the debate over the tariff made it clear that "most congressmen had no idea what the effect of the proposed bill might be on revenues" (*Taxation and Political Change*, pp. 76–7). Yet, soon after Hayne's peroration, the Senate voted by a narrow majority to postpone the pension expansion bill under consideration indefinitely. When the House voted in the next session of the Twenty-first Congress to proffer additional pension benefits to the militia, state troops, and volunteers of the Revolutionary service and to grant the widows and children of deceased pensioners the balance of their benefits, the Senate again took no action. *RD* (21/1), p. 405, May 3, 1830; *RD* (21/2), p. 745, Feb. 17, 1831.

[52] *RD* (22/1), pp. 2498 and 2372, Apr. 5 and 3, 1832, Johnston and Bouldin, respectively; Davis, pp. 2386–7, Apr. 4; House passage, p. 2713, May 2. All of the House members voting from New York, Massachusetts, Maine, Connecticut, Vermont, New Hampshire, Pennsylvania, New Jersey, Rhode Island, Delaware, Louisiana, Missouri, Illinois, Indiana, and Kentucky were in favor the pension bill. Of the 126 affirmative votes, only 35 came from southern and western states [Virginia (5), North Carolina (3), Tennessee (2), Ohio (8), Kentucky (9), Louisiana (3), Indiana (3), Illinois (1), and Missouri (1)]. House members from the states of South Carolina, Georgia, Alabama, and Mississippi

that Congress's removal of the pension program's poverty requirement would allow the nation to reward "untiring industry and frugality" instead of indolence, intemperance, and dissipation[53] – in the political parlance of today, "personal responsibility and opportunity" or "work, not welfare."

The debate over expanding the pension system was equally acrimonious in the Senate in 1832. Regional disagreements over inclusion and exclusion for benefits revealed how fully the locus of the political conflict over the Revolutionary entitlements had shifted from their mere existence to their programmatic boundaries of desert and reward, which obviously were socially constructed and therefore manipulable by members determined either to deny or to bring home benefits to a rapidly expanding electorate. When John Robinson of Illinois advocated pensions for those who fought in the Northwest Territory and in the Indian Wars, the senators from Tennessee took exception to any exclusion of men fighting the tribes of the Southwest, asking what possible difference there could have been between those engaged in the Revolutionary War on one side of the mountains and on the other. Theodore Frelinghuysen of New Jersey replied that Congress had to discriminate somewhere, whereupon Hugh White of Tennessee and Alexander Buckner of Missouri responded that the nation's respect could not be extended to the militias of the East without including those in West, whose toils had secured the very land that the Government held. Senator Hayne sarcastically suggested that if volunteers were to be entitled to pensions, he saw no reason why wagoners and boatmen should be excluded, or farmers. In fact, since the obvious purpose of the bill was to take money out of the public purse, perhaps the Government should just give a pension to everyone who had *lived* in the time of the Revolution. Hayne's complaint that New England received a far greater share of Federal pensions than his state prompted Samuel Foot of Connecticut to charge that nearly half of the population of South Carolina were Tories.[54] Hayne made sure that the final version of the pension bill would include the officers and soldiers of the militia, volunteers, and state troops of the southern states, then voted against it

voted unanimously against the bill. All of the 48 negative votes came from Maryland, Virginia, North Carolina, South Carolina, Georgia, Alabama, Mississippi, Tennessee, and Ohio.

[53] Remarks of Representative Henry Hubbard of New Hampshire, *RD* (22/1), p. 1925, Feb. 29, 1832. The notion of pensions as rights also subtly infused the debate, though no firm consensus was reached as to whether an additional "debt" to the veterans was still outstanding.

[54] *RD* (22/1), pp. 761–6, Apr. 11, 1832; Hayne, p. 708, Apr. 5; Foot, p. 924, May 11.

as it was approved by a majority of the Senate on May 19, 1832, by a vote of 26 to 19.[55] Just before the bill passed, Henry Clay of Kentucky denied once more that such an "act of justice" for the brave men who survived of the gallant band that had secured the nation's independence should be "identified with the tariff."[56]

The sectional quarrels over Federal pensions that took place in the late 1820s and early 1830s clearly were implicated in the larger contemporary debate over nationalization. Yet, it would be difficult to demonstrate with any precision where arguments about the Revolutionary pension system gave way to, or actually represented, arguments over states' rights. Warren Davis, for example, warned fellow House members against expanding the pension system in language that simultaneously decried the practice of selective entitlement and the increasing power and activity of the national government:

[T]his system of transferring property by legislation, of giving pensions and gratuities to individuals, companies, corporations, and States; of squandering, like a young heir, the public lands, which belonged to the people, on deaf and dumb

---

55 "An Act supplementary to the 'Act for the relief of certain surviving officers and soldiers of the Revolution,'" June 7, 1832, *RD* (22/1), Appendix, p. xvii; Senate passage, *RD* (22/1), p. 933. The 1832 act extended the May 1828 grant of full pay for life to surviving officers, noncommissioned officers, musicians, soldiers, Indian spies, mariners, and marines who had served during the Revolution for a total of two years in the Continental Army or state troops, volunteers, militia, or Navy, who were not already entitled to benefits under the 1828 act. It originally required applicants to relinquish all other Federal pensions to claim its benefits, but was amended in 1833 to exempt invalid pensioners from that restriction. The sectional distribution of the Senate vote was similar to that of the House. The senators voting from New York, Massachusetts, Maine, Connecticut, Vermont, New Hampshire, Pennsylvania, New Jersey, Rhode Island, Delaware, Illinois, Indiana, and Ohio unanimously favored the bill. Those from Maryland, Virginia, North Carolina, South Carolina, Georgia, Tennessee, Alabama, Mississippi, and Missouri voted unanimously against it. The senators from Kentucky and Louisiana split on the issue.

56 *RD* (22/1), p. 930, May 11, 1832. According to Dall Forsythe, Clay had reopened the tariff debate in Congress with reduction proposals in January 1832 in the hope of securing some support from the South for his presidential bid, but failed in that effort when he rejected a compromise amendment from Hayne. *Taxation and Political Change*, pp. 99–100. The Tariff of 1832 was enacted within days of the Pension Act (which Clay voted in favor of). The linkage between tariffs disadvantaging particular areas of the nation and military pension expenditures advantaging others would contribute to sectional conflict throughout the remainder of the nineteenth century. See, e.g., Richard Franklin Bensel, *Sectionalism and American Political Development* (Madison: University of Wisconsin Press, 1984), pp. 60–73. Once the individual income tax became a primary source of national revenue, however, disagreement over entitlement expenditures became more interest group-oriented and interpersonal, particularly when national fiscal stress suggested selective benefit *reductions* for some of the variously entitled.

asylums, and other local institutions; of destroying commerce and agriculture, to benefit a comparatively small number of capitalists, who had embarked their funds in manufactures; of making gifts to States and sections of the Union, for roads and canals; would degrade and demoralize the people by making them dependent on the Government; would emasculate the free spirit of the country.[57]

Both pro- and antipension members of the Twenty-second Congress explicitly took issue with selective entitlement as a policy device, albeit from different perspectives that were premised upon the outcomes that had resulted from its use. Northern advocates of the 1832 supplementary pension bill, like Rufus Choate of Massachusetts, argued that Congress's previous pension laws had been *too* selective, unjustly denying many deserving veterans benefits granted to others. Southerners on the other side of the issue, including Warren Davis and Robert Hayne, accused pension advocates of not being selective *enough*: that is, of employing an unprincipled, ad hoc, "add-a-group" approach arbitrarily to entitle *too many* veterans to pensions, thereby benefiting the "receiving States" at the expense of the "paying" ones.[58] Antagonists from the West argued against the 1832 bill's enlargement of the pension system because it would not extend as far as their own constituents – veterans of battles with Indians on the frontier. Clearly, any growth of the Revolutionary pension system would expand the reach of the central state apparatus. However, participants on both sides of the debate registered too much concern over problems arising from selective entitlement per se for it to be concluded that they were not as concerned about the appropriate *use* of state power as they were about its location.

Not surprisingly, enactment of the liberal Pension Act of 1832 resulted in another period of explosive Federal expenditures and abuse.[59] It was "thought incredible that there should be so many Revolutionary soldiers alive."[60] More than 24,000 claims were submitted in the six months after the act's passage, causing Secretary of War Lewis Cass to estimate in a January 1833 report to Congress that nearly 23,000 pensions would be granted in that year for a total expenditure of some $5,368,275, far more than anticipated (Figure 3.9). Beyond expressing concern over soaring

---

57 *RD* (21/1), p. 2396, Apr. 4, 1832.
58 Choate, *RD* (22/1), pp. 2446–58, Apr. 9, 1832; Hayne, *RD* (21/1), p. 401, Apr. 29, 1830.
59 Based upon Dewey's figures, pension expenditures comprised 19.46 percent of total U.S. Government expenditures in 1833 and 17.64 percent in 1834. *Financial History of the United States*, pp. 169, 246.
60 Glasson, *Federal Military Pensions*, p. 83.

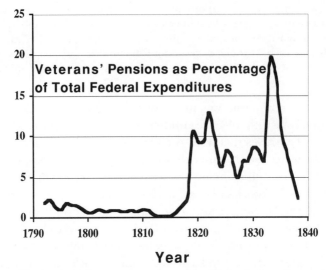

FIGURE 3.9. Veterans' pensions as a percentage of total Federal expenditures, 1792–1838. Calculated with data from *The Statistical History of the United States From Colonial Times to the Present* (New York: Basic Books, 1976), p. 1106, and "Statements showing amount of revolutionary pensions paid annually from 4th March, 1789, to 31st December, 1838," 342 S. doc. 307, 25th Cong. 3rd sess.

costs and fraud, Cass initiated a statutory reorganization of the Pension Bureau to guarantee the authority and accountability of its head, who as a mere "clerk" controlled annual disbursements of some $2,500,000. A more formal bureaucratic structure was required both to manage the increasing scope of the government's programmatic business and to encourage adherence to fading standards of virtuous behavior.[61] Meanwhile, as some members of Congress became vocal about the size of the pension establishment and a lack of associated controls, efforts continued to expand the system to accommodate new groups. John Quincy Adams, who as president had called for the Pension Act of 1828, noted in April 1834 that Revolutionary claimants not only seemed immortal, but

[61] Congress responded to Cass's recommendations in March 1833, providing for a commissioner of pensions who would be appointed by the president and the Senate, and would execute the pension laws under the direction of the secretary of war. The Pension Office became a bureau of the Department of the Interior when it was established in 1849. Land entitlements also contributed to the increased workload and administrative misbehavior in the General Land Office, leading to executive branch growth and reorganization. See Chapter 4. "Letter from the Secretary of War," *House Doc.* 22/2, vol. 1, no. 34, Jan. 7, 1833; Glasson, *Federal Military Pensions*, p. 86; Crenson, *Federal Machine*, pp. 136–7, 162–5.

appeared to multiply with the passage of time. Yet even after pension frauds led to well-publicized exposés and numerous indictments for forgery and perjury in 1834 and 1835, Congress declined to enact measures for the reform of the Revolutionary pension system.[62] Instead, with another hefty surplus in the Treasury, it extended Federal benefits once more in 1836, granting half-pay for life to the widows and orphans of men who had died or would die from wounds received in the military service of the United States. Rather than subject itself to "the charge of injustice or ingratitude towards its faithful sustainers," the Government performed one more "act of sheer justice" for its "most meritorious citizens," furthering the growth of the state and a policy legacy of selective beneficence as it ensured the lasting gratitude of the surviving widows, children, and grandchildren of the patriot soldiers "gathered home to their fathers."[63]

The historical and institutional contexts of the Revolutionary pension laws made their passage not only possible but logical. The need to secure an effective fighting force made pension entitlements the policy solution of choice for a new and determined American state. That the Continental Congress had little authority to enact officers' pensions and no means of funding them did not prevent these early benefits from becoming important social policy precedents. The establishment of a putative program of service pensions, coupled with contemporary understandings about representation and legislative obligation, created powerful expectations of the state that would not simply disappear when governing circumstances changed.

For many who had sought to create the new nation, the Revolution became the shaping event of their lives, and they invariably measured

---

[62] *Memoirs of John Quincy Adams*, ed. Charles Francis Adams (Philadelphia: J. B. Lippincott & Co., 1876), vol. 9, p. 124, April 7, 1834; Glasson, *Federal Military Pensions*, pp. 87–91. Glasson (p. 90) notes that in 1834, more than fifty years after the end of the war, there were approximately 40,000 Revolutionary pensioners receiving benefits under the invalid acts, the Pension Act of 1818, and the Pension Act of 1832, compared with the Pension Bureau's estimate of a total individual enlistment in the Revolutionary Army, including the militia, of 184,038.

[63] "An Act granting half pay to widows and orphans where their husbands or fathers have died of wounds received in the military service of the United States in certain cases, and for other purposes," July 4, 1836, *RD* (24/1), Appendix, p. xlvii; remarks of Representative Ratliff Boon of Indiana, *RD* (24/1), p. 4285. The Pension Act of 1836 was not the last of the Revolutionary pension legislation. Further benefits for surviving patriots were granted during the Civil War, while specific pension provisions for Revolutionary widows culminated in the War of 1812 Pension Act of 1878. Glasson, *Federal Military Pensions*, pp. 92–3.

the developing Republic's health against their memories of the original patriotic uprising.[64] In the wake of the nation's second war for independence, it was natural for an anxious people to reflect upon the first one they had fought, for victory in the War of 1812 had "renewed and reinstated the national feelings and character which the Revolution had given."[65] When James Monroe, the last president from the Revolutionary generation, suggested a way to enshrine that nationalistic fervor in a legislative monument to the nation's citizen-soldiers, an overwhelming majority of Congress seized the moment. Overcoming decades of resistance to selective state benefits, and forgoing its historic commitment to acknowledge and adjudicate the claims of the people on an individual basis, Congress's programmatic recognition of America's aging veterans reconstituted civic virtue and representation for a new age. Creating a pension program for worthy patriots seemed an ideal way "to build on the existing consensus, to complete the unfinished business, [and] to demonstrate the constructive uses of national power."[66]

It would be difficult to overestimate the magnitude of the changes in the American polity that the Revolutionary pension system helped to bring about. First, that system contributed to the growth and development of an array of national institutions. The pensions and pension expectations created by state actors from the 1780s on facilitated the establishment of the military forces essential to building and sustaining the nation, allowing the new American state to govern at the center and at the periphery. Men serving the nation in subsequent nineteenth-century wars were not promised service pensions when they enlisted, but surviving

---

[64] Robert H. Wiebe, *The Opening of American Society: From the Adoption of the Constitution to the Eve of Disunion* (New York: Alfred A. Knopf, 1984), pp. 183–4. See also pp. 16, 46, 98–9, and 235–6 regarding the sanctity of the Revolutionary gentleman's honor code.

[65] Albert Gallatin to Matthew Lyon, May 7, 1816, cited in White, *The Jeffersonians*, p. 10. See also Jean V. Matthews, *Toward a New Society: American Thought and Culture, 1800–1830* (Boston: Twayne Publishers, 1991), pp. 16–17.

[66] Stephen Skowronek, *The Politics Presidents Make: Leadership from John Adams to George Bush* (Cambridge, MA: Belknap Press of Harvard University Press, 1993), p. 86. As Skowronek notes, Monroe's habit of dressing in the clothing of the Revolutionary era reminded everyone who saw him of his past service to the nation, providing a symbolic linkage between the past and his nationalistic administration's sponsorship of new works. Beyond strengthening the state, the sight of things associated with the Revolution also reminded Americans of the importance of resistance to tyranny and repression at a time when revolutionary movements were sweeping through countries on other continents. Pauline Maier, *American Scripture: Making the Declaration of Independence* (New York: Alfred A. Knopf, 1997), pp. 187–8; see also Harry Ammon, *James Monroe: The Quest for National Identity* (New York: McGraw-Hill Book Company, 1971), pp. 368, 371–8, 385–95.

veterans of those conflicts not unreasonably looked to precedent and expected that pension benefits would be forthcoming from a grateful American state. Federal pensions indeed were legislated for most of the veterans of each of those wars, but not until they spent decades lobbying Congress in a frustrating effort at national recognition, just as the Revolution's veterans had.[67] After members of the Union's forces had won the Civil War, the state's obligation to entitle them to public benefits was cast by advocates as the highest conceivable moral and legal obligation. The Union veterans' investment in preserving the nation had been so great as to create a sacred debt: one that could never sufficiently be repaid.[68]

Beyond building the military, the pensions for Revolutionary veterans spurred the development of central fiscal and administrative systems. The petitions and claims that inspired the invention of programmatic entitlement as a policy device also contributed to the development of the congressional committee system, and to more modern modes of representation and legislative behavior.[69] The petition's eventual demise was in large part due to the politics of slavery in the 1830s and Congress's imposition of a gag rule on related constituent communications. That citizens inundated Congress with all manner of appeals and demands from 1789 on, however, including thousands of petitions and claims related to Revolutionary military service, helped to bring about the end of legislative adjudication as a core congressional practice.[70] In 1855, after years of anguished debate over the appropriate forum for the resolution of citizens'

---

[67] War of 1812 veterans were not granted service pensions by Congress until 1871 (see Chapter 5). Indian War and Mexican War veterans received service pensions in 1892 and 1887, respectively. Glasson, *Federal Military Pensions*, pp. 114–17.

[68] Stuart C. McConnell, *Glorious Contentment: The Grand Army of the Republic, 1865–1900* (Chapel Hill: University of North Carolina Press, 1992), pp. 157–61. McConnell's rich account of late-nineteenth-century pension politics indicates quite a bit of continuity with the pension politics of the early nineteenth century. Like the debates over Revolutionary pensions, arguments over the provision of Civil War pensions featured both conflict and confusion over claims that were need-based versus rights-based and geographic contests over pensions rooted in tariff politics.

[69] In addition to the committees detailed previously, the House established standing committees on Revolutionary pensions in 1825 and invalid pensions in 1831. The Senate established a Committee on Private Land Claims in 1826.

[70] An exasperated John Quincy Adams wrote in February 1832: "There ought to be no private claims business before Congress. . . . It is a judicial business, and legislative assemblies ought to have nothing to do with it. One-half of the time of Congress is consumed by it, and there is no common rule of justice for any two of the cases decided. A deliberative Assembly is the worst of all tribunals for the administration of justice." *Memoirs of John Quincy Adams*, vol. 8, p. 480.

claims, Congress finally was brought to establish a special federal Court of Claims, with which it shared responsibility for determining claims against the United States until World War II.[71]

Finally, the entitlements of the Revolutionary pension system shaped American understandings about law, legality, and citizenship in the early decades of the nation's existence. They figured significantly in the working out of key constitutional provisions, influenced the meaning of property, and informed contemporary beliefs about distributive justice and redistributive obligation. Last, but certainly not least, they affected the ways in which people were included in the polity and participated in public life. Americans learned early on that at some times and for some purposes, they could become citizens of the nation, endowed with certain programmatic rights, instead of being consigned to local systems of public care or left to fend for themselves. If Congress's selective creation of military pension benefits did not portend the disaster that Senators Smith and Macon warned of, those early pension entitlements nonetheless played a vital role in the constitution of the American nation.

[71] Shinomura, "History of Claims," pp. 627, 649–82; William M. Wiecek, "The Origin of the United States Court of Claims," *Administrative Law Review* 20 (1968): 394–404. In Shinomura's analysis, the period between the Civil War and World War II was a transitional one in which citizens increasingly came to view private claims as legal rather than political matters. Because Congress was reluctant to part with its traditional authority, a "hybrid" model of claims determination emerged. Congress continued to consider some claims, particularly tort and moral claims, while gradually authorizing other categories of claims to be determined by the judiciary. Only after it became overwhelmed with the pressing national and international concerns of the twentieth century, argues Shinomura, did Congress turn over almost all authority for claims determination to the federal courts, providing a continuing appropriation for the payment of judgments.

4

The "Public" Lands and Public Welfare

Tenantry is unfavorable to freedom. It lays the foundation for separate orders in society, annihilates the love of country, and weakens the spirit of independence. The tenant has, in fact, no country, no hearth, no domestic altar, no household god. The freeholder, on the contrary, is the natural supporter of a free government, and it should be the policy of republics to multiply their freeholders, as it is the policy of monarchies to multiply tenants.

Thomas Hart Benton, May 16, 1826[1]

To suggest that the enactment of pensions for Revolutionary veterans and their survivors created a welfare state during the formative years of the nation would be an exaggeration. So, too, would be a claim that these pensions resulted in central state building that was unremitting or uniform. The pension entitlements of the early national period were nonetheless critical to the path of American political development, for they inaugurated a vital Federal role in the well-being of individual citizens. In doing so, they created avenues for reconstructive assaults on the nation's original decentralized institutional order and initiated the United States into the ways of fragmented, categorical policymaking. The implementation of Federal pension laws both necessitated and justified the growth of national fiscal and administrative systems. Meanwhile, state actors acquired a powerful means of simultaneously appealing directly to an expanding electorate and refining the terms of their citizenship through public benefit programs. The creation of such an instrumental and ideological nexus between the Federal Government and individual citizens was a significant departure at a time when local allegiances still superseded loyalty to national institutions of public authority. Enabling

---

[1] *Register of Debates in Congress, 1825–1837* [hereafter *RD*] (19/1), p. 727.

the Government to govern in new and unanticipated ways, it brought about a shift of power toward the center of what had been designed to be a radically deconcentrated, federally organized state.[2]

Federal military pensions were not the only programmatic entitlements through which that nexus was articulated, for the founding of the new nation resulted in the creation of a public domain in addition to the U.S. Treasury. From the moment independence was declared, and particularly as the contours of America expanded, the public lands were viewed as an asset that could be utilized to accomplish a wide variety of national policy purposes. Federal lands constituted a potent agent of nationalization from the early days of the Confederation, for where the exercise of the most basic functions of national governance (diplomacy, war, and finance) required the approval of nine of the thirteen state delegations before 1789, the U.S. Congress largely was able to govern directly in the West, raising revenue and creating new states. Financially and administratively, the public domain became the new national government's greatest asset, if not its only asset – one that presented a singular opportunity for the fledgling Government to "test and expand its powers."[3] National legislative bodies availed themselves of that opportunity both before 1789 and after, utilizing land to create entitlements as a means of recruiting people to serve the state's purposes.

One of the earliest and most remarkable proposals for the use of America's western lands was the Second Continental Congress's August 1776 offer of citizenship and acreage to Hessian mercenaries and other members of the British army willing to leave the service of the Crown for the United States. Angered that Parliament had invited American troops to desert and even compelled "people, taken at at sea, to serve

[2] Stephen Skowronek, *Building a New American State: The Expansion of National Administrative Capacities* (Cambridge: Cambridge University Press, 1982), pp. 5–10, 19–23.

[3] Daniel Feller, *The Public Lands in Jacksonian Politics* (Madison: University of Wisconsin Press, 1984), p. 5. It should be noted that Congress's authority was not quite plenary. As is discussed later, the states' cession of their western lands was not complete until 1802. Moreover, while the idea was that the Federal Government should manage Indian affairs and regulate Indian trade with the tribes, actors from individual states continued to challenge Congress's sole and exclusive right to deal with Native American tribes throughout the 1780s, rendering intergovernmental relations problematic in at least one domestic policy area even as the U.S. Federal system was created. See Peter S. Onuf, *The Origins of the Federal Republic: Jurisdictional Controversies in the United States 1775–1787* (Philadelphia: University of Pennsylvania Press, 1983), pp. 3–20; Francis Paul Prucha, *American Indian Policy in the Formative Years: The Indian Trade and Intercourse Acts 1790–1834* (Cambridge, MA: Harvard University Press, 1962), pp. 30–43.

against their country," Congress had its offer printed in German on to-
bacco wrappers in the hope that it would fall into the hands of enemy
soldiers.[4] More typical of future American land entitlements, however,
was the program of land grants enacted for Congress's own new nationals: the officers and soldiers who served in the Continental Army for the
duration of the Revolution. Although the Government would actually
have no land at its disposal until years after the war ended, the need to
recruit and retain a force capable of winning the war inspired the Continental Congress to assume that land bounties, like half-pay pensions,
could be "provided by the United States," with their cost simply "paid
and borne by the states in the same proportion as other expenses of the
war."[5] If the Revolution failed, there obviously would be no demand for

[4] *Journals of the Continental Congress, 1774–1789*, vol. V (June–October 1776), ed.
Worthington Chauncey Ford (Washington, DC: GPO, 1904–) [hereafter *JCC* (V, June–
October 1776)], pp. 653–5, 705–9, August 14, 27, 1776; *JCC* (X, January–May 1778),
pp. 405–9. The Continental Congress's "secret" resolution of August 14 promised that
all "foreigners" choosing to leave the armies of "his Brittanic majesty in America" to
become "members of any of th[e] states" would be "protected in the free exercise of
their respective religions, and be invested with the rights, privileges and immunities of
natives, as established by the laws of th[o]se states." Congress would "provide, for every
such person, 50 Acres of unappropriated lands in some of th[o]se states, to be held by
him and his heirs in absolute property." That resolution was amended thirteen days later
to distinguish among and between the officers and soldiers, granting 1,000 acres to a
colonel, 800 acres to a lieutenant colonel, 600 acres to a major, 400 acres to a captain,
300 acres to a lieutenant, 200 acres to an ensign, 100 acres to noncommissioned officers,
and "to every other officer or person" in the foreign corps not specifically named land
"in the like proportion to their rank or pay in said corps." Foreign officers were also to be
rewarded with additional lands in proportion to the number of soldiers they "br[ought]
over." Congress increased its offer in April 1778, promising deserters additional acreage,
livestock, and six weeks' rations; it also asked the states to reserve, as expediently as possible, "a sufficient quantity of lands to answer the purposes expressed" at no charge to
the United States. Rhode Island, Connecticut, and New Jersey voted against the latter
resolution, as did individual members of the Massachusetts Bay, Maryland, and South
Carolina delegations, including Henry Laurens. The Continental Congress's offers to
foreign enlistees may have been in retaliation for an earlier British offer of 200 acres of
land, plus 50 acres for each family member, to those who would serve in the Revolution
on the side of the Crown. Only one such land grant to a foreigner was ever made, in 1792.
Paul Wallace Gates, *History of Public Land Law Development* (Washington, DC: GPO, 1968),
p. 251; Payson Jackson Treat, *The National Land System 1785–1820* (New York: E. B. Treat
& Co., Publishers, 1910), p. 228.
[5] *JCC* (V, June–October 1776), pp. 763, 788, September 16, 20, 1776; Gates, *Public Land
Law Development*, p. 251. The September 1776 resolutions graduated the amounts of
the land bounties according to military rank, ranging from 500 acres for a colonel to
100 acres to each noncommissioned officer and soldier. Bounty lands were also rendered
nonassignable. Congress also resolved to extend the bounty provisions on August 12,

lands still in the possession of the Crown. If it succeeded, the land grants could surely be furnished somehow. Either way, Congress would not have to concern itself with their actual provision until after the conclusion of the war.[6]

The United States acquired its independence from Great Britain along with a fee-simple right of dominion over the western lands extending to the Mississippi River from Great Britain in the 1783 Treaty of Paris. However, the Native Americans who previously had held claim to the entire continent, and who still lived within the contemporary territorial limits of the United States, resisted U.S. attempts to force them to give up their lands at the close of the Revolution. The consolidation and expansion of the United States was complicated further by European legal doctrine establishing that Native Americans retained a right of occupancy (or "right of soil"), giving them the use, enjoyment, and profitable possession of their land as long as they occupied it. Stymied, the Confederation Government declared that it had an exclusive right to purchase or inherit this right of occupancy when the Native Americans decided to sell or no longer lived on the land, but making such an assertion was hardly the same thing as actually achieving national ownership and sovereignty.[7]

In some respects, the legislation entitling certain Army veterans to grants of public land was very similar to the Revolutionary pension enactments of the 1770s and 1780s. Overtly discriminatory in nature, it distinguished between officers and soldiers just as the half-pay pension legislation had. It also discriminated *among* officers, so that the largest rewards were conferred upon those of the highest rank. Yet, the conflicts that initially arose over the enactment of the categorical bounty land program had less to do with the social implications of its inequitable distribution scheme than with the fact that its implementation would require the states to offer up material resources that some of them would be

1780, granting major generals 1,100 acres and brigadier generals 850 acres [*JCC* (XVII, May–September 1780, pp. 726–7)].

[6] Treat, *National Land System*, p. 233.

[7] The acquisition and administration of the public lands and the "management" of the Native Americans were thus domestic policy issues that were inextricably intertwined. As George Washington put it, "the Settlmt. of the Western Country and making a Peace with the Indians [we]re so analogous that there c[ould] be no definition of the one without involving considerations of the other." Reginald Horsman, *Expansion and American Indian Policy, 1783–1812* (East Lansing: Michigan State University Press, 1967), pp. 3–38; Francis Paul Prucha, *American Indian Treaties: The History of a Political Anomaly* (Berkeley: University of California Press, 1994), p. 226; George Washington to James Duane, September 7, 1783, cited in Prucha, *American Indian Policy*, p. 28.

hard pressed to supply. Under their colonial charters, only seven of the original thirteen states – Massachusetts, Connecticut, New York, Virginia, North Carolina, South Carolina, and Georgia – held claim to portions of the western wilderness that could be used after the Revolution to create military land grants (or, for that matter, be sold to retire state war debts). The other six states thus had good reason to fear that after the war they would "be left to sink under an enormous debt," while the others could "replace all their expenditures from the hard earnings of the whole confederacy." They contested the enactment of veterans' land entitlements until it was guaranteed that the United States as a whole, not the states acting in their individual capacities, would make good on the promise of bounty lands.[8] Protracted interstate conflict over the boundaries and disposition of western lands, along with problems with Indian and foreign claims, impeded the ratification of the Articles of Confederation and delayed the conveyance of most of the states' western lands to the United States until almost two decades after the war. As a result, there was no effective system for the provision of military bounty lands in place until 1796, when the Fourth U.S. Congress finally made a tract in Ohio available for the location of the Revolutionary bounties. By then, many veterans, officers and soldiers alike, had sold their military land rights along with their pension certificates for a fraction of what they would eventually have been worth.[9]

---

[8] Feller, *The Public Lands in Jacksonian Politics*, pp. 3–4; "Representation of the Legislative Council and General Assembly of the State of New Jersey," *JCC* (XI, May–September 1778), p. 650; *JCC* (XIV, April–September 1779), pp. 619–22; Rudolf Freund, "Military Bounty Lands and the Origins of the Public Domain," *Agricultural History* 20 (January 1946): 10. Maryland pointedly refused to ratify the Articles of Confederation until the landed states had ceded their western claims to the United States, rejecting the suggestion that it could simply buy land for military bounties from other states. As Maryland's delegates in Congress put it, "an Expectation was formed by the People of our State that what was conquered from an Enemy at joint Expence of Blood and Treasure of the whole should become their joint property but as Claims had been set up opposite to our Ideas of natural Justice it became a wise people rather to prepare for the worst ... than trust to the mercy of a few Venders...." The Continental Congress compromised in 1776 in order to pacify Maryland and other landless states, promising money bounties to those enlisting for three years and reserving land bounties for those soldiers and officers who would sign up for the full duration of the war or until they were honorably discharged. Maryland continued to demand that western lands acquired from Great Britain become a "common stock" for the benefit of the nation until individual states began ceding their lands to the United States.

[9] Jerry A. O'Callaghan, "The War Veteran and the Public Lands," *Agricultural History* 28 (October 1954): 163–5; Freund, "Military Bounty Lands," pp. 10–18; Gates, *Public Land*

The importance of the Revolutionary veterans' land entitlements derived partly from their use as a benefit that would ensure the enlistment
of a fighting force with the capacity to win the war for independence. As
Paul Wallace Gates observed, the promise of land bounties in advance
of enlistment was a "frank acknowledgment that patriotism, the emer-
gency of the moment, and the wages the government offered were not
sufficient to induce men in the numbers needed to offer their services. It
was also an acknowledgment that land was not always easy to obtain, was
much in demand, and that a land bounty might prove more attractive
than anything else the government could promise."[10]

Because land grants also were enacted for veterans *after* particular
military engagements, however – sometimes *well* after – they cannot be
understood merely as compensation promised in exchange for service.
Although Gates and other scholars long have characterized the Revolution's land bounties as "military" policies that served as a precedent for
enlistment bonuses of the future, these programmatic entitlements had
much broader significance as an original strain of national social welfare
policy that, like early veterans' pensions, judiciously entitled groups of
American citizens to individual-level public benefits. They gave rise to
military and civilian expectations that extended well beyond the legislative confines of particular veterans' programs. When enacted selectively,
as they often were, they also created conflict and dissension among and
between groups of military personnel, leading men who were entitled to
lesser land benefits, or not entitled to land at all, to petition and lobby
Congress for inclusion in land grant programs. That Congress often did
not respond favorably, and sometimes did not respond at all, infuriated
citizens accustomed to political representation premised upon a legislative obligation to listen.

Congressional actors framed their creation of pension benefits for
Revolutionary veterans as a singular policy response to the exigencies of
the war for independence (and, later, to the ostensibly unique postwar
life circumstances of the Revolution's patriots). The creation of veterans'
land entitlements, by contrast, required congressmen to formulate an

Law Development, p. 59. The original legislation granting land bounties had forbidden the
sale of bounty warrants, but the Confederation Congress moved to authorize their sale
in 1788. That Congress did not hasten to satisfy the Revolutionary veterans' land claims
(particularly the officers') in form or substance, despite the formal creation of the public
domain in 1783, is discussed in more detail later.
[10] *Public Land Law Development*, p. 249.

exception to the general policy for the "disposal" of the public lands. That policy directed the public domain's sale in exchange for cash, to benefit the nation collectively, and it was at the heart of the agreement that facilitated the creation of the United States. As noted previously, unresolved questions about the disposition of western lands posed a serious impediment to national unification. In an effort to end the protracted squabbles over the states' release of their western lands and secure the ratification of the Articles of Confederation, the Continental Congress pledged in 1780 that any lands ceded to the nation would be "disposed of for the common benefit of the United States." The State of New York accordingly ceded its western territory in 1781 as proof of its "earnest desire to promote the general interest and security, and more especially to accelerate the federal alliance." When three years later a second state, Virginia, was finally moved to cede some of its territory, it did so in language that explicitly articulated the individual states' understandings about the nation's future use of the public lands.[11] All lands not reserved for other purposes were to be

considered as a common fund for the use and benefit of such of the United States as have become, or shall become, members of the Confederation or federal alliance of the said States, Virginia inclusive, according to their usual respective proportions in the general charge and expenditure, and shall be faithfully and bona fide disposed of for that purpose, and for no other use or purpose whatsoever.[12]

Given the staggering national debt that plagued the United States by the end of the Revolution, this vision of the public domain as a common fund or capital asset that could be used to extinguish the nation's

---

[11] Feller has observed that the language of the Virginia Deed of Cession "contained the seeds of a controversy that would trouble the Union decades later and that still continues, though in muted tones and under very different circumstances, today": the question of whether Federal ownership of the public domain in the western states could be reconciled with their guaranteed rights of "sovereignty, freedom, and independence." *Public Lands in Jacksonian Politics*, p. 5.

[12] Resolution of the Continental Congress, September 6, 1780; Deed of Cession between the State of New York and the Congress of the United States of America, 1781; Deed of Cession between the State of Virginia and the Congress of the United States of America, 1784; all cited in Thomas Donaldson, *The Public Domain: Its History, with Statistics* (Washington, DC: GPO, 1884), pp. 64, 66–7, 68–9. See also Onuf, *Origins of the Federal Republic*, pp. 75–125, regarding the intricacies of the New York and Virginia cessions. As Onuf notes, the western land cessions "represented a first step in resolving state inequalities without attacking the states themselves, while simultaneously underwriting the expansion of congressional power through the creation of a nation domain" (p. 154).

liabilities was appealing.[13] Not surprisingly, the Confederation Congress formulated an optimistic plan for the systematic disposal of western lands and the establishment of territorial governments, which it codified in the Ordinance of 1785.[14] The plan garnered significant approval, but it would be difficult to implement, in part because of competing visions of the public domain's future.

Revolutionary veterans holding land warrants expected Congress to utilize some of the public domain to fulfill its wartime promises and satisfy their claims. Although the Newburgh addresses of March 1783 had ignored the issue of bounty lands to press Congress for pension benefits, some of the main actors in the Newburgh conspiracy advocated the formation of a new state for military veterans on the Ohio River. Almost 300 officers from New England had sent George Washington a petition in June 1783 asking Congress to assign and mark out "a Tract or Territory suitable to form a distinct Government (or Colony of the United States)" that would in time be admitted to the Confederation. Washington, in turn, had pushed the plan before Congress, observing that he was "perfectly convinced" that the district of unsettled land being

---

[13] This method of utilizing the public domain posed an attractive alternative to financier Robert Morris's controversial scheme to establish a central fiscal apparatus through customs duties. See Chapter 2 herein and Richard H. Kohn, *Eagle and Sword: The Federalists and the Creation of the Military Establishment in America, 1783–1802* (New York: Free Press, 1975), p. 55.

[14] The ordinance ordered that the public domain be surveyed, divided into rectangular townships 6 miles square, and then subdivided into thirty-six numbered, square-mile (640 acre) "sections" or lots. Natural resources of the Republic such as mines, salt licks and springs, and mill seats were to be set aside, as were five sections in each township: four for "federal" lots, and one for the "maintenance of public schools" (another remarkable departure from Congress's general land policy, as well as from its sphere of authority under either the Articles of Confederation or the U.S. Constitution that would shortly be ratified). Once surveyed, the townships were to be sold at public auction at a price of $1 per acre, with half of them offered whole and half by individual section so that citizens of modest means might have an opportunity to become landowners. Congress waited impatiently for the surveying to be completed, for the debts of the nation "pressed heavily upon few outward assets." Treat, *National Land System*, pp. 22–40; Peter S. Onuf, *Statehood and Union: A History of the Northwest Ordinance* (Bloomington: Indiana University Press, 1987), pp. 21–8; Malcolm J. Rohrbough, *The Land Office Business: The Settlement and Administration of American Public Lands, 1789–1837* (New York: Oxford University Press, 1968), pp. 8–9, 10. Rohrbough notes that "[w]ith the exception of the school reservations, efforts to preserve the resources of the public domain proved futile; Congress eventually gave up and opened these to unlimited exploitation. The ordinance correctly identified the objects of national interest and tried to secure them ... [but] the execution was faulty, and the results were disappointing" (p. 8). Problems in preserving the natural resources on Federal lands persist in the twenty-first century.

requested could not "be so advantageously settled, by any other Class of Men, as by the disbanded Officers and Soldiers of the Army, to whom the faith of Government ha[d] long since been pledged." Such a plan of colonization "would connect our Governments with the frontiers, extend our Settlements progressively, and plant a brave, a hardy and respectable Race of People, as our advanced Post, who would be always ready and willing (in case of hostility) to combat the Savages, and check their incursions." Reckoning that the very name of such a "formidable" settlement would "awe the Indians," Washington recommended its establishment as "the most likely means to enable us to purchase upon equitable terms of the Aborigines their right of preoccupancy; and to induce them to relinquish our Territories, and to remove into the illimitable regions of the West."[15]

The idea of sending veterans and other citizens to serve as a kind of paramilitary force on the nation's periphery held serious appeal for Federal officials. Some nine-tenths of the U.S. population, after all, lived on the land in the 1780s, wedded to farming and a way of life known by contemporaries as the "household factory."[16] Many people, military men and civilians alike, stood ready to move south and west in search of new opportunities and land that they could call their own. It was relatively easy for congressmen and presidents to envision creating land entitlements for them as a means of simultaneously achieving multiple policy goals. Land benefits could render the nation's assistance to people clamoring for property and help to settle the claims of veterans. They also could extend the nation and national sovereignty, shielding America's new borders against the incursions of other nations, domestic and international, that had designs upon the continent. The idea of using the American people as a force with which to extend the empire of the United States would persist in the minds of decision makers and the public for decades to come, inspiring policies and programs that would affect the lives and fortunes of many citizens and citizens-to-be.[17]

[15] Freund, "Military Bounty Lands," pp. 13–15; Letter from George Washington to the President of Congress, June 17, 1783, in *The Writings of George Washington*, ed. John C. Fitzpatrick (Washington, DC: GPO, 1931–), vol. 27, pp. 16–18.

[16] Bruce Laurie, *Artisans into Workers: Labor in Nineteenth-Century America* (Urbana: University of Illinois Press, 1997), pp. 16–17.

[17] Regarding the protean concept of "empire" for late-eighteenth- and early-nineteenth-century Americans, see Peter S. Onuf, *Jefferson's Empire: The Language of American Nationhood* (Charlottesville: University Press of Virginia, 2000), pp. 57–61.

George Washington and other contemporary commentators attributed Congress's failure to take action on the Revolutionary officers' proposal to form a veterans' state to the delay in western land cessions, but that was not the only factor behind its inaction. Some members of Congress were concerned that a landed gentry might arise in the West because of wealth derived from military land grants. Thomas Jefferson, chair of the congressional committee appointed to prepare a plan for the temporary government of the western territory, worried specifically that the location of military land bounties might "continue a distinction between the civil & military which it would be for the good of the whole to obliterate as soon as possible." Aware that prominent members of the hereditary Society of the Cincinnati were behind the Army plan to create a new state from bounty lands, Jefferson drafted a land ordinance in 1784 that required equal male suffrage, barred the settlement of citizens with hereditary titles, and reiterated the Continental Congress's 1776 prohibition on the sale of military land warrants (a measure designed to thwart speculation). The amended version of the ordinance that Congress finally adopted omitted Jefferson's clauses concerning universal suffrage and hereditary title, but required veterans to wait on their land claims until the Northwest was surveyed and then to locate them within a special military reserve.[18]

Military veterans were not the only Americans with designs upon the property that comprised, or could be extracted from, the public domain. As soon as the Revolution ended, increasing numbers of people had begun to move southward and westward to settle on lands regardless of their legal ownership. Though an age-old practice, "squatting" was a big problem for a new government charged with defending the nation's territorial claims and keeping peace with Indian tribes whose lands were being usurped by the nation's citizens.[19] A troubled Confederation Congress issued a proclamation in 1783 that prohibited trespassing and barred the acquisition of Native American lands by purchase or other means without express congressional permission and, in the 1785 Treaty

---

[18] Freund, "Military Bounty Lands," pp. 12–18 (Jefferson cited on p. 16); Rohrbough, *Land Office Business*, pp. 5–8; draft ordinance, *JCC* (XXVI, January–June 1784), pp. 118–20; Ordinance of May 20, 1785, *JCC* (XXVIII, January–June 1785), pp. 375–81.

[19] According to Everett Dick, the term "squatter" was first used in Congress in 1806 to denote settlers who had moved onto property they did not own and made improvements. *The Lure of the Land: A Social History of the Public Lands from the Articles of Confederation to the New Deal* (Lincoln: University of Nebraska Press, 1970), p. 51. See also Onuf, *Statehood and Union*, pp. 28–33.

of Fort McIntosh, committed the United States to the removal of white trespassers from Native American lands. Congress also forbade illegal intrusions on the public lands by proclamation in 1785, authorizing the secretary of war to remove squatters and other trespassers ordered to depart immediately. Even after the nation's troops repeatedly burned squatters' cabins, uprooted their crops, destroyed their fences, dispossessed them, and forcibly ejected them from their encampments, however, the migration and encroachment of defiant, formally landless settlers continued unabated.[20] Many of them surely expected to purchase the land that they inhabited once it was surveyed and available for sale. Others recognized that the Government lacked an effective means of controlling their advances. Either way, there seemed to be plenty of land for the taking.[21]

The Native Americans who had held the original claims to the land within the new U.S. borders, and who still inhabited much of it,[22] also had a vision of the "public" lands at the turn of the nineteenth century:[23]

[20] *JCC* (XXV, September–December 1783), pp. 602, 694; Gates, *Public Land Law Development*, p. 67; Rohrbough, *Land Office Business*, pp. 4, 14–16.

[21] Though land ownership was quickly discarded as a legal requirement for voting in the early Republic, it was still valued as a symbol of full citizenship and independence. Andrew Cayton also notes that while squatters technically had no legal right to occupy particular lands, "their conception of property ownership depended more upon actual possession than legal titles. Further, they had little respect for a distant national authority and felt no obligation to sacrifice their individual interests so that the national debt could be reduced." Their concern was with local custom and individual rights, and "not the aggrandizement of Congress." *The Frontier Republic: Ideology and Politics in the Ohio Country, 1780–1825* (Kent, OH: Kent State University Press, 1986), p. 3; see also Dick, *Lure of the Land,* pp. x–xi.

[22] Well over a million Native Americans, living in villages maintained by subsistence farming and supplemental hunting and gathering, had inhabited the area east of the Mississippi River and south of the Great Lakes and the St. Lawrence River valley when European explorers arrived and initiated the "Indian" or fur trade. Increasing European demand for furs led to game depletion, problems related to alcohol abuse, and bloody skirmishes over access to furs and to markets among rival tribes and between colonial militias and tribal warriors. Whole tribes along the northern and southern Atlantic coasts were exterminated by the end of the French and Indian War in 1763, when a victorious Britain extracted ownership of certain Indian tribal lands, seized Canada, and proclaimed an official boundary for white purchase and settlement within the thirteen colonies, transforming conflicts over the land's products into conflicts over the possession of the land itself. Anthony F. C. Wallace, *The Long, Bitter Trail: Andrew Jackson and the Indians* (New York: Hill and Wang, 1993), pp. 16–33.

[23] An exchange between a Shawnee chief and U.S. Commissioner Richard Butler during a treaty conference in January 1786 illustrates the Native Americans' vision of the "public" domain. The Shawnee chief stated, "God gave us this country [and] we do not understand measuring out the lands, it is all ours." Butler replied: "We plainly tell you that this country belongs to the United States – their blood hath defended it, and will forever protect it.

one that did not feature their expropriation from "Indians" "destined" to be deprived of their ancestral holdings and "removed" to distant, discrete "reservations."[24] The fact that many Native Americans had sided with the British during the Revolution did not imply that they all had sought or made peace with the United States by the end of the war in 1783, or that they considered themselves to have been defeated militarily, however much the United States might have "looked upon itself as a conqueror and counted the Indians among the conquered."[25] Nor did European treaties recognizing the sovereignty of the United States over the lands east of the Mississippi (and, later, the trans-Mississippi West) automatically nullify the Native Americans' right to occupy much of that territory – a legal and practical reality that soon would be recognized by Congress, a succession of U.S. presidents, and the federal courts.[26] If the

---

Their proposals are liberal and just; and you instead of acting as you have done, and instead of persisting in your folly, should be thankful for the forgiveness and offers of kindness of the United States." Having thought the matter over, the chief responded, "Brethren, our people are sensible of the truths you have told them. You have everything in your power – you are great, and we see you own all the country." The Shawnee then signed the treaty and were allotted some lands to live upon. Richard Butler's account of the treaty negotiation, cited in Horsman, *Expansion and American Indian Policy*, pp. 22–3.

[24] See President Jackson's Message to Congress of December 8, 1829, in which he discussed the "condition and ulterior destiny" of Indian tribes. Asserting that the Government's policy of "lavish" compensation for their lands had caused them to recede "further and further to the West," retaining savage habits rather than being reclaimed to a civilized life, Jackson advocated a Federal policy of "removal" to a reservation set aside somewhere west of the Mississippi. It was too late, Jackson said, "to inquire whether it was just in the United States to include them and their territory within the bounds of new States whose limits they could not control. That step c[ould] not be retraced." *RD* (21/1), Appendix, pp. 14–16.

[25] Prucha, *American Indian Treaties*, p. 41. See also Onuf, *Jefferson's Empire*, pp. 39–41; and Horsman, *Expansion and American Indian Policy*, p. 4. Horsman observes that some Native Americans in 1783 would hardly have known that a revolution had taken place, and few could have comprehended "how the signing of a treaty in Paris between the English and the Americans could result in the transfer of their villages and hunting grounds to the new United States."

[26] Horsman, *Expansion and American Indian Policy*, pp. 4–38; Prucha, *American Indian Treaties*, p. 226. Horsman writes that between 1783 and 1786, Congress's policy for dealing with the Northwest Native American tribes was a high-handed one, which presumed both that they lacked even a right of soil in the land they lived on and that they would cede their lands as a punishment for fighting on the British side of the Revolution. It was only when that policy failed in practice that Congress came to recognize, as Prucha likewise has observed, that neither the condition of U.S. military forces nor the "humanity and justice" demanded by the national character of the American Republic recommended the acquisition of land by force, no matter how appealing such a route might seem to frontiersmen for decades to come (pp. 12–38, 171).

United States wanted clear title to the public domain, it would have to be established either by negotiating treaty and purchase agreements with the tribes or through military action ending in absolute conquest. Though the nation initially took what it pragmatically decided was the high road – "conciliation of the Indians by negotiation, a show of liberality, express guarantees of protection from encroachment beyond certain set boundaries, and a fostered and developed trade"[27] – its efforts did not restrain the depredations of acquisitive whites or ensure that Native Americans would receive adequate Government compensation for their "right of occupancy in the soil."[28] In the long run, neither the American state nor its citizens paid any heed to the Native Americans' view of the land that they occupied as members of distinct, if domestic, political communities.[29]

These disparate visions of the public domain – land as "cash cow," land for the taking, land for the entitlement of worthy people and purposes, land as ancestral home – would color the thoughts and actions of

[27] Prucha, *American Indian Policy*, p. 44.

[28] Jefferson's term, cited in Prucha, *American Indian Treaties*, pp. 227–8. Jefferson included a statement of respect for the Native Americans' right of occupancy in the constitutional amendment he proposed to ratify the Louisiana Purchase, maintaining the position he had taken as secretary of state that they should have "full, undivided and independent sovereignty as long as they choose to keep it, [which] might be forever." Regarding the peculiar place of Native Americans in the early Republic, see Rogers M. Smith, *Civic Ideals: Conflicting Visions of Citizenship in U.S. History* (New Haven, CT: Yale University Press, 1997), pp. 131–2, 144–6.

[29] Two cases came before the U.S. Supreme Court in the early 1830s involving the Cherokees in Georgia, who declared themselves an "independent nation," and the State of Georgia, whose legislature had authorized the annexation of Cherokee land and the end of their self-rule. The Court declared itself without jurisdiction in the first case because the Cherokees were neither a state nor a *foreign* nation. Yet, observing that the "condition of the Indians in relation to the United States [wa]s perhaps unlike that of any other two people in existence," Chief Justice John Marshall recognized the Cherokees as "a distinct political society, separated from others, capable of managing its own affairs and governing itself." *Cherokee Nation* v. *Georgia*, 5 Peters 1, 16 (1831). In the second case, which concerned a Vermont minister's violation of a state law requiring white residents on Cherokee land to have a state license, Marshall called Native American tribes "domestic dependent nations" and ruled that as the land belonged to the Cherokees and they formed a distinct, independent political community, the laws of Georgia could "have no force, and . . . the citizens of Georgia . . . no right to enter, but with the assent of the Cherokees themselves, or in conformity with treaties and with acts of congress." *Worcester* v. *Georgia*, 6 Peters 515, 561 (1832). It was the latter decision about which President Jackson is reported to have said, "John Marshall has made his decision and now let him enforce it." Georgia state officials defied the Court's decision by refusing to release minister Worcester (pardoned by the governor of Georgia a year later) and by maintaining the state's hold on Cherokee land. Sheldon Goldman, *Constitutional Law: Cases and Essays* (New York: Harper & Row, Publishers, 1987), p. 28.

westward-looking governments, white citizens, and Native Americans for decades to come. Together, they would shape the role played by the public lands in American social provision. When the new U.S. Government assembled in 1789, it found the issue of the public domain to be extremely pressing and the national policy legacy addressing it already committed in three critical directions: toward the establishment of an effective system of land sales, toward a solution to the problem of the public domain's illegal occupation, and toward "special" grants of the public lands for particular policy purposes like military enlistment and educational enhancement.[30] The need to resolve the Indian question was implicated throughout, as was an increasingly obvious need for state building at the national level of government. As the nineteenth century unfolded, the United States would have to build a more effective army, a larger and more capable bureaucracy, and the central fiscal capacity necessary for paying off war debts and acquiring even more land from foreign nations and Native American tribes ill prepared to resist the nation's "manifest destiny."[31] In all of this, entitlements would play a vital role.

Public Lands and Early Nation Building, 1789–1811

Despite the Confederation Congress's commitment to treat the public domain as a "common fund," land sales did not produce much revenue for

---

[30] The Confederation Congress had introduced the principle of national land grants for education in the Land Ordinance of 1785, which specified that the sixteenth section of every township surveyed should be set aside for the establishment of schools. Such grants may have followed the New England colonial precedent of supporting local education, but they were probably also intended to stimulate land sales. In its instructions to the Board of Treasury concerning lands sales in the Northwest in the Ordinance of 1787, the Confederation Congress directed that every twenty-ninth section of every township should be set aside for purposes of religion, in addition to every sixteenth section for education. Treat, *National Land System*, pp. 265, 31; Donaldson, *The Public Domain*, p. 209.

[31] Describing the future prospects of the United States in 1784, Thomas Hutchins, geographer of the United States, declared that the new nation's inhabitants, "far from being in the least danger from the attacks of any other quarter of the globe, w[ould] have it in their power to engross the whole commerce of it, and to reign, not only lords of America, but to possess, in the utmost security, the dominion of the sea throughout the world, which their ancestors enjoyed before them." As Henry Smith Nash observed, Hutchins's prophecy "left little to be added by the philosophers of Manifest Destiny in the 1840s." Belief in a continental destiny quickly became a central element in the developing American nationalism after the Revolution ended. Hutchins, *An Historical Narrative and Topographical Description of Louisiana, and West-Florida* (Philadelphia, 1784), pp. 93–4, cited in Smith, *Virgin Land: The American West as Symbol and Myth* (Cambridge, MA: Harvard University Press, 1950), p. 9.

the nation between the Ordinance of 1785's enactment and the adoption of the Constitution in 1789. Nor did sales proceed in the neutral manner that the Government originally had intended. In its eagerness to generate revenue, the Confederation Congress decided to circumvent its prescribed method of lands sales before its program of surveying was even complete, selling extensive tracts to eastern speculators at prices far below the minimum price established in the Ordinance of 1785.[32] The idea behind this policy departure was that sales of large tracts to groups of capitalists would simultaneously realize cash and shift administrative burdens from the Confederation to the land's new owners. It was reasoned that even if purchasers acquired their tracts below the nominal price by paying in depreciated government securities (then accepted by the Treasury at face value), bulk sales would still decrease the nation's outstanding indebtedness substantially and would obviate the expense and delay of government surveys. Unfortunately, up-front payments by speculators turned out to be unexpectedly small, as did the revenues collected by other land sales. Both sales and land surveys, already slowed by internal dissension and Native American unrest, lapsed completely upon the death of U.S. Geographer Thomas Hutchins in 1789. When Treasury Secretary Alexander Hamilton took over the management of the public land system that year, it stood compromised and out of use, lacking only the imminent default of the aforementioned speculators and the Government's rescue of them to render it completely discredited.[33]

---

[32] In 1787, the Ohio Company of Associates, a group of Revolutionary veterans with strong ties to the Society of the Cincinnati, contracted to buy 1.5 million acres of land on the Ohio and Muskingum rivers at a price of less than 10 cents an acre (since the U.S. Treasury accepted depreciated certificates at par). The Scioto Company, composed of certain members of Congress, bought 5 million acres along the Ohio River east of the Scioto on the same terms. In 1788, John Cleves Symmes (a member of Congress from New Jersey) and associates also bought 1 million acres in Ohio at the same bargain rate. The list of shareholders in each group of speculators "read like the business (and political) register of New Jersey, Connecticut, Massachusetts, and New York, and included Assistant Secretary of the Treasury William Duer, a Scioto promoter who had to resign his office in part because of the conflict of interest." Almost every Revolutionary army officer owned shares in the Ohio Company. Freund noted that it was through the Ohio Company that "some of the dreams of the army plan of 1783 came true." Kohn, *Eagle and Sword*, p. 100; Freund, "Military Bounty Lands," p. 15; see also Kaplan, "Veteran Officers and Politics," pp. 31–4, 41–3, 55–7; Cayton, *Frontier Republic*, pp. 19–27; Roy M. Robbins, *Our Landed Heritage: The Public Domain, 1776–1936* (Princeton, NJ: Princeton University Press, 1942), pp. 10–11; Rohrbough, *Land Office Business*, p. 11.

[33] Rohrbough, *Land Office Business*, pp. 11–13; Feller, *Public Lands in Jacksonian Politics*, p. 7. Petitioned by the Ohio Company for relief in 1792, Congress "took a broad view of

Hamilton's recommendations on the public lands, included in his 1790 analysis of the nation's resources and economic prospects, identified "two leading objects of consideration": the "facility of advantageous sales" and the "accommodation" of individuals who resided in, or who would emigrate to, the West. Although Hamilton found it desirable and practical for the Federal government to try to achieve both policy goals, he argued that advantageous sales, rather than the welfare of citizens, should be the Government's primary focus of attention "as an operation of finance."[34] He thus distinguished between three classes of prospective buyers, whose needs dictated the development of separate sets of administrative arrangements: "moneyed individuals and companies," who would buy to sell again; "associations of persons" intending to settle western lands themselves; and "single persons [and] families" who either already resided in the West or would move there.[35]

the situation," deciding that the company's $500,000 down payment – one-third of the purchase price it had contracted to pay – was sufficient compensation for the land it had received. Some considered Congress's alteration of the contract in the face of the Ohio Company's prospective nonperformance a "national grant for the encouragement of [military veterans'] settlement on the frontier." Symmes made his first payments on his tract of land, then proceeded to sell off land that did not legally belong to him to settlers who later would have to depend upon Congress to help them out of their predicament. No down payment was required of the "ill-starred" Scioto Company, which sold rights to some 3 million acres to French citizens and then folded before its survey was complete or title conveyed, leaving numerous French immigrants without money or land. A "sympathetic" Congress passed several relief measures between 1795 and 1806, granting over 25,000 acres of land to the immigrants who had been duped. Treat, *National Land System*, pp. 47–65.

[34] Given that one of the sections of the Public Debt Act of August 4, 1790, applied the proceeds from the sale of the public lands "toward sinking and discharging" the nation's debts, a majority of Congress likely agreed.

[35] A "General Land Office" at the seat of the Federal Government would serve the first group, the capitalists and corporations that would make "large purchases," while subordinate offices located in the Northwest and Southwest would accommodate the needs of the other two classes of buyers. With the price of land set at 30 cents per acre, the entire sales operation was to be managed by three commissioners (either newly appointed or ex officio) of the General Land Office, who would supervise commissioners charged with the management of the subordinate offices. Although Hamilton also recommended the appointment of a surveyor general who would have the power to appoint deputy surveyors in each of the western governments and districts, he advocated discarding the uniform requirement of surveys prior to sales in favor of a system that permitted the presurvey sale of land in indiscriminate locations by special contract. "Plan for Disposing of the Public Lands," communicated to the House of Representatives, July 22, 1790, *American State Papers, Class VIII, Public Lands* [hereafter *ASP, Public Lands*], vol. 1, p. 8. As Treat noted, Hamilton proceeded to develop his plan for the disposition of the public lands as if no previous system existed, dismissing the Ordinance of 1785 without

The House had asked Hamilton for his advice on land policy, but it took a preoccupied and effectively itinerant Congress until early 1796 to consider the issue of the public domain in earnest.[36] By then, the consideration that Hamilton had deemed of secondary importance, that of accommodating settlers or small-tract purchasers, had come to figure as prominently in congressional debates as the issue of how to fill the coffers of the U.S. Treasury. Not surprisingly, members favoring the sale of small tracts to settlers often came from states nearest the frontier. William Findley of Pennsylvania, for example, asserted that it was in the interest of the nation to try to "encourage industrious farmers": a policy "not only good for Government," but one that "tends to make the people happy." John Williams of New York agreed: he "thought it of the first consequence that the country should be settled with industrious freeholders." Virginian Robert Rutherford, a self-proclaimed "child of nature [and] inhabitant of the frontier, as untaught as an Indian," urged his colleagues to adopt a policy assisting the "industrious, respectable persons" who were "real settlers," warning that capitalist monsters from Europe were ready to join those in the United States to swallow up the country. The rage of speculators, as Findley noted, "seemed to have no bounds."[37]

consideration. *National Land System*, p. 70. Though Hamilton is typically characterized as the person responsible for the adoption of a general revenue policy toward the public domain, he did not advocate bringing in more revenue into the U.S. Treasury than would be necessary to establish credit, for a surplus would have removed one very plausible reason for enacting a protective tariff. Nor did he completely ignore the needs of settlers in recommending a minimum tract size and price per acre. A primary goal of Hamilton's plan thus seems to have been balance: both to establish the public domain as a principal source of national revenue and to dispose of western lands in a manner that would guarantee a stable economic and social order. See Robbins, *Our Landed Heritage*, p. 14.

36 Philadelphia was designated only a temporary capital until Congress exercised its Article I, Section 8 authority to locate a permanent seat for the Federal Government. By 1796, the site on the Potomac had been chosen by President Washington, but land sales there had been so dismal that reputable creditors refused to accept purchased lots as collateral for loans, requiring an act of Congress to guarantee them. Maryland and Virginia eventually provided the loans that would finance the work required to construct the nation's original public buildings. Congress met in what is now Washington for the first time in 1800. James Sterling Young, *The Washington Community, 1800–1828* (New York: Columbia University Press, 1966), pp. 15–21.

37 *AC* (4/1), pp. 339, 346, 328–9, 414, Feb. 15, 18, Mar. 3, 1796. As is discussed later, "real" or "actual" settlers increasingly were framed as a group that should be favored by public land policy as the moral opposite of speculators. Treat suggests that the exposure and arrest of two men representing a company of speculators for attempting to bribe certain House members into favoring a grant of some 20 million acres of land in Michigan in

Although the notion of legislation aimed at benefiting settlers had begun to appeal strongly to some House members, it was scuttled in the Senate. The Land Act of 1796 set the bar high for potential buyers, pegging the price of public land at a minimum of $2 per acre and the minimum tract size at 640 acres. Importantly, it also established credit terms for the first time. Contrary to expectations, the new land law neither tempted many speculators, generated much income for the Federal government, nor facilitated further settlement of the west.[38] As a result, Congress progressively liberalized the terms of its sales policy, halving the minimum purchase unit from 640 to 320 acres in 1800 and again to 160 acres in 1804, extending credit for up to four years in 1800, waiving all interest except on late payments in 1804, and establishing remote offices so that land sales could be conducted near the tracts to be sold.[39] In addition, relief legislation was enacted in 1806 to extend payment deadlines, allowing members of Congress to avoid the unpleasantness of enforcing forfeiture provisions upon constituents as their final payments became past due on lands purchased on credit. Additional relief acts followed in 1809 and 1810.[40] As Daniel Feller has observed, the passage of

early 1796 both caused a significant increase in congressional interest in the question of the public domain and "undoubtedly caused Congress to hold fast to its position against large sales to speculators." *National Land System*, pp. 77–9. Yet, there was a strong connection between the Federal land officials and the land business. Rufus Putnam, for example, who served as surveyor general under President Washington, had previously been the principal representative of the Ohio Company of Associates in the Northwest Territory. Many of the Government's surveyors were also speculators. Rohrbough, *Land Office Business*, pp. 20–1.

[38] "An Act providing for the sale of Lands of the United States in the Territory northwest of the river Ohio, and above the mouth of the Kentucky river," *AC* (4/2), pp. 2906–10, May 18, 1796; Treat, *National Land System*, pp. 80–7; Benjamin Horace Hibbard, *A History of the Public Land Policies* (New York: Macmillan Company, 1924), pp. 60–9; Gates, *Public Land Law Development*, pp. 125–6. As Treat notes, the terms of the Land Act of 1796 were essentially similar to those of the Ordinance of 1785 and the first general land act enacted by the U.S. Congress.

[39] "An Act to amend the act, entitled 'An act providing for the sale of lands of the United States, in the Territory Northwest of the Ohio, and above the mouth of the Kentucky river,'" *AC* (6/1), pp. 1515–22, May 10, 1800; "An Act making provision for the disposal of the public lands in the Indiana Territory; and for other purposes," *AC* (8/1), pp. 1285–93, Mar. 26, 1804.

[40] "An Act to extend the time for making payment for the public lands of the United States," *AC* (10/2), pp. 1831–2, Mar. 2, 1809; "An Act to extend the time for making payments for public lands of the United States, in certain cases," *AC* (11/1 and 2), pp. 2566–7, Apr. 30, 1810. The House debate over the 1810 Relief Act [*AC* (11/1 and 2), pp. 1999–2006] demonstrated a split between advocates of the general revenue policy and advocates of settlement. Richard Johnson of Kentucky defended the land

a relief act for the benefit of delinquent public land purchasers became something of an annual ritual by the outbreak of the War of 1812.[41] Taking a new, proactive approach to land-related indebtedness, these relief acts programmatically released particular groups of citizens from their legal obligation to meet previously established payment deadlines. Though they still were required to pay for their land eventually, these citizens' treatment by the state was discernibly different than that accorded other people in debt, who were left to petition Congress individually in hope of some kind of assistance.

The arguments made in the House in 1796 in favor of small-tract purchasers reflected the fact that petitions and memorials praying for land grants, reduced land prices, and the perfection of land titles had begun to flow into Congress with regularity. Inhabitants of the Mississippi Territory, for example, sent the members of the Eighth Congress multiple memorials asking for free land for "actual settlers" there, arguing that land grants would bring a "great increase of population" to their territory. Their request was denied in early 1804 on the recommendation of a special House committee, which observed that "bounties" of that sort had "uniformly been refused by the United States."[42] In 1805, Jean Noel Destrihan, speaker of the House of Representatives of the new Territory of Orleans, sent Congress a memorial from that body praying for local lands to be conveyed to settlers who had inhabited and cultivated them prior to the Louisiana Purchase. In a clear critique of Federal land sales policy, Destrihan noted that "the former Governments of France and Spain, under whose dominion this country has successively passed, did not consider the vacant lands as a source from which revenue was to be derived, but as a means of increasing the population of the country, encouraging

debtors: "Are these men speculators? No, sir; I shall take pleasure in recording on the Journals my vote of indulgence to the people who have settled on little farms for which they have paid their last shilling, and who are about to be deprived, unless we interfere, of that land they have improved by their own labor" (p. 2001). The easy credit terms established by the Land Act of 1800 in fact inspired many people to go into debt to buy huge amounts of western land. Only $3,000,000 was owed to the United States for payments on public land purchases in 1815, but by the time of the Panic of 1819, when Revolutionary pension expenditures threatened to bankrupt the Government, that amount had risen to $16,794,795. Cayton, *Frontier Republic*, p. 115.

[41] *Public Lands in Jacksonian Politics*, pp. 12–13; Robbins, *Our Landed Heritage*, pp. 27–8. For a detailed account of administrative expansion associated with the implementation of the land system between 1800 and 1812, see Rohrbough, *Land Office Business*, pp. 26–50.

[42] "Applications for Donations to Actual Settlers in the Mississippi Territory communicated to the House of Representatives, January 23, 1804," *ASP, Public Lands*, vol. 1, p. 181.

its agriculture, and gaining the affection of its inhabitants." Destrihan begged Congress to recognize the peculiar situation of Louisiana citizens deprived of proof of land ownership by political upheaval and fire. In the absence of irrefutable legal evidence, however, Treasury Secretary Albert Gallatin would only recommend that some of their claims be recognized.[43]

Individual citizens also sent Congress petitions asking for grants of free land. The diversity and ingenuity of their requests, and the justications that they offered for them, demonstrate that the citizens of the early Republic felt quite free to approach their elected representatives to ask for laws comporting with their experience and interests. Their petitions provide a wonderful snapshot of life in the early Republic and demonstrate the extraordinary range of demands that the nation's new legislature was required to deal with.

In 1806, for example, the Ninth Congress was asked to render judgment on a petition from the children of the late John Ward and "an Indian woman, with whom he cohabited as his wife." Ward had been captured by the Indians when very young and, not surprisingly, had conformed to their ways. However, he had urged his children, should they survive him, to seek out his white relatives, "endeavor to make a settlement among them, and adopt the civilized mode of living, as being preferable to that of the savage state." The children followed this advice after their father's death, locating and settling near his brother in Ohio, but they had no means of purchasing land. They turned to Congress to ask for a grant of land, noting that necessity would require them to return to the Indians if they did not receive it. The House's newly formed Committee on Public Lands acknowledged its interest in Ward's children's cause, but said that it could find no precedent or principle recognized by Congress that would warrant compliance with their request.[44]

The Ninth Congress also responded negatively to the 1806 petition of Frances Menissier, who asked for a section of land in Ohio. Menissier informed Congress that for six years, at his own "considerable expense," he had engaged in wine-making experiments in Cincinnati, the success

---

[43] "Land Titles in the Territory of Orleans – The Culture of Sugar – And the Endowment of Public Schools communicated to the Senate, December 31, 1805," *ASP, Public Lands*, vol. 1, pp. 250–2.

[44] "Application to Confirm to Certain Indians the Lands They Occupy in Ohio communicated to the House of Representatives, January 24, 1806, *ASP, Public Lands*, vol. 1, p. 256.

of which rendered him "able to raise such a quantity of the same species of vine as is common in France, as to supply the whole State of Ohio with good wine, for medicinal and other purposes, at one-fourth of the price for which imported wines c[ould] be obtained." Given these efforts, he prayed that Congress would provide him with a donation of land as "an encouragement for the cultivation of the vine," but the House Committee on Public Lands recommended against it. According to information it had received "through other channels," Menissier's claims of vinicultural prowess were exaggerated, and the section of land he asked for was already sold – circumstances that alone warranted the denial of his petition. The committee also felt compelled to note "another ground of refusal, equally applicable to all such cases," in anticipation of "applications of a similar nature":

The encouragement asked for by the petitioner is neither more nor less than a direct bounty on the culture of the vine – it being asked not in money, but in land, does not change its nature. The public lands are the common property of the people of the United States, and the proceeds of the sales thereof ought to be applied only to national purposes, for which, if this source of revenue did not exist, the Government would be bound to provide by a tax on the people. As every donation of public land, or diminution of its price, for the encouragement of any species of labor, must, by lessening this source of revenue, increase the demand of the Government on the people, it is the same in effect to them, whether the encouragement is given in a grant of money or land; if we would not give the former, we ought to withhold the latter.[45]

The committee's language clearly indicates the vision of the public domain held by a majority of the Ninth Congress, along with that majority's commitment to the general sales policy established for its disposal. Both stood in stark contradiction to the petitioners' sense that the public lands could serve dynamic, vitally important functions beyond the generation of revenue.[46]

The issue of the illegal occupation of western lands was probably as active on the congressional agenda as the development of a national system of land sales between 1789 and the outbreak of the War of 1812. Many Americans urged the enactment of a "preemption" law that would grant

---

[45] "Cultivation of the Vine communicated to the House of Representatives, February 3, 1806," *ASP, Public Lands*, vol. 1, pp. 256–7.

[46] On the dynamic role of law and property in the nineteenth century, see James Willard Hurst, *Law and the Conditions of Freedom in the Nineteenth-Century United States* (Madison: University of Wisconsin Press, 1956).

squatters preferential rights to settle on and improve public lands, then later buy them at a modest price without having to compete for them at auction – another kind of programmatic entitlement.[47] They believed that the settlement and improvement of portions of the public domain constituted a form of public service and should be rewarded.[48] As Gates observed, citizens' petitions for preemption rights, "sometimes filled with pathos and usually with marked dislike of the speculator, ran the gamut of emotion." Some petitioners requested Congress's indulgence because of the depredations of Indians on their (illegally founded) communities. Others cited poverty, and the dangers and hardships "attendant on the first settlers of an uncultivated frontier forest." Still others warned that if they did not become entitled to preemption rights, they might have to abandon American soil to seek land in Spanish dominions.[49] To some members of Congress, especially those from western states, the enactment of preemption legislation seemed the answer to a number of prayers. Legalizing at least some of the squatting that was occurring could increase the populations of their states, enhancing their positions within Congress and the Republic itself. Moreover, the American people wanted land. Surveys and land sales were not progressing quickly enough. Adventurous souls were crossing the frontier regardless of Federal policy, and the Government needed an effective means of staking its claim to regions beyond its immediate borders. To many congressmen, the fact that portions of the public domain had already been promised to military veterans meant that a precedent for land entitlements benefiting citizens had already been established.

[47] A statute programmatically allowing persons otherwise illegally settling on often choice public land to purchase it at the Government's minimum price, exempt from market forces and the criminal penalties for squatting (some of which were monetary), must be considered a legal entitlement. Unfortunately, some scholars do not recognize this, because preemption laws did not convey lands to settlers as outright gifts. James Oberly, for example, asserts that preemption "merely put off the time when a buyer had to pay for his land." *Sixty Million Acres: American Veterans and the Public Lands before the Civil War* (Kent, OH: Kent State University Press, 1990), p. 24.

[48] See, e.g., "Pre-emption Rights Northwest of the Ohio communicated to the House of Representatives, May 12, 1796"; "Pre-emption Rights in the Northwestern Territory communicated to the House of Representatives, on the 25th of February, 1801"; "Pre-emption Rights in Indiana and Mississippi communicated to the House of Representatives, March 11, 1806"; and "Pre-emption Titles in the Mississippi Territory" (a memorial of the House of Representatives of the Mississippi Territory) communicated to the Senate, November 7, 1808," *ASP, Public Lands*, vol. 1, pp. 68, 111, 261, 597.

[49] *Public Land Law Development*, p. 221.

Majorities of the early U.S. Congresses, however, still believed in adhering to the general revenue policy. As a consequence, the Government could not officially sanction intrusions upon the public domain, however ineffectual its attempts at deterrence might have been.[50] After the 1794 victory of General "Mad" Anthony Wayne's forces at Fallen Timbers, Britain's surrender of its western posts, and the 1795 Indian cession of a huge tract of tribal land in the Treaty of Greenville[51] had unleashed a new flood of settlers into the back country, Arthur St. Clair, governor of the Northwest Territory, had warned Congress that urgent action was required. If not "disposed of" soon, such numbers of people would take possession of the public lands that they might not easily be removed.[52] Congress had responded by reiterating its preference for orderly land sales in the Land Acts of 1796, 1800, and 1804. It also enacted legislation making persons found guilty of settling upon public land in the new Louisiana Territory subject to fines of up to $1,000 and imprisonment for up to a year,[53] staunchly dismissing the many petitions of citizens claiming or requesting preemption rights. The Intrusion Act signed by President Jefferson in 1807 extended the Government's penalties to people settling illegally on any portion of the public domain after its enactment. It permitted squatters already on public land to remain there until the land was sold, but only if they would sign a formal statement acknowledging that they were mere tenants and had no rightful claim to it. Those who would not do so were made subject to criminal prosecution, fines of $100, and prison sentences of up to six months. As Gates put it, the

---

[50] Gates, *Public Land Law Development*, p. 219. A bill featuring a preemption provision was reported in the First U.S. Congress but was not enacted.

[51] Native Americans ceded the southern two-thirds of what is now Ohio and part of present-day Indiana in exchange for $20,000 worth of goods, the promise of a $9,500 annuity of "like useful goods, suited to the circumstances of the Indians," and the right to hunt in ceded territory "without hindrance or molestation, so long as they demean[ed] themselves peaceably, and offer[ed] no injury to the people of the United States." Prucha, *American Indian Treaties*, p. 93, citing *Indian Affairs: Laws and Treaties*, volume 2, *Treaties*, comp. Charles J. Kappler (Washington, DC: GPO, 1904), pp. 39–45.

[52] St. Clair to the secretary of state, January 1796, in *Territorial Papers of the United States*, ed. Clarence Edwin Carter (Washington, DC: GPO, 1934), vol. 2, pp. 542–9, 548.

[53] "An Act erecting Louisiana into two Territories, and providing for the Temporary Government thereof, 1804 *AC* (8/1), pp. 1293–1300, Mar. 26. In addition to imposing penalties including fines and imprisonment, the act authorized the president to employ "such military force as he may judge necessary" to remove squatters from the public lands.

legislation was "a peculiar measure to be enacted by an agrarian-minded administration."[54]

Peculiar or not, the Intrusion Act was almost certainly perceived by the public as illiberal and unfair, since laws enacted during the same time period programmatically granted special preemption rights to particular groups of squatters, especially those who engaged in favored occupations or moved onto lands within particular areas. For example, squatters who had built (or were in the process of building) gristmills or sawmills within the public domain north of the Ohio River became entitled to purchase the sites on which they were located (up to 640 acres, at $2 per acre) by the Land Act of 1800.[55] Congress also granted preemption rights to all persons inhabiting and improving public land in the Mississippi Territory in the Land Act of March 3, 1803, entitling them to purchase tracts of unspecified size on credit terms. The act also established grants of 640 acres of land for those who had settled in that area before the Spanish troops finally left in 1797.[56] A number of acts were passed between 1799 and 1804 that granted preemption rights to people who had purchased land from speculator (and former congressman turned territorial judge) John Cleves Symmes, for which he had no clear title. Federal law also began to offer preemption rights to squatters residing in certain areas where Government land sales were delayed, including Georgia and Michigan.[57] These and other special Federal dispensations

54 "An Act to prevent settlements being made on lands ceded to the United States, until authorized by law," *AC* (9/2), pp. 1288–90, Mar. 3, 1807; Gates, *Public Land Law Development*, p. 220.

55 Act of May 10, 1800, *AC* (6/1), pp. 1515–22. In Treat's view, preemption rights were granted to mill owners on account of the "public service" they had performed, having been "forced" to settle on public lands before the completion of surveys. *National Land System*, p. 99.

56 "An Act regulating the grants of land, and providing for the disposal of the lands of the United States, south of the State of Tennessee," *AC* (7/2), pp. 1593–1601, Mar. 3, 1803. Subsequent legislation extended the deadlines by which payments could be made on preempted lands. Though they were denied, numerous petitions were also received by the Eighth Congress from settlers in the Mississippi Territory suggesting that the population there would increase greatly if outright donations of public land were made. See "Applications for Donations to Actual Settlers in the Mississippi Territory," communicated to the House of Representatives, January 23, 1804, *ASP, Public Lands*, vol. I, p. 181.

57 Preemption rights were, for example, offered to persons living in the Georgia cession in 1803 and 1808, as well as in 1808 to settlers who had taken up residence in Michigan by 1804. The granting of limited preemption rights in areas where land sales were delayed became a common practice of the United States by 1820. Treat, *National Land System*, pp. 383–5.

not only selectively entitled particular groups of frontiersmen to public benefits on a programmatic basis, but rewarded them for engaging in precisely the same "lawless" behavior that rendered other citizens deviant and subjected them to criminal prosecution, fines, and imprisonment. While this privileging of particular groups in the face of the Intrusion Act might not have suggested that a universal preemption law would soon be forthcoming, it surely did not discourage squatting. Coupled with the Government's widely known inability to rout trespassers from the public domain, the preemption enactments of the early nineteenth century almost certainly encouraged citizens and immigrant citizens-to-be to ignore government prohibitions to move south and west, petitioning Congress for their own particular preemption rights and lobbying for the passage of a general preemption act.[58]

President Jefferson, after all, was well known for his sympathy with the pioneer and for his expansionist desires. In his second inaugural address in March 1805, delivered after the Louisiana Purchase had appended a vast new area to the nation, he had asked, "who can limit the extent to which the federative principle may operate effectively?"[59] Jefferson looked forward to the proliferation of free republican states, bound together by harmonious interests and a common dedication to the "principles of justice" under the United States' new constitutional regime. In his vision, the expanding union would become an empire of liberty, at least for those benefiting from the expansion of white male citizenship. Westward expansion promised to guarantee the maintenance of a virtuous, agrarian republic in perpetuity, free of unnatural concentrations of population, wealth, and power, because territorial control of western rivers and harbors would facilitate the development of a system of inland commerce that the port cities of the eastern seaboard would serve but not dominate.[60]

It was not resistance to national expansion that hampered the creation of land grants and general preemption rights for citizens before the War of 1812. Rather, it was disagreement over how best to achieve

---

[58] Broad preemption legislation indeed was enacted in 1830 and 1841. See Chapter 5.

[59] "Second Inaugural Address," 4 March 1805, James D. Richardson, *A Compilation of the Messages and Papers of the Presidents 1789–1897* (Washington, DC: Bureau of National Literature and Art, 1901).

[60] Onuf, *Jefferson's Empire*, pp. 53–4, 56, 69; Smith, *Civic Ideals*, p. 165–6; Stephen Skowronek, *The Politics Presidents Make: Leadership from John Adams to George Bush* (Cambridge, MA: Belknap Press of Harvard University Press, 1993), p. 79.

it. Federalists held that the union's growth should never run ahead of
the Government's ability to enforce its authority against foreign and domestic threats. Believing the nation to be at risk from the disproportion
between its military force and strategic objectives, they were certain that
"further expansion would weaken the bonds of union, exposing and exacerbating interregional conflicts of interest." Federalist foreign policy
thus urged the United States to "consolidate authority in a central government that commanded the resources of the continent" before it "reck-
lessly risked the enmity of the great European powers." Jefferson and his
Democratic-Republican brethren saw the situation differently. They rejected the consolidation of authority that they believed had destroyed the
British Empire in favor of an extended, decentralized polity dedicated to
ostensibly equal rights, reciprocal benefits, and relentless improvement.
In Peter Onuf's words, they were "reform-minded proponents of an idealized world order, made fully and finally compatible with natural rights,
free exchange, the progressive diffusion of civilization, and the rights of
self-government within and among confederated states."[61]

Martin Shefter has suggested that the Jeffersonians' behavior with
respect to the public domain reflected the fact that they were very much
a party of notables. Once their political position was secured, they were
able to provide privileged access to public benefits for the classes they
represented while using public authority "to discipline the groups that
were excluded from the Jeffersonian regime." Hence their sale of public
lands only in large lots to commercial farmers, while Federal marshalls
evicted subsistence farmers who were squatting on the public domain.[62]
For partisan reasons, these practices may have made sense. Congress's
enactment of selective benefit programs, and its selective attention to the
petitions of the people during the Adams and Jefferson administrations,
were nonetheless seriously at odds with contemporary beliefs about the
obligations of representation.

In 1796, the Fourth Congress finally had utilized a portion of the public domain to create what became known as the United States Military
District in the Northwest Territory (later Ohio) for the provision of Revolutionary veterans' land bounties, allowing the nation's original patriots until 1800 to secure and locate their warrants. That deadline was

---

[61] *Jefferson's Empire*, pp. 55–6.
[62] *Political Parties and the State: The American Historical Experience* (Princeton, NJ: Princeton
University Press, 1994), p. 66.

extended to 1802 in 1799, but by the end of 1801, some 552,605 out of the 1,612,605 acres of warrants issued remained unlocated.[63] Far from being inhabited by "a brave, . . . hardy and respectable Race of People" ready and willing to "combat the Savages," as George Washington had anticipated, large portions of the military reserve remained unoccupied. Veterans used their warrants as land-office money, exchanging their land entitlements for cash. Many had sold their warrants to speculators as soon as they were rendered salable by the Confederation Congress in 1788. An early study of Revolutionary land bounties estimated that some 100 men controlled 1.4 of the approximately 2 million acres that the United States had granted to veterans in the Ohio Military District. The result was that many veterans believed that they had been defrauded of their rights. They would spend years petitioning Congress for a resolution of their claims and pursuing settlements in litigation brought against the United States.[64]

The fact that the Revolutionary veterans' land grants did not encourage western settlement did not dissuade Congress from the practice of establishing land bounties as a means of inducing enlistment. Long before the claims of the Revolution's heroes were satisfied, the Twelfth Congress would return to the public domain and to selective entitlement in order to raise the forces required to fight a second war for independence. Its 1811 decision to entitle soldiers willing to enlist in the Army to portions of the public domain, but to *omit officers* from the new program of land benefits, would raise the same questions about which citizens should get "what, when, and why"[65] that the issue of the Revolutionary officers' lost pension certificates and land warrants still generated. The resolution of these questions, along with essentially similar ones that would be raised in debates over the establishment of new preemption rights and free

---

[63] "An act regulating the grants of laud [sic] appropriated for military services . . . ," *AC* (4/2), p. 2935, June 1, 1796; Treat, *National Land System*, pp. 240–2. Congress would pass twenty-six acts extending the period for obtaining Revolutionary warrants and perfecting locations between 1799 and 1864, with the last warrant issued in 1886, more than a century after the bounties were originally legislated by the Continental Congress.

[64] Freund, "Military Bounty Lands," pp. 8, 18; William Thomas Hutchinson, "The Bounty Lands of the American Revolution" (Ph.D. diss., University of Chicago, 1927), cited in O'Callaghan, "The War Veteran and the Public Lands," p. 165; "Annual Report of the Commissioner of the General Land Office," December 13, 1847, S. ex. doc. (30/1), vol. II, no. 2, p. 23.

[65] This allusion is, of course, to Lasswell's definition of politics as "who gets what, when, how." See Harold D. Lasswell, *Politics: Who Gets What, When, How* (New York: McGraw-Hill Book Company, 1936).

homesteads, would expand the Government's role in the well-being of American citizens, increase the role and presence of Federal administrators in the localities, and play a central role in configuring the partisan and sectional conflicts that eventually would culminate in the Civil War.

Soldiers, Settlers, and "Others": The Public Domain and Land Entitlements, 1811–1830

The War of 1812 was a watershed event with respect to the development of the American continent. Where before the war the United States had faced seaward, a second victory over Great Britain firmly reoriented the nation toward the frontier, transforming Federal land policy into one of the most critical issues of national governance. As Daniel Feller has observed, politicians and citizens alike understood that "public land policy addressed certain fundamental problems of American development, problems that affected not only the West but the whole society, problems that even touched the integrity of the Union itself."[66]

Although both the Confederation government and early U.S. Congresses had attempted to establish uniform national systems for the acquisition and disposition of public lands, their development and implementation had been fraught with difficulty. The elaborate policy that national leaders had adopted after 1786 to deal with U.S. expansion over Native American lands, featuring the acknowledgment of a Native American right of occupancy, formal (if forced) purchases of land by negotiation and treaty, the establishment of definite boundary lines, and the regulation of trade and intercourse with the tribes, was largely a failure. It did not cultivate peace between whites and Native Americans or facilitate the commingling of civilizations that the eighteenth-century Enlightenment view of the Indian anticipated. Nor did it prevent the confiscation of Native American lands as white demand for land reached unprecedented heights.[67] Faced with the inevitable question of whether to use

---

[66] *The Public Lands in Jacksonian Politics*, p. xi.

[67] Horsman, *Expansion and American Indian Policy*, pp. 170–3. See also Jean V. Matthews, *Toward a New Society: American Thought and Culture, 1800–1830* (Boston: Twayne Publishers, 1991), pp. 71–93, for an account of the ways in which "man" and human nature were viewed in early-nineteenth-century America. Matthews notes that after 1800, Enlightenment views of an essentially universal human nature gave way to greater preoccupation with human differences. There was significant interest in the Native American as a natural phenomenon of the New World, especially among eastern whites who were no longer physically threatened by them. Though they were considered culturally inferior,

U.S. military force against its own citizens or Native Americans on the western frontier, the Government chose the latter, forgoing a policy of assimilation for one of Indian "removal."[68] Public policies aimed at relocating and "civilizing" the tribes reinforced the belief that Native Americans were "incompetent cultural inferiors, whose legal claims against white encroachments were being indulged, not recognized as true rights."[69]

That the United States would be breaking old promises and making false new ones in assigning new Native Americans to new lands west of the Mississippi was clear to many observers. Alexis de Tocqueville, for example, chided the U.S. Government for acting in bad faith by "promis[ing] a permanent refuge to th[o]se unhappy beings in the West" when it was "well aware of its inability to secure it to them."[70] He noted that America's destructive conduct toward its aboriginal people was singularly attached to the "formalities of law":

Provided that the Indians retain their barbarous condition, the Americans take no part in their affairs; they treat them as independent nations and do not possess themselves of their hunting-grounds without a treaty of purchase; and if an Indian nation happens to be so encroached upon as to be unable to subsist upon their

educated Americans often accorded Native Americans an "essential natural equality with whites." Thus the Government reflected eastern elite opinion, which encouraged intermarriage between whites and Native Americans as a method of assimilation along with Native American adoption of "white norms of marriage, family descent, individual property, and the work ethic." There was no room in Jeffersonian America for cultural pluralism, however. If Native Americans persisted in clinging to their own ways, they would have to be removed. The fate of the Republic depended on the vision of a continent, as John Quincy Adams put it in 1811, "destined by Divine Providence to be peopled by one *nation*, speaking one language, professing one general system of religious and political principles, and accustomed to one general tenor of social usages and customs" (cited in Matthews, *Toward a New Society*, p. 89).

68 Meanwhile, the U.S. Government was attempting to acquire tribal lands in Spanish Florida through a process of infiltration, violence, and extermination. Andrew Jackson's controversial exploits at the behest of President Monroe, which involved the slaughter of members of an independent Native American nation and execution of British subjects at a Spanish fort, succeeded in convincing Spain to sell Florida to the United States and relinquish its claims to Oregon for $5 million and a repudiation of American claims to Texas and California. The treaty with Spain barely passed in the Senate, but Florida was annexed and became a U.S. territory in 1822. Due to the efforts of Secretary of State John Quincy Adams, the $5 million purchase price was paid not to Spain but to American citizens who had claims against that nation – establishing Adams's reputation as a wily diplomat. Virginia Bergman Peters, *The Florida Wars* (Hamden, CT: Archon Books, 1979), pp. 47–64; John Mayfield, *The New Nation 1800–1845* (New York: Hill and Wang, rev. ed., 1982), pp. 47–9.

69 Smith, *Civic Ideals*, p. 181.

70 *Democracy in America*, ed. Phillips Bradley (New York: Vintage Books, 1955), vol. 1, p. 366.

territory, they kindly take them by the hand and transport them to a grave far from the land of their fathers.[71]

Federal policy deprived the Indians of their rights or exterminated them "with singular felicity, tranquilly, legally, philanthropically, without shedding blood, and without violating a single great principle of morality in the eyes of the world." It would be impossible, de Tocqueville observed, "to destroy men with more respect for the laws of humanity."[72]

Former Senator James Barbour, secretary of war under John Quincy Adams, also pointed to the hypocrisy of removal. Submitting a plan for establishing an Indian territory in the trans-Mississippi West to Congress in 1826, Barbour stated that it was impractical and, like earlier policies, destined to be reneged upon if the desire for land "continue[d] to direct [U.S.] councils." Declaring that the Government's previous policies had "essentially failed," Barbour asked whether it could

be a matter of surprise that the [tribes] hear, with unmixed indignation, of what seems to them our ruthless purpose of expelling them from their country, thus endeared? They see that our professions are insincere; that our promises have been broken; that the happiness of the Indian is a cheap sacrifice to the acquisition of new lands; and when attempted to be soothed by an assurance that the country to which we propose to send them is desirable, they emphatically ask us, What new pledges can you give us that we shall not again be exiled when it is your wish to possess these lands? It is easier to state than to answer this question.[73]

Criticism notwithstanding, the lure of the land and national expansion, coupled with southern intransigence over including people of color in their populations, came to outweigh concern about the morality of the Republic's actions during the 1820s. As more and more Americans turned their imaginations and energies toward the process of subduing and populating the continent, there was growing acceptance of the idea that Native Americans were a race of "noble savages" destined to become extinct upon the advent of a superior people. Such a belief justified the Native Americans' lack of entitlement to their homeland and Federal policies disposing of that homeland for the benefit of other subjects of the new American state.[74]

---

[71] Ibid., p. 369.

[72] Ibid.

[73] Barbour, "Preservation and Civilization of the Indians," *ASP, Class II, Indian Affairs* [hereafter *ASP, Indian Affairs*], vol. 2, p. 647.

[74] Reginald Horsman, *Race and Manifest Destiny: The Origins of American Racial Anglo-Saxonism* (Cambridge, MA: Harvard University Press, 1981), pp. 189–207; Matthews, *Toward a New Society*, pp. 137, 89–93.

Of course, the question of precisely *how* the public lands would be disposed of, and for *whose* benefit, had loomed large since the days of the Revolution, and attempts to establish a consistent sales policy for the public domain had not sufficed to constrain exercises in national policymaking running counter to it. Those exceptions to what was supposed to be a general rule – including military land bounties, selective preemption enactments, and land grants aimed at certain people and purposes – ensured that more cycles of demand and protest over the disposition of the public domain would be forthcoming. There would be appeals for other categorical Federal land policies, accusations of pork barreling and legislative impartiality, sectional inequity and conflict, and counterdemands for fairness and universality in the distribution of land benefits. The drive to acquire land from Native Americans and other peoples and nations would continue unabated until the "tide" of the white American population flowed to "the distant shores of the Pacific."[75] As was the case with the Revolutionary pension program, the issue was no longer the propriety of selective entitlement per se or the utilization of U.S. assets in the process, but rather that of precisely *who* the U.S. Government should entitle to public benefits and *how* it should do so.

The fact that land entitlements technically avoided cash benefits to give away portions of an entity considered the "public" domain (lands variously acquired from Native Americans and "others," albeit partially purchased, meant that they often were perceived as distributive rather than redistributive policies. In this respect, they were somewhat less controversial than the Revolutionary pensions concurrently on the congressional agenda. In other respects, however, land benefits raised questions that were *more* difficult for presidents and Congress to resolve than pension questions, for the public domain's acquisition and disposition was inextricably linked to other critical Federal policy issues, including foreign affairs, the protective tariff, a national bank, internal improvements, and, eventually, slavery.[76]

---

75 James Barbour, "Preservation and Civilization of the Indians," p. 648. Barbour's prediction continued: "Before this resistless current the Indian must retire, till his name will be no more."

76 The tariff, a national bank, Federal internal improvements, and a land policy designed to control the rate of western settlement were advocated by proponents of the so-called American System of policies. These issues dominated political debate for decades following the War of 1812. See Major L. Wilson, *Space, Time, and Freedom: The Quest for Nationality and the Irrepressible Conflict 1815–1861* (Westport, CT: Greenwood Press, 1974).

The creation of land entitlements involved decisions elevating the needs and deeds of certain virtuous citizens over the Republic's need for cash (and the desires of the land speculators who ostensibly could afford to supply it). For those decisions to be made, virtue had to be defined and recognized. The question of *how much* virtue was required to trigger the state's substantive beneficence also had to be answered. Stories invoking widely held cultural values and moral archetypes offered Federal actors a potent means of explaining their preferences. Strategically crafted and deployed, "causal stories" were indeed essential in justifying the Government's conferral of land benefits and associated costs.[77] Just as the issue of Federal military pensions was framed to counterpose the selfless citizen-soldier and the ruthless mercenary, and just as the issue of Federal disaster relief had begun to counterpose innocent victims of fate and blameworthy victims of fault,[78] Federal land policy could be constructed to pit the virtuous "actual settler" against the self-serving speculator.[79] Initially, the story of the actual settler did not suffice to convince Congress to divert too far from its policy of selling the public domain.[80] However, that story gained serious explanatory power as congressmen and presidents encountered the problems of building and

Obviously, a complete history of the public domain is beyond the scope of this book, which investigates the relationship between the programmatic, statutory entitlement of categories of citizens and state and nation building. For more comprehensive treatments of Federal land policy, see Gates, *Public Land Law Development*; Treat, *National Land System*; Hibbard, *Public Land Policies*; Robbins, *Our Landed Heritage*; Feller, *Public Lands in Jacksonian Politics*; Raynor G. Wellington, *The Political and Sectional Influence of the Public Lands 1828–1842* (Cambridge, MA: Riverside Press, 1914); and George M. Stephenson, *The Political History of the Public Lands from 1840 to 1862: From Pre-emption to Homestead* (New York: Russell & Russell, 1917).

[77] See Deborah Stone, *Policy Paradox and Political Reason* (Glenview, IL: Scott, Foresman & Co., 1988), chapter 8; and "Causal Stories and the Formation of Policy Agendas," *Political Science Quarterly* 104 (1989): 281–300.

[78] Michele L. Landis, "Let Me Next Time Be 'Tried by Fire': Disaster Relief and the Origins of the American Welfare State 1789–1874," *Northwestern University Law Review* 92 (1998): 967–1034; and "Fate, Responsibility, and 'Natural' Disaster Relief: Narrating the American Welfare State," *Law and Society Review* 33 (1999): 257–318.

[79] See Feller, *Public Lands in Jacksonian Politics*, pp. 29–31, for a discussion of the ritualized rhetoric pitting the settler against the speculator – a dichotomy that, while essentially fallacious, had great moral force.

[80] Onuf has suggested that policymakers were extremely hostile to speculators not because they expected all land purchasers to be settlers, but because speculators threatened to usurp the Government's role in controlling the western land market. That threat had serious political implications for the new nation. "If Congress could not create, alienate, and guarantee land titles, it could not, for all practical purposes, govern at all." *Statehood and Union*, pp. 33–4.

legitimizing the white yeoman Republic of the early to mid-nineteenth century.[81]

Because a capable military was essential to the existence of that Republic, veterans' land bounties had an important role to play. Shortly before the War of 1812 was declared against Great Britain, Congress established land grants of 160 acres (as well as small cash bonuses) for all "effective able-bodied men," aged eighteen to forty-five, who were willing to enlist in the Army as soldiers and noncommissioned officers for a minimum of five years. Congress upped its offer to 320 acres of land in 1814 when the war was going badly and enlistments lagged.[82] That soldiers enlisting at the end of the war were entitled to double the amount of land given to those who served for its duration became a source of criticism and protest. In addition to the fiscal inequity involved, the disparate benefit levels seemed to impute less virtue and deservingness to the men who had served the longest. Citizens lost no time in pointing this out to Congress and asking for a remedy, as an 1818 petition from a group of men from Hampden County, Massachusetts, shows:

Your petitioners are not disposed to question the policy or expediency of any of the laws which have been passed by your Honorable Body for compensating the soldier who served during the late war. No doubt the exigencies of the Country fully warranted the alterations that were from time to time made. But, your petitioners would humbly ask your honors to lay the subject before you & would ask whether justice, expediency, & sound policy (looking forward to the probability

[81] See Smith, *Civic Ideals*, pp. 165–7.

[82] "An Act for completing the existing Military Establishment," December 24, 1811, and "An Act to raise an additional Military Force," *AC* (12/1), pp. 2227–8 and 2229–34, Jan. 11, 1812; "An Act making further provision for filling the ranks of the Army of the United States," *AC* (13/3), pp. 1837–8, Dec. 10, 1814; "An Act to provide for designating, surveying, and granting the Military Bounty Lands," *AC* (12/1), pp. 2292–3, May 6, 1812. Like the Revolutionary bounties, the lands were to be located in military reserves; the president was directed to survey three areas totaling no more than 6 million acres of land "fit for cultivation, not otherwise appropriated, and to which the Indian title [wa]s extinguished" in the Michigan, Illinois, and Louisiana (later Arkansas) territories. Congress substituted another 1.5 million acres in Illinois and 500,000 acres in Missouri for the lands in Michigan when they were discovered to be of poor quality. Because the Illinois, Missouri, and Arkansas territories were quite remote from other western areas being settled at that time, scholars have usually interpreted Congress's purpose in creating these military districts as an attempt to create another "screen" of military veterans between older U.S. settlements and the Native Americans. Gates, for example, suggested that it would have taken "courage and something more than physical strength and a land warrant to migrate so far away from Maine, New Jersey, or New York." *Public Land Law Development*, p. 263; see also Hibbard, *History of the Public Land Policies*, pp. 119–20.

or rather certainty of future wars) do not require that those who early enlisted &
bore the burden and heat of the war should be compensated in money or land
equal to those who entered the service at the eleventh hour.[83]

Apparently to ensure that no one would read self-interest into their petition, the men signed it under the closing "citizens who have not been
soldiers in the late war."

As far as the Army's soldiers were concerned, the establishment of a discernibly inequitable land bounty program was almost certainly preferable
to the Madison administration's proposal to create a program of direct
national conscription if voluntary enlistments continued to be insufficient.[84] Congress's steadfast refusal to entitle Army *officers* to land before,
during, or immediately after the War of 1812 in the face of the instabil-
ity of the officer corps, the Government's sustained desire to establish a
population of veterans on the frontier, and the well-known precedent of
the Revolutionary officers' land bounties was less comprehensible. Bills
reported in 1815 and 1816 proposed to grant officers' land benefits but,
significantly, only to those officers who had been "deranged" or dismissed
from the nation's service in a highly controversial reduction in force[85]

---

[83] Petition of Sundry Citizens of Hampden County, Massachusetts, February 6, 1818,
HR15A-G8.2, Records of the U.S. House of Representatives, Record Group 233, National
Archives, Washington, DC. This was not the only kind of complaint registered about Army
land bounties. Note, for example, the petition requesting higher disability pension rates
sent to Congress by former sailors Frederick Earnest and Frederick Williamson, each of
whom had lost an arm in combat at sea. Earnest and Williamson pointed out that they
would have been better off if they had served in the Army instead of the Navy, for "had
they been acting on shore as soldiers they would upon their discharge have been entitled
to a bounty in land altho not wounded." 6 January 1818, HR15A-G9.1, NARA.

[84] John Whiteclay Chambers II, *To Raise an Army: The Draft Comes to Modern America*
(New York: Free Press, 1987), pp. 32–5.

[85] Agricultural and military historians mystified by Congress's long-standing refusal to offer
land to the War of 1812's officers have long tended to overlook the fact that the bounty
bills reported in 1815 and 1816 did not propose to entitle all of the war's officers to
benefits, but only those who had served and subsequently been dismissed from the
Army following the Peace of Ghent. Even Paul Gates, author of the encyclopedic *History
of Public Land Law Development*, could only speculate over Congress's treatment of the
1812 officers' exclusion from benefits. "Perhaps," he wrote, "it was the size of the military
bounties given officers of the Revolution and the large estates they had made possible
that discouraged Congress in 1811 from offering any land to officers" (p. 262). Hibbard
declared more severely that "[t]he land bounty acts during and following the War of 1812
show[ed] a complete lack of understanding of the proper use of land, assuming that
there is a proper use as a reward for military service and the proper way of administering
it. . . ." He also questioned Congress's original exclusion of enlisted men younger than
eighteen and older than forty-five from benefits. "Probably there was no sinister intention
involved," but "[w]hy, forsooth, should not these patriots be located as well as those of

that cut the size of the officer corps from a wartime high of 3,495 to 656.[86] The protracted debate over the second of these bills is illuminating with respect to contemporary attitudes toward the Army's officers, and the kinds of battles that historically have ensued over exclusionary categories of desert.

Kentuckian Richard Johnson, chair of the House Committee on Military Affairs, was behind the idea of selectively entitling only the disbanded officers to land. Describing the painstaking committee deliberations that had produced the proposal, Johnson pointed to the policy precedent of the Revolutionary pensions, noting that whereas "[t]he memorable Congress of '83, which closed the Revolution, gave half-pay for life to the officers, or five years whole pay," the new bill "propose[d] only a donation in land." It was true that no such promise had been made to the officers, but the Government's obligation to provide land to its deranged officers was not diminished, he argued, if members of Congress thought they deserved it. In his view, patriotism was worth rewarding, for officers' land bounties would serve as a "cheap, but effectual" means of preparing the Republic for later wars, imparting moral power ("by such illustrious examples of honor, virtue, gratitude, and justice"), physical power ("by uniting all hearts and all hands in support of a Government inspiring such confidence"), and intellectual power ("by extending the means of support and cultivation to the indigent and distressed"). That the proposed legislation would not benefit at least 300,000 sea fencibles,

---

regular army age? To this question there was no answer." *History of the Public Land Policies*, p. 119. Congress passed legislation granting bounties to those men who had enlisted as soldiers regardless of age or subsequent promotion shortly after the war, but the War of 1812's officers would not receive bounties until the 1850s, in the wake of the Mexican War. See Chapter 5 herein.

[86] *AC* (14/1), p. 1800; *ASP, Public Lands*, vol. 6, pp. 302–3; *AC* (14/1), p. 979. The reduction in force generated a significant amount of resentment among Army officers not only because of its size, but moreover because in implementing it, the Madison administration had neither adhered to the seniority rule nor confined its discharges to the extra forces raised between 1808 and 1814. Instead, for the first time, the administration had requested and utilized confidential reports on the officers' relative merits, and had terminated the careers of many senior commanders, including almost all of the remaining veterans of the Revolution, the Confederation Army, and the "American Legion" who had secured much of the land north of the Ohio for the nation in the Battle of Fallen Timbers. Most officers apparently accepted their discharge without protest, but others who remained discontented formed an association, published their grievances in the press, and complained bitterly to their representatives (and social equals) in Congress. See William B. Skelton, *An American Profession of Arms: The Army Officer Corps, 1784–1861* (Lawrence: University Press of Kansas, 1992), pp. 61–4.

rangers, militiamen, and volunteers who had served in the late war was surely understandable. To do so would require some 50 million acres of land, a "serious encroachment upon the national domain" that would greatly reduce revenues from its sale, and a "prodigal waste" of national resources that those groups of veterans had never expected and had never claimed. What those veterans *had* expected and demanded, Congress had provided: legislation granting half-pay pensions for five years to their widows and children, which Congress "ha[d] the power to extend," should that "provision be considered inadequate."[87]

That Congress was being petitioned by Continental Army officers for an equitable settlement on their lost commutation certificates and, more generally, by Revolutionary officers and soldiers demanding the creation of a service pension program was a factor in the Committee on Military Affairs' decision to propose the officers' land bounty bill in 1816. Noting how onerous the committee's duties had become because of the diversity of "expectations of different classes of individuals," Johnson specifically acknowledged Revolutionary veterans' claims, asserting that the committee had "endeavored to embrace the cases of all who were entitled to consideration, without injury to the Republic," including the "surviving officers and soldiers of the Revolution . . . unable to gain a livelihood by labor." That the Government had contracted no legal obligation to grant land to the late Army's discharged officers was not, in Johnson's view, an argument against the bill, for it would "reflect more honor upon Congress to give where it [wa]s merited, without legal obligation." Congress should not inquire into whether it had "promised" to "make donations to the officer," for "a tender father never stops to inquire whether he is bound by contract to aid and relieve a worthy son; nor does a man of noble feelings inquire whether he is bound by contract to extend the hand of assistance to a friend in distress."[88]

---

[87] Remarks of Richard Johnson, *AC* (14/1), pp. 979–86, Feb. 15, 1816. The Fourteenth Congress granted half-pay for five years to the widows and orphans of Army officers, noncommissioned officers, soldiers, and musicians, and the officers and soldiers of the militia, including the rangers, sea fencibles, and volunteers, provided that the men had enlisted for either a year or eighteen months and had died either during the War of 1812 or later, as a consequence of wounds received in the service. "An Act making further provision for military services during the later war, and for other purposes," *AC* (14/1), pp. 1837–9, Apr. 16, 1816. Service pensions for War of 1812 veterans were not enacted until 1871, despite continued agitation heightened by the precedent set by the Revolutionary pension legislation of 1818–32.

[88] Remarks of Richard Johnson, *AC* (14/1), pp. 985–6, Feb. 15, 1816. Johnson's remarks suggest that he was trying to finesse the contemporary distinction between debts of

Despite the growing norm of deference to committee expertise,[89] many of Johnson's colleagues disapproved of the proposed bill. The idea of entitling the Army's disbanded officers to land bonuses while ignoring the veteran officers who remained in the service was incomprehensible. Many believed that the latter group had "rendered more service to the country, and ha[d] stronger claims on her bounty than those who ha[d] been deranged." As House member Oliver Comstock of New York put it, the "imperfection" of the new provision was "manifest," for it "exclude[d] from its benefits the most meritorious class of the Army." The respective merits of the officers composing the late Army had been evinced in the selection of officers for the Peace Establishment. What had induced any of the officers to enter the service, and had multiplied the number of candidates for military office to "an extent beyond that which it was proper to gratify and employ? . . . [P]atriotism, the love of fame, and the laudable desire of rendering benefit to the country." Justice certainly did not dictate that the disbanded officers be entitled to land, for the Government had neither "failed to perform its engagements with the officers" nor "subjected itself to the imputation of bad faith." Congress had "complied with every legal and moral obligation imposed on [it]" with respect to the deranged officers. Nor did "sound policy" suggest that such grants should be made.[90] The notion that the illiberality of Congress's conduct toward the deranged officers would result in the refusal of officers to serve in future conflicts was no more than a "fanciful picture." Not gratuities, but an "honorable sense of duty, and an ardent and long cherished attachment to those eternal principles of civil and religious liberty, guarantied

---

gratitude and debts of justice, or between moral and legal obligation. See Chapter 3 for a discussion of this distinction with respect to the Revolutionary pension legislation.

[89] Joseph Cooper, *The Origins of the Standing Committees and the Development of the Modern House* (Houston: Rice University Press, 1970), pp. 51–61; see also the remarks of Micah Taul, *AC* (14/1), p. 989, Feb. 15, 1816. Taul pointed to his refusal to defer to the Committee on Military Affairs' recommendations as a means of signaling that his opposition to the land bounty proposal was serious. He usually distrusted his own judgment "when it [wa]s different from that of any of the standing committees of the House. The members composing those committees are selected for their capacity and particular knowledge of the business to be referred to them. . . . [I]t is to be presumed that every measure, before it is reported to the House, undergoes a very nice scrutiny. . . . In opposing, therefore, any measure recommended by them, you have to encounter 'fearful odds' indeed." Fearful odds notwithstanding, Taul found the selective bounty provision "impolitic" and urged that it be stricken out. See the later discussion.

[90] Note the distinction that Comstock drew between Congress's adjudication of legal claims and legislative policymaking.

us by our excellent political institutions, w[ould] be among the powerful motives that w[ould] secure forever to the Government their best services and affection."[91]

Comstock and other House members opposed to the selective land bounty provision did not stop at contrasting the merits of the discharged officers and those of the officers retained in the Army, but went on to portray the discharged officers as less deserving of Federal benefits than the Army's soldiers, members of the militia, volunteers, and many other Americans. Citing the gross inequity of the Army's pay rates for officers and soldiers as justification for the land bounties established for soldiers,[92] Wilson Lumpkin of Georgia noted that while the Army's soldiers had endured danger and hardship, many officers had lived in "luxury and dissipation" during the war, "spending their time in idleness and pleasure, at their recruiting stations, and frequently their conduct was such, that they were so little respected by the community where they were stationed, that they scarcely enlisted a man." He had "no doubt they injured the cause they were in honor bound to support ... living upon the Government, without rendering the smallest benefit to it." And how could he vote to benefit "regular officers, some of whom ha[d] been worse than useless to the Government, while the arduous and important military services" of the militia's officers and those who fought with them were "passed over, entirely neglected?"[93]

Micah Taul of Kentucky also rejected the idea that the nation was "exclusively" indebted to the Army for victory, for "disaster had succeeded disaster in such rapid succession" that the nation literally had been "clad in mourning" until the militia had provided the war's "first ray of hope." If suffering was to be rewarded, Congress should "begin with the non-commissioned officers and privates of the militia," for "[c]omparatively speaking, the situation of the officer during the late war was enviable" and "the situation of the soldier wretched, deplorable." He "would not make a donation of land to the officer, without making a similar donation to the soldier." However, Taul "d[id] not think either entitled to it," for

[91] Remarks of Oliver Comstock, *AC* (14/1), pp. 987–8, Feb. 15, 1816. Rufus Easton, delegate for the Missouri Territory, went further than Comstock, warning that if Congress bestowed bounties exclusively upon the disbanded officers, the nation would have "officers by the thousands" in future contests, "but few soldiers, to fight the battles of this beloved country." *AC* (14/1), p. 996.

[92] Lumpkin quoted the Army's monthly pay rates as follows: major generals, $245; brigadier generals, $132; colonels, $93; majors, $64; captains, $43; soldiers, $8. *AC* (14/1), p. 1039.

[93] Remarks of Wilson Lumpkin, *AC* (14/1), pp. 1038–42, Feb. 20, 1816.

he doubted the basic authority of Congress to dispose of the public lands in such a way. It had become, he argued, "too common a practice under almost all governments to reward a few at the expense of the many. Let us not, if possible, fall into this error. If we are to exercise our charity, let us find fit objects; for ill-directed or misplaced charity, is worse than no charity at all."[94]

The disbanded officers' bounty provision was defeated by a slim margin of 74 to 60 on February 15, 1816, but it was reconsidered a few days later when a majority of the House voted to entitle *Canadian* officers and soldiers who had supported the American war effort to land grants in Indiana.[95] John Hulbert of Massachusetts fumed at the incongruity of allowing refugees, *traitors*, to fare "sumptuously at the nation's table, while [its] own citizens, who ha[d] constantly adhered to [their] Government, [we]re left, like dogs, to pick up the crumbs that f[e]ll from the same table." He denounced the grants for the Canadians as an "exceptionable and odious provision," "perverse" in principle and "dangerous" in example, a "foul stain, an indelible blot on the annals of American legislation."[96] Nonetheless, the Fourteenth Congress enacted legislation entitling the Canadian officers and soldiers to land, while still another House vote spurned land grants for the disbanded American officers by a margin of 77 to 59.[97] The proposal was revived yet again when the military services bill reached the Senate in the form of an amendment sponsored by James Wilson of New Jersey, who argued that beyond being just and a means of forming a military barrier on the frontier against "the incursions of the savages," such a "gratuity" was sanctioned by Revolutionary war precedents. Moreover, "public opinion, so far as it could be collected, called for this, or some other expression of the national gratitude to the disbanded officers." Wilson's reasoning was not persuasive.

94 Remarks of Micah Taul, *AC* (14/1), pp. 989–91, Feb. 15, 1816. Rufus Easton also contended that the selective entitlement of the disbanded officers would be misdirected. "This is, or ought to be, a Government of equal rights – equal protection should be extended to all, and equal and exact justice measured out to all alike." Was the nation "to give to the rich, to disbanded officers, to the aristocratic branch of the community, who sought with eagerness the honor of holding [its] commissions, and the truly unfortunate to remain wholly unprovided for?" *AC* (14/1), p. 994.

95 "An Act granting bounties in lands and extra pay to certain Canadian volunteers," *AC* (14/1), p. 1800, March 5, 1816.

96 *AC* (14/1), pp. 999–1006, Feb. 16, 1816. Proponents of the land entitlements for the disbanded officers pointed to the precedent set by the Continental Congress in offering land grants to foreigners willing to desert and fight for the nascent United States.

97 *AC* (14/1), p. 1051, Feb. 21, 1816.

The amendment failed by a vote of 15 to 10, leaving the Senate to reconsider the question of which of the War of 1812's officers, if any, should be entitled to land benefits. Trying a new tack, the Committee on Military Affairs was instructed to "inquire into the propriety of granting bounty lands to such of the disbanded officers of our late army as have been *disabled* by wounds while in the public service, and of granting the same quantity of land to each soldier who has served during the late war, and been honorably discharged."[98]

These struggles to invent and reinvent appropriate categories of desert in 1816 are extremely revealing. Either a majority of the Fourteenth Congress was not ready to adopt a programmatic approach to dealing with the demands of the Army's officers, or its members found themselves unable to craft an entitlement program that embodied an acceptable categorical resolution of those veterans' demands. Their refusal to create post hoc War of 1812 officers' land bounties also seems to have been influenced by other factors. One important consideration was their projected cost, which was exacerbated by the enormity of the national debt in 1816.[99] Some members asserted that the entitlements would be a "cheap" form of public policy because they would require land rather than money. However, that argument was shattered by the calculation that at the current selling price of $2 dollars per acre, passage of the bill might result in the loss of some $2 million of Federal land sales revenues at a time when Congress was considering the imposition of a direct tax of $3 million on the people of the United States.[100] The proposed land

[98] Remarks of James Wilson, March 19, 1816; Senate vote, March 20; Lacock's motion, March 27; Senate resolution, March 29 (emphasis added); *AC* (14/1), pp. 210–11, 213, 251–3. By December 1816, Acting Secretary of War George Graham would warn Congress that the law granting Canadian volunteers bounty lands needed to be amended in order to "guard the public against imposition." Graham complained that only one week's voluntary service was required to entitle parties to land bounties, and it appeared that numerous frauds had been practiced. *ASP, Claims,* p. 499.

[99] The total indebtedness of the United States on January 1, 1816, was $127,334,000. Aggregate U.S. Government spending during the years 1812–15 nearly equaled the spending of the previous two decades, with yearly deficits ranging from a low of $10.4 million in 1812 to a high of $23.6 million in 1814. Total expenditures in those years equaled $20.2 and $34.7 million, respectively. Davis Rich Dewey, *Financial History of the United States* (New York: Longmans, Green, and Co., 1915), pp. 165, 141–2.

[100] Remarks of Wilson Lumpkin, February 20, 1816, referring to the House's passage, six days earlier, of a bill that became "An Act supplementary to the act to provide additional revenues for defraying the expenses of Government and maintaining the public credit, by laying a direct tax upon the United States ...," *AC* (14/1), pp. 1042, 1858–63, Apr. 26, 1816. Lumpkin said: "For my part I cannot reconcile it to my feelings, to vote a

bounty program may also have been galling given the fact that the vast majority of men bearing arms in the War of 1812 – some 86 percent – did so in local units that were not directly under control of the U.S. Government or its officers.[101]

Many of the arguments made against selective land benefits in the Fourteenth Congress precisely anticipated those that would be articulated two years later in the Fifteenth Congress as it proceeded to enact the categorical 1818 Pension Act.[102] Where that law was enacted and rapidly expanded, however, disbanded officers' land bounty bills failed year after year, despite intense lobbying by both interested officers and state legislatures. In 1831, an exasperated House Committee on Public Lands would introduce yet another land bounty measure, arguing somewhat legalistically that the disbanded officers had expected and believed that land bounties were due them at the end of the second war for independence "as an expression of the feeling of the government for their sufferings and privations, as well as a reward for their services and sacrifices." That the officers still believed the Government owed them land grants, the committee said, was "evidenced by the reiteration of their claims." Moreover, many of those brave and patriotic men and their heirs were "known to be in reduced circumstances," a condition requiring that their claims upon the justice and liberality of the country could "no longer be neglected or postponed." However "just, politic, and expedient" the 1831 bill might have seemed to the Committee on Public Lands, though, no land bounty legislation was forthcoming from the Twenty-first Congress.[103] Not even the addition of disability or poverty as criteria of deservingness would

---

direct tax of three millions of dollars indiscriminately on the people, and then, in the next vote give away two millions of their property, or money; for in reality I view it as the same thing." This was the third such tax passed by Congress. The first, aimed at raising $3 million, was enacted in the summer of 1813; a second tax worth twice that amount in revenues was enacted in September 1814. Congress likely was also well aware of the problems facing the General Land Office in implementing the bounty legislation for soldiers alone. See Rohrbough, *Land Office Business*, pp. 78–84.

[101] Chambers, *To Raise an Army*, pp. 34–5.

[102] Pension opponents Nathaniel Macon of North Carolina and James Barbour of Virginia both served as senators in both the Fourteenth and Fifteenth Congresses, as did pension advocate Robert Goldsborough of Maryland. Macon voted in favor of Senator Wilson's amendment to revive the categorical land bounty provision, but Barbour voted against it. No vote was recorded for Goldsborough.

[103] "On the application to grant land to officers disbanded from the Army after the War of 1812–'15, and to the heirs of those who died or were killed in service," communicated to the House of Representatives, Mar. 1, 1831, *ASP, Public Lands*, vol. 6, pp. 302–6.

suffice to convince a majority of Congress of the merits of creating land entitlements for the disbanded War of 1812 officers, despite the precedent set by the establishment and expansion of the Revolutionary pension system.[104]

Public Land Policy and Sectionalism

The Twenty-first Congress's failure to act on the disbanded officers' claims surely reflected its reluctance to recognize those officers as uniquely deserving, along with fear that the enactment of benefits for them might result in demands upon the state from other groups for similar treatment. But Congress's rejection of the bounty proposal in 1831 was also undoubtedly symptomatic of the degree to which Federal land policy had become enmeshed in sectional conflicts over the distribution of national wealth, population, and power by the late 1820s and early 1830s.[105] The Government's repeated decrees against squatting had not caused an exodus of "intruders" from the public domain. Instead, its repeated enactment of selective preemption laws had only heightened demands for a general preemption law from the hardy, presumptively virtuous woodsmen who were expanding the contours of the nation by settling the frontier. Deluged with petitions demanding various forms of legislative action and relief, Western congressmen sought recognition that settling the West was a national service deserving of substantive benefits, including universal preemption rights, grants to the states for education and internal improvements, the enactment of relief measures for debtors who had bought land under the nation's credit sales system, and a reduction in the national minimum land price. In their view, the future of the West was dependent upon changes in land policy favorable to settlement. Federal cooperation was not simply a matter of good policy, but one of "justice and right."[106]

---

[104] That many of the discharged officers were also veterans of the Revolution may have been a factor in Congress's repeated refusal to grant them land. It is interesting to note, however, that arguments made against the passage of the supplementary Revolutionary pension act of 1832 warned against setting another precedent that would be looked to by the War of 1812's officers, who "had already put forth their claim" for a "reward, not indeed in money, but in land." See, e.g., remarks of John Bell of Tennessee, Apr. 9, 1832, *RD* (22/1), p. 2461.

[105] Feller, *Public Lands in Jacksonian Politics*, p. 189. This and the next several paragraphs draw especially upon Feller's rich account of the rise of sectional conflict over the disposition of the public lands during the early nineteenth century.

[106] Ibid., 17.

Thus it was that in 1824, after Congress had lowered the minimum price of Federal land to $1.25 per acre, abolished the credit system, and reduced the minimum tract size to 80 acres,[107] Missouri Senator Thomas Hart Benton introduced the ultimate Western measure: a bill proposing to subject lands unpurchased after five years to reauction at a considerably reduced minimum price of 50 cents per acre, and to grant 80 acres of land to all "actual settlers" willing to fulfill a three-year residency requirement. The bill initially was tabled, but its subsequent resubmission in a modified form, proposing the annual reduction or "graduation" of the price of unsold Federal lands and free tracts for settlers, would dominate debate over the disposition of the public domain for decades. As Feller has observed, Benton's 1826 declaration that the public domain belonged to the people and not to the Government offered a "simple, comprehensive explanation for Western embarrassments: an oppressive, unconstitutional, irrational land system, based upon greed and Eastern hostility to Western growth."[108] It was only "right and proper" that

the first settlers, who ha[d] made roads and bridges over the public lands at their own expense, and with great labor and toil, should be allowed a privilege greater than other purchasers. . . . [H]e who renders a benefit to the public, who

---

[107] "An Act making further provision for the sale of the Public Lands," *AC* (16/1), pp. 2578–80, Apr. 24, 1820. Congress also passed Relief Acts for the benefit of land debtors in 1821, 1822, and 1823. The Relief Act of March 2, 1821, allowed debtors to relinquish portions of the land they had bought and have the payments made on it applied to their remaining land; it also forgave all accrued interest and gave a reduction of 37.5 percent on the outstanding amount due if debtors completed payments on their original purchases by September 30, 1822. The Relief Acts of 1822 and 1823 extended the time period in which debtors could file applications to relinquish land. See Gates, *Public Land Law Development*, pp. 140–2. As Gates notes, the Panic of 1819 undoubtedly played a role in pushing Congress to reduce the minimum sales price of the public lands and enact relief measures. At its peak in December 1819, the outstanding debt from land bought on credit was $22,000,657. By contrast, total Federal expenditures for 1819 amounted to $21,511,000. Dewey, *Financial History of the United States*, p. 169.

[108] Feller, *Public Lands in Jacksonian Politics*, pp. 75–7, cited phrase on p. 77. "Happily," Benton told his colleagues, "I speak to those who understand and anticipate me. I speak to statesmen, and not to compting clerks; to Senators, and not to *Quæstors* of provinces; to an assembly of legislators, and not to a keeper of the King's forests. I speak to Senators who know this to be a Republic, not a Monarchy; who know that the public lands belong to the People, and not to the Federal Government; who know that the lands are to be 'disposed of' for the common good of all, and not kept for the service of a few." In Benton's view, the best way to maintain the American Republic was to put the lands in the hands of the people, for freeholders would comprise a "race of virtuous and independent farmers, the true supporters of their country." He cited the following poem as authority [*RD* (19/1), pp. 727–8 (emphasis in the original)]:

by his enterprise and industry, has created to himself and his family a home in the wilderness, should be entitled to his reward.[109]

To nationalists like President John Quincy Adams, however, it was right and proper to maintain a Hamiltonian general revenue policy toward the public domain. Adams recognized that a copious supply of funds would be required to consummate his vision of the United States as a "united American nation striding toward economic, intellectual, and moral achievement under the fostering care of a benevolent central government."[110] Aided by a treasury surplus and falling interest payments on the national debt, the income generated from land sales would finance an ambitious scheme of Federal public works projects extending from the Atlantic to the Pacific Ocean, which would in turn enhance the value of the remaining lands, increasing their selling price.[111]

The manufacturing North Atlantic states also favored keeping the price of public lands high, for it was in their best interests to retard the western emigration of the population that supplied them with cheap labor. However, they were much less sanguine than President Adams about the prospect of allowing land revenues to flow into the U.S. Treasury. In addition to the fact that such a flow might aid in the payment of the debt, reducing the need for the high protective tariffs that promoted American manufactures, it would provide the Federal Government with a large measure of control over development in the states. As New Jersey Senator Mahlon Dickerson baldly put it, direct Federal spending eventually would "so far decrease the powers of the State Governments, and increase those of the United States Government, as to destroy the federative

> What constitutes a state?
> Not high-rais'd battlements, nor labored mound,
> Thick wall, nor moated gate;
> Nor cities proud, with spires and turrets crown'd,
> Nor starr'd and spangled courts,
> Where low-born baseness wafts perfume to pride:
> But MEN! high-minded men,
> Who their *duties* know, but know their RIGHTS,
> And, knowing, *dare* maintain them.

[109] House Committee on Public Lands, "Pre-emption Rights in the Choctaw District in Mississippi," *ASP, Public Lands*, vol. V, p. 401.

[110] Feller, *Public Lands in Jacksonian Politics*, p. 72. Concerning Adams's election due to a nationalist coalition drawn from the New England, mid-Atlantic, and western states and his outline for a "nationalist program of monumental proportion," see also Skowronek, *Politics Presidents Make*, pp. 115–19.

[111] Wellington, *Political and Sectional Influence of the Public Lands*, pp. 3–5.

principle of our Union, and convert our system of confederated republics into a consolidated government." Dickerson and some of his congressional colleagues consequently advocated the adoption of a policy of "distribution," whereby Federal lands would be sold and the proceeds distributed on some equitable basis to the states rather than deposited in the treasury.[112]

Although distribution might have provided the old states of the South with cash disbursements partly offsetting the impact of the tariff, many southern members of Congress, particularly Old Republicans, were more interested in retiring the national debt and limiting the nation's fiscal capacity in order to preserve states' rights. They saw the debt as a potent instrument of centralization for consolidation-minded presidents and congressmen willing to "undermine the Constitution by bribing the states out of their principles with their own taxpayers' money."[113] In their view, the public land legislation of recent years had demonstrated how the public domain had been employed to justify Federal intrusion in matters of subnational policy like internal improvements and education. Moreover, Rufus King's radical proposal to dedicate Federal land revenues to the emancipation and relocation of slaves could only be understood as "a departure from the conditions and spirit of the compact between the several states ... calculated to disturb the peace and harmony of the Union."[114] Fearing a nationalist assault on slavery and the plantation system, Virginians John Randolph and Littleton Tazewell, among

---

[112] Dickerson, a Report "from the committee to whom was referred the resolution proposing to divide among the States annually a portion of the revenues of the General Government ...," S.doc. 95 (19/1) 128. The distribution proposals of the mid-1820s came in a variety of forms. Some advocated distributing the net proceeds of land sales to the states according to population with no strings attached – essentially, an early form of revenue sharing. Others sought to target land revenues for particular purposes. One 1826 proposal in the House, for example, urged the distribution of funds to the states for common schools. Senator Henry Johnson of Louisiana urged that land revenues be invested in a permanent fund, with the interest income on it distributed among the states according to their representation in the House, half to be used for internal improvements and half for education. Coupling the land question with that of slavery, Rufus King of New York suggested that the proceeds of future land sales should be used for the emancipation of slaves and their removal, with free blacks, from the United States, a proposal that had no friends in the South. Gates, *Public Land Law Development*, pp. 5–9; Wellington, *Political and Sectional Influence of the Public Lands*, pp. 5–6.

[113] Feller, *Public Lands in Jacksonian Politics*, p. 74.

[114] Robert Hayne, Feb. 28, 1825, *RD* (18/2), pp. 697–8.

others, began to advocate the cession of the Federal lands back to the states.[115]

As Congress debated the proper direction that Federal land policy should take in the mid- to late 1820s, a "veritable mania" for land swept the frontier regions, and demands for inexpensive or donated land were heard throughout the nation. Five of the seven public land states' governors declared themselves for graduation or cession, and the legislatures of Alabama, Louisiana, Missouri, Indiana, Illinois, and the Florida and Arkansas Territories all petitioned Congress for various reforms of the land system – graduation, cession, preemption rights and free lands for settlers, the abolition of the credit system, additional relief for land debtors, and the sale of land in smaller tracts.[116] Articulating an early argument for the public provision of subsistence benefits to all citizens, nascent labor organizations also began to urge Congress to place "all the Public Lands, without the delay of sales, within the reach of the people at large." They argued that all men had a natural birthright in the soil, but while that right was subject to the control of others, men might "be deprived of life, liberty, and the pursuit of happiness."[117]

It appeared that no one was enamored with the operation of the Federal land system. From the first, land sales had never met Congress's expectations, either in terms of acres sold or revenue generated. Squatters occupied Native American lands and portions of the public domain unimpeded by a Government that could condemn, but not control, their depredations. Citizens approaching their elected representatives saw their petitions for land grants and preemption rights go unanswered. The Federal land benefits already established, however well intentioned, had caused relentless social and political controversy. Congress had repeatedly been required to grant relief to land debtors, admitting the weakness and inconsistency of its own policies and imposing an administrative nightmare on a General Land Office already beset by operational difficulties, meager budgetary allotments, and widespread accusations of corruption.[118]

---

[115] S.doc. 99 (19/1) 128; *RD* (19/1), May 26, 1826, p. 782; *RD* (20/2), Feb. 10, 1829, pp. 58–9.

[116] Feller, *Public Lands in Jacksonian Politics*, p. 77.

[117] "Memorial to Congress," *Mechanics' Free Press*, Oct. 25, 1828, p. 1, in *A Documentary History of American Industrial Society*, ed. John R. Commons et al. (Cleveland: Arthur H. Clark Company, 1910), vol. V, pp. 43–5.

[118] Rohrbough, *Land Office Business*, pp. 156–99.

Clearly, some sort of change was called for. Yet the gulf between eastern and western viewpoints in Congress, as Feller notes, seemed "fundamental and unbridgeable, for each thought that existing policy unfairly
favored the other."[119] In January 1830, Senator Robert Hayne exhorted
the newly elected Twenty-first Congress concerning the magnitude of the
Federal land problem:

Every gentlemen who has had a seat in Congress for the last two or three years, or
even for the last two or three weeks, must be convinced of the great and growing
importance of this question. More than half of our time has been taken up with
the discussion of propositions connected with the public lands; more than half
of our acts embrace provisions growing out of this fruitful source. Day after day
the changes are rung on this topic, from the grave inquiry into the right of the
States to the absolute sovereignty and property in the soil, down to the grant of
a pre-emption of a few quarter-sections to actual settlers.... No gentleman can
fail to perceive that this is a question no longer to be evaded; it must be met –
fairly and fearlessly met. A question that is pressed upon us in so many ways; that
intrudes in such a variety of shapes; involving so deeply the feelings and interests
of a large portion of the Union; insinuating itself into almost every question of
public policy, and tinging the whole course of our legislation, cannot be put aside,
or laid asleep. We cannot long avoid it; we must meet and overcome it, or it will
overcome us.[120]

Hayne correctly perceived the centrality of the public domain in chart-
ing the course of the nation's future. Missouri's admission to the union
in 1820 had temporarily struck a balance of power within the union, but
the governing conditions that resulted were anything but calm or static.
Dramatic changes had taken place in state and society in the decades since
independence had been declared and won. If a new vision of American
nationality rooted in white Christian male dominance existed by the time

---

[119] *Public Lands in Jacksonian Politics*, p. 81.

[120] *RD* (21/1), Jan. 19, 1830, pp. 31–2. It was this speech, made in response to Connecticut
Senator Samuel Foot's proposal to suspend land sales temporarily and abolish the office
of the surveyor general, that began the legendary Webster–Hayne debate. Benton had
opened fire on Foot's resolution when it had come before the Senate the previous day,
characterizing it as nothing more than a "horrid policy of making paupers by law." The
tariff – a "most complex scheme of injustice, which taxe[d] the South to injure the
West, to pauperize the poor of the North"– had been "bad enough, but it [wa]s a trifle,
a lame, weak, and impotent contrivance, compared to the scheme which [wa]s now on
the table" – "cruel legislation which would confine poor people in the Northeast to work
as journeymen in the manufactories, instead of letting them go off to new countries,
acquire land, become independent freeholders, and lay the foundation of comfort and
independence for their children." *RD* (21/1), Jan. 18, 1830, p. 24.

of Jackson's election to the presidency, little agreement existed upon how to sustain it.[121] Partial solutions would be found in the definitions of property and civil rights that came with the expansion of the United States during the 1830s and 1840s, but the acquisitive achievements of the nation led by Jackson and Polk would come at a price. Just how high a price remained to be seen.

[121] Smith, *Civic Ideals*, pp. 198–9.

5

Expanding a Nation, Dissolving a Union

Are you endowed with reason? Then you must know that your right
to life hereby includes the right to a place to live in – the right to a
home. Assert this right, so long denied mankind by feudal robbers
and their attorneys. Vote yourself a farm.

National Reform circular, 1846[1]

Hard choices faced the Twenty-first Congress with respect to Federal land
policy. To begin with, it fell to that Congress to consider legislation implementing President Jackson's 1829 plan to "remove" Native Americans
to a location west of the Mississippi River. Jackson and other advocates
attempted to defuse criticism of the removal plan by asserting that it
was legally and morally justified, but that did not prevent Congress from
being deluged by hundreds of petitions and memorials from outraged
religious groups and benevolent societies. A Removal Act passed by narrow margins in both chambers,[2] but only after a protracted and bitter
debate in which New Jersey Senator Theodore Frelinghuysen accused
the United States of having seized more Indian land than it knew what
to do with.[3] As if to prove his point, most of the land bills introduced
in the Twenty-first Congress inspired little more than stalemate. A select
committee was appointed by the House to draw up a "distribution" bill
giving the proceeds of land sales to the states, but the matter failed to

---

[1] Reprinted in John R. Commons, ed., *A Documentary History of American Industrial Society*
(Cleveland: Arthur A. Clark Company, 8 vols., 1910), vol. VII, pp. 305–7.

[2] The vote on the Indian Removal Act was 28 to 19 in favor in the Senate and 102 to 97
in favor in the House. *Register of Debates in Congress, 1825–1837* [hereafter *RD*] (21/1),
Apr. 24 and May 24, 1830, pp. 383, 1133.

[3] *RD* (21/1), Apr. 9, 1830, p. 311; Anthony F. C. Wallace, *The Long, Bitter Trail: Andrew
Jackson and the Indians* (New York: Hill and Wang, 1993), pp. 65–70. For Frelinghuysen's
complete arguments against removal, see *RD* (21/1), pp. 309–20, 325, 380–1.

go any further.[4] A drastically amended version of Benton's proposal to "graduate" or lower the price of Federal lands was approved by a slim margin in the Senate, only to be tabled indefinitely by the House. Davy Crockett's proposal that the Government cede back certain "waste" lands in Tennessee also received short shrift. Its demise led some congressmen to conclude that efforts toward a general "cession" law returning the public lands to the states were hopeless, and perhaps detrimental to the cause of those advocating moderate change in the national land system.[5]

In the face of these failures, a preemption measure sailed through both houses of the Twenty-first Congress so easily that it appeared as if the Government had never opposed illegal settlement on public land, let alone made it a criminal offense. The Preemption Act of 1830 granted preemption rights to those squatters who already were cultivating and living on portions of the public domain in 1829. President Jackson signed the law in the face of vehement protest by General Land Office Commissioner George Graham, who declared himself "opposed in principle to the whole bill." Beyond the disruptive effect that it would have on the administration of the entire land system, Graham worried about the law's effect as a policy precedent, arguing that it was likely to make the settler of 1830 feel "entitled to the rights accorded the settler in 1829."[6] Senator Samuel

---

[4] As noted in Chapter 4, the Twenty-first Congress was deeply divided regarding supplementary pension legislation for veterans of the Revolution, defined by Senator Hayne as just another "scheme for the distribution of public money" that would keep tariffs up by postponing the retirement of the national debt. *RD* (21/1), p. 401. All eight southeastern senators voted against Clay's land revenue distribution bill in 1832 and 1833, when an amended version passed only to go down to a pocket veto by President Jackson. By 1836, the issue had been transformed into an almost purely partisan one, with Whigs in the Twenty-fourth Congress voting overwhelmingly for distribution and Democrats, who held a sizable majority in the House, against it. Where some southerners advocated distribution as an opportunity to recoup revenues lost to the tariff, others viewed it as an attempt to bribe the South and West into accepting high tariffs. Daniel Feller, *The Public Lands in Jacksonian Politics* (Madison): University of Wisconsin Press, 1984), pp. 143–83; Helene Sara Zahler, *Eastern Workingmen and National Land Policy, 1829–1862* (New York: Columbia University Press, 1941), pp. 115–16.

[5] Though the notion that the federal land system violated the rights of the states and the true meaning of the Virginia Cession, the Northwest Ordinance, and the Constitution "was a Western commonplace" in the late 1820s, arguments for cession sank like a stone in the Twenty-first Congress. Eastern politicians found the western states' demands for multiple favors in addition to the entire public domain disgusting and pretentious. Feller, *Public Lands in Jacksonian Politics*, p. 125. Regarding sectional politics and the failure of the graduation and cession bills, see pp. 131–6.

[6] "An Act to grant pre-emption rights to settlers on the Public Lands," May 29, 1830, *RD* (21/1), Appendix, pp. xlvii–xlviii; John Moore (Graham's chief clerk) to

Bell of New Hampshire registered the same objection: even if the proposed legislation was a selective and retroactive measure, benefiting only those people already occupying Federal land, such a provision could only encourage future violation of the laws regulating the public land system. How could it fail to tempt other intruders to trespass upon the public domain in the expectation that they, too, would be given the right to purchase illegally settled land at the minimum price without competition? And how could Congress fail to establish new preemption rights when they demanded them? "We cannot, and we will not," Bell warned, "refuse them the same privilege, when they ask us, which we now propose to grant. Any person who has witnessed the effect of precedents in this body, must see that this precedent will be acted upon."[7]

In objecting to the statute Graham and Bell not only accurately predicted what would happen after the preemption Act of 1830 was passed, but also identified the problem that the state creates for itself in enacting all selective entitlements: that of contending with the demands generated, at least in part, by the interpersonal and intergroup comparisons that such laws inspire. In the absence of entitlement programs, or when entitlements are essentially universal, there is no basis for making such comparisons or for developing expectations that the state will be forthcoming with particular substantive benefits. Once selective entitlements are enacted, however, their differential treatment of different "types" of citizens renders the state liable to defend – or extend – its overtly discriminatory, programmatic categories of deservingness. Missouri Senator David Barton actually tried to justify the passage of the 1830 Preemption Act on the basis of problems created by previous preemption laws. Since "Congress had on various occasions deemed it necessary to depart from

Representative Clement Clay and Graham to President Andrew Jackson, cited in Malcolm J. Rohrbough, *The Land Office Business: The Settlement and Administration of American Public Lands, 1789–1837* (New York: Oxford University Press, 1968), p. 205. Introduced within days of Hayne's speech on the difficulty of the land question (see Chapter 4), the preemption bill was approved quickly in the Senate by a vote of 29 to 12 and moved almost as quietly through the House, passing by a vote of 100 to 58. Yet, as late as 1826, the House Committee on Public Lands still argued that legal prohibitions against settlement on the public lands before they were marketed and sold should be strictly maintained, declaring preemption a "subversive" idea. Feller attributes the 1830 preemption bill's passage largely to a half-sectional, half-partisan alliance of southern and western Congressmen. "Settlers on Public Lands and the Right of Pre-emption," communicated to the House of Representatives, January 18, 1826, *ASP, Class VIII, Public Lands*, vol. IV, pp. 332–3; Feller, *Public Lands in Jacksonian Politics*, pp. 129–31.

7 *RD* (21/1), Jan. 4, 1830, pp. 8–9.

the provisions of the [Intrusion] act of 1807, and grant pre-emption rights to actual settlers on the public lands," Barton argued, "great inequality" had been created that Congress was obligated to "destroy."[8]

Whether or not Barton and the other members of the Twenty-first Congress who voted for the 1830 Preemption Act admitted that it would create precisely the same kind of inequality that earlier selective preemption measures had, such an outcome was inevitable, for it was not truly a general or universal preemption statute.[9] The act merely forgave previous violations of Federal antitrespass law and granted retrospective benefits to a particular category of citizens. Though it was certainly more universal than earlier preemption laws, it neither repealed the provisions of the Intrusion Act, authorized further illegal settlement of the public lands, nor granted future squatters preemption rights. That end seemed to be in sight, however. As one jubilant Florida newspaper reported, there was "no doubt that Congress w[ould] be induced to extend its provisions."[10] How could it refuse? The new legislation had started the land system "down a road from which it was impossible to turn back." Though the preemption Act of 1830 had not completely shattered "the fragile fiction that pre-emption was a special favor granted to recognize particular services and sufferings," it had rendered Federal sanctions against squatting, already moribund, effectively "dead beyond hope of resurrection"[11]

---

[8] *RD* (21/1), Jan. 4, 1830, p. 9. Barton also argued that it was a "notorious fact, that it was [the squatters'] poverty, and not their disregard of the laws, or their want of patriotism, that drove them to encounter the privations of a pioneer life.... [N]o practical injury could be done by laws which tend to place the lands in the hands of those whose occupation it is to till them, and who are generally least able to buy them, rather than in the hands of those who already have not only lands, but the means of buying more, and speculating upon the more poor and more interesting part of mankind, who actually cultivate the earth." Barton apparently found Western settlement important enough to overlook the fact that the 1830 Act was both selective and supportive of illegal behavior. Bell, by contrast, thought it "would be better to repeal all laws on [the] subject [of preemption], and to permit a general scramble," than to pass the 1830 law. *RD* (21/1), Jan. 4, 1830: Barton, p. 9, Bell, p. 8.

[9] Cf. Paul Wallace Gates, *History of Public Land Law Development* (Washington, DC: CPO, 1968), p. 225; Rohrbough, *Land Office Business*, pp. 200–20.

[10] Tallahassee *Floridian and Advocate,* July 13, 1830, cited in Rohrbough, *Land Office Business,* p. 205.

[11] Feller, *Public Lands in Jacksonian Politics,* p. 129. Feller contends that the law of 1830, which he terms a "general" preemption act, destroyed the connection between the grant of preemption rights and "particular sufferings and services" – i.e., the connection between rights and the reasons for granting them. I disagree with this interpretation. Although the 1830 Preemption Act undoubtedly paved the way for increasingly general or universal policies, it still conferred preemption rights selectively, as did subsequent

and guaranteed that demands for a general preemption law would be forthcoming.[12]

Congressional disagreement slowed progress toward the enactment of such a law.[13] Advocates of preemption rights argued that they would prevent "unequal and ruinous" competition for land between speculators and yeoman pioneers at land sales. By contrast, opponents of preemption like Henry Clay, a speculator himself, denounced legislative concessions to squatters – citizens Clay termed "lawless rabble." Some congressmen viewed preemption laws as a form of illegitimate class legislation because of the selective benefits they bestowed. Still others squabbled over particular preemption proposals' categories of desert and reward, arguing that if public property was to be distributed, it should also go to widows and orphans, the aged and infirm, and poor citizens *unable* to travel west.[14] Reflecting the racism and nativism of the day, an overwhelming majority of the Senate became intent upon restricting preemption rights to whites

statutes employing the hardships of frontier life as both rhetorical justification and criteria of desert. See the later discussion.

[12] That the implementation of the 1830 Preemption Act was a complete fiasco for any number of reasons contributed. Conflicts arising between the General Land Office and Congress over matters of statutory interpretation, stringent bureaucratic requirements placed upon squatters wishing to exercise their preemption rights, delays in surveying due to a lack of appropriations, the death of George Graham and President Jackson's subsequent removal and replacement of his successor, the inability of squatters to pay for the lands they occupied, and the consequent abuses of speculators only exacerbated the pressure on Congress to enact a more "user-friendly" (not to mention New West–friendly) preemption policy. Rohrbough, *Land Office Business*, pp. 205–12; Gates, *Public Land Law Development*, pp. 226–8.

[13] A new Intrusion Act was passed in 1833 to prevent squatting in eastern Iowa. However, legislation passed in 1832 allowing preemptions in other areas on tracts as small as 40 or 80 acres. In 1834, Congress extended the provisions of the 1830 Preemption Act to benefit all squatters occupying and cultivating Federal lands by 1833. In the wake of the Panic of 1837, inundated by a stream of petitions demanding further preemption rights and pushed by President Van Buren, Congress enacted another temporary provision, establishing preemption rights on much of the public domain for a period of two years for every settler who was either the head of a family or twenty-one years old and who personally resided on Federal land at the time of its passage in 1838. That act was, in turn, extended in 1840 in a more liberal piece of legislation that granted setters residing on one parcel and cultivating another the right to buy either of them. Gates, *Public Land Law Development*, p. 228–39.

[14] See, e.g., "Application of Alabama for a Reduction of the Price of the Public Lands and Pre-emption Rights to Settlers," communicated to the Senate, Jan. 16, 1834, *ASP, Class VIII, Public Lands*, vol. VI, p. 657; remarks of Henry Clay, Jan. 27, 1838, *The Congressional Globe* [hereafter *CG*] (25/2), Appendix, p. 134, 135–6; remarks of Hugh White, Feb. 2, 1837, *CG* (24/2), p. 147–8; remarks of John Davis, Feb. 9, 1937, *CG* (24/2), Appendix, p. 309–12.

"so as to exclude persons of color." Many Senators thought they should be denied to aliens or "foreigners" as well.[15]

Finally, on September 4, 1841, the Twenty-seventh Congress and President John Tyler formally abandoned the view that all settlement on unoffered public land constituted criminal trespass. The "log cabin" law that they enacted still was not general or universal, for it sanctioned only *prospective* (not retrospective) acts of settlement on certain surveyed portions of the public lands by certain classes of individuals.[16] Nonetheless, it was far more extensive, and inclusive, than previous preemption laws had been. For all intents and purposes, Congress had officially transformed squatting on the public domain from a criminal, if common, practice to a statutorily guaranteed legal right.[17] In doing so, it had simultaneously transformed depraved, lawless squatters into legitimate, brave frontiersmen: the virtuous "actual settlers" of the Jeffersonian agrarian ideal.[18]

---

[15] *CG* (26/2), Appendix, pp. 18–27.

[16] "An Act to appropriate the proceeds of the sale of the public lands, and to grant preemption rights," September 4, 1841, *U.S. Statutes at Large*, vol. V, pp. 453–8. The final version of the act entitled U.S. citizens and those who declared their intent to become citizens to preemption rights without reference to race. As the act's title indicates, it was actually a hybrid distribution-preemption measure. In addition to granting preemption rights to certain individuals, it provided that each new state would receive 500,000 acres of land for the construction of internal improvements and 10 percent of the net proceeds from the sale of lands within its borders. The remainder of the revenues from lands sold were to be distributed to all of the states (including the new "public land" states) on the basis of their representation in Congress, provided that the tariff was not raised above the 20 percent level (in which case distribution would cease). The final vote on the bill was divided along almost strictly partisan lines, with Whigs almost unanimously in favor and Democrats opposed. A contemporary observer said that Congress previously had "never seen so much log-rolling and lobbying and caucusing and putting on the screws." Raynor G. Wellington, *The Political and Sectional Influence of the Public Lands, 1828–1842* (Cambridge, MA: Riverside Press, 1914), pp. 96–104, quoted passage p. 102; see also Roy M. Robbins, *Our Landed Heritage: The Public Domain, 1776–1936* (Princeton, NJ: Princeton University Press, 1942), pp. 72–89.

[17] Robbins, *Our Landed Heritage*, p. 89; Gates, *Public Land Law Development*, p. 238. It would take another decade for qualified preemption rights to be granted on unsurveyed Federal land, and then only in particular locations for specified periods of time. Nonetheless, statutes entitling people to preemption rights continued on an expansionary trajectory, paralleling – as well as fueling and justifying – the expansionist tendencies of the United States.

[18] As one advocate put it in the Senate, the "main object of the bill was not to protect those who were called trespassers and violators of the law, but to say to the hardy cultivator of the land ... that he should be safe in the possession of the fruits of his labor." Implicit in this statement is the labor theory of value: where the land in its natural state was essentially unproductive, the settler's labor gave it economic value. According to Mary Young, this theory was implicit in all arguments favoring lower prices to settlers. See

Causal Stories and Continental Ambitions

This discussion of the evolution of Federal preemption legislation is by no means intended to imply that the enactments of 1830–41 were solely the result of the expansionary logic of entitlement policies or, for that matter, that the passage of that legislation may be completely understood in isolation, extracted from the context of the extraordinarily complex politics of that time. Far from it: Federal land policy both greatly affected, and was greatly affected by, the intricate personal, sectional, and partisan conflicts that shaped the path of development of Jacksonian America. The land question was an issue that not only directly affected the welfare of communities and individuals, but also involved alternative visions of the national future.[19] By the end of the 1830s, disparate sectional views on the appropriate use of the public lands had been transformed into distinct partisan differences. Where Whigs saw the western domain as a kind of endowment that could aid the Government in directing the nation along the road to social and economic improvement, Democrats envisioned the public lands as a resource that could facilitate individual freedom and enterprise unfettered by governmental interference. Where Whigs advocated the measured, government-orchestrated development of a mixed economy, Democrats urged the accelerated growth of an agrarian republic through individual action. Despite these differences, however, both parties continued to invoke familiar oppositional agrarian archetypes to perpetuate the notion that conflicts over the disposition of the public lands were essentially conflicts over how policies could best be crafted to allow the nation's deserving actual settlers to triumph over money-grubbing speculators.[20] Whigs and Democrats alike pronounced

CG (26/2), Appendix, p. 19; and Young, "Congress Looks West: Liberal Ideology and Public Land Policy in the Nineteenth Century," in *The Frontier in American Development: Essays in Honor of Paul Wallace Gates*, ed. David M. Ellis (Ithaca, NY: Cornell University Press, 1969), pp. 74–112, 79.

[19] Feller, *Public Lands in Jacksonian Politics*, p. 191. Readers are referred to Feller's rich study for a more comprehensive account of the politics of the public land system during the early nineteenth century.

[20] Feller, *Public Lands in Jacksonian Politics*, pp. 189–97; Joel H. Silbey, *The Partisan Imperative: The Dynamics of American Politics Before the Civil War* (New York: Oxford University Press, 1985), pp. 59–61; Allan Kulikoff, *The Agrarian Origins of American Capitalism* (Charlottesville: University of Virginia Press, 1992), pp. 80–90; see also Silbey, *The American Political Nation, 1838–1893* (Stanford, CA: Stanford University Press, 1991), pp. 72–89. In his 1832 annual message to Congress, a newly reelected President Jackson announced his belief that national land policy should shift from revenue generation to graduation so that the public lands could be "sold to settlers in limited parcels at a price

themselves for the settler, who, like the citizen-soldier, "portrayed the American not as he was but as he wished to think of himself"[21] in both politics and public policy.

Allan Kulikoff has observed that, partisan differences aside, both Democrats and Whigs praised the farmer in a language of white male citizenship in a concerted effort to preserve the small-scale farm, headed by a white man, within a system of private property. To do so at a time when radicals had begun to seek some citizenship rights for women and agitate against slavery was essentially to take a stand against political rights for women and blacks. Silences about race and gender contributed to intraparty unity across free labor and slave regions that were growing further apart, while Native Americans merited notice only when they figured as a savage impediment to settlement by virtuous white male farmers.[22] In Rogers Smith's words, this was the "high noon of the white republic." Ascriptive doctrines blending liberal, republican, paternalist, racist, and nativist rationales provided Federal actors with powerful justifications for "broken treaties, military conquest, near-genocidal removals of Native Americans, and ever-deepening systems of involuntary servitude."[23]

The truth was that the sharp dichotomy posited between the settler and the speculator had always been largely false. Land speculation was a common investment activity among men of means regardless of their sectional or partisan orientation. Language elevating the morality of the actual settler in Jacksonian political rhetoric likely served, as some scholars have suggested, as a kind of purgative "by which men reaffirmed their fidelity to an ideal they were perhaps all too conscious of violating."[24] Always resonant, the image of the yeoman farmer in his bucolic Republic took on even greater meaning as Jacksonian America faced the

---

barely sufficient to reimburse to the United States the expense of the present system, and the cost arising under our Indian compact." *RD* (22/2), Dec. 4, 1832, Appendix, p. 5.

[21] Feller, *Public Lands in Jacksonian Politics*, p. 197.

[22] Kulikoff, *Agrarian Origins*, pp. 80–1.

[23] Rogers M. Smith, *Civic Ideals: Conflicting Visions of Citizenship in U.S. History* (New Haven, CT: Yale University Press 1997), p. 200.

[24] Feller, *Public Lands in Jacksonian Politics*, p. 197; Marvin Meyers, *The Jacksonian Persuasion: Politics and Belief* (Stanford, CA: Stanford University Press, 1960), pp. 121–41. See also Silbey, *The Partisan Imperative*, p. 60. Silbey observes that the elaboration of congruent ideological constructs in otherwise divergent partisan rhetoric constitutes an attempt to establish party legitimacy through an appeal to widely shared views in society.

incursions and dislocations of a "market revolution."[25] As more and more Americans experienced the force of market relations in their ordinary lives, even those who were successful – the "haves" who adroitly negotiated the extraordinary social and economic changes of the period – yearned nostalgically for a vanishing, seemingly less complex, more morally pure past.[26] Land largely functioned as a commodity, and as a means of acquisition and socioeconomic ascent, but it was commonly, and vividly, depicted as a source of personal solace and refuge, along with agriculture as the most honorable occupation.[27] Rhetorical appeals to a fictive agrarian ideal held a prodigious power to soothe.

The agrarian ideal also held enormous symbolic potential for state actors when they could invoke it in law, the authoritative discourse of the state. Though official articulations of the yeoman farmer myth undoubtedly reflect Jacksonian culture and politics at large, the persistence with which the "actual settler" literally made his way into the pages of the *United States Statutes at Large* reveals more than individual-level anxiety over societal change. The legal enshrinement of the virtuous settler in statutes creating land entitlements was a vital part of the Government's struggle to advance and justify its own "anxious aggrandizement" and the policies of aggressive expansionism that it utilized to expand its domain, for far more than manifest destiny, it was manifest *design* that brought about the acquisition of the territory that is now the United States.[28]

Just as the American state employed the idea of manifest destiny for the purpose of ennobling and legitimizing the chauvinism, aggressiveness,

---

[25] Charles Sellers, *The Market Revolution: Jacksonian America, 1815–1846* (New York: Oxford University Press, 1991). See also Michael Paul Rogin, *Fathers and Children: Andrew Jackson and the Subjugation of the American Indian* (New York: Alfred A. Knopf, 1975), pp. 251–2.

[26] Sellers, *Market Revolution*, pp. 119–22, 152–71, 237–40; Jean V. Matthews, *Toward a New Society: American Thought and Culture, 1800–1830* (Boston: Twayne Publishers, 1991), pp. 10–16, 109–10. Matthews notes that by the late 1820s, even the American farmer was criticized for destroying nature, using slash-and-burn techniques to produce a few bumper crops, make a quick profit, and then move on.

[27] Meyers, *Jacksonian Persuasion*, pp. 134–5, citing Harriet Martineau, *Society in America* (New York, 1837). See also Rogin, *Fathers and Children*, pp. 78–9. Alexis de Tocqueville's observation on the situation is also apt: "It seldom happens that an American farmer settles for good upon the land which he occupies; especially in the districts of the Far West, he brings land into tillage in order to sell it again, and not to farm it; he builds a farmhouse on the speculation that, as the state of the country will soon be changed by the increase of population, a good price may be obtained for it." *Democracy in America*, ed. Phillips Bradley (New York: Vintage Books, 1955), vol. 2, p. 166.

[28] Thomas R. Hietala, *Manifest Design: Anxious Aggrandizement in Late Jacksonian America* (Ithaca, NY: Cornell University Press, 1985).

and coercive tactics that were the essential components of its continental expansion, so, too, did it employ the myth of the pioneer or actual settler.[29] Of all of the symbols available to nineteenth-century American leaders, few held as much potential for sanctioning the growth of centralized state power or for rendering applications of that power morally pure. Like pension entitlements for patriot citizen-soldiers, actions taken in the name of the actual settler – whether purchases of extraordinary amounts of unmapped terrain, the removal and slaughter of aboriginal people, skirmishes and wars fought against new-found "enemy" nations, or the creation of land grants and preemption rights – helped to reconstruct a state engaged in acts of warfare as a benevolent, "welfare"-oriented state that was justified in its efforts to conquer space.[30] The pervasiveness of the settler myth in the public policy of the early to mid-nineteenth century demonstrates the extent to which the American state attempted to convince both citizens and itself that the United States would be able to enter "the great nation of Futurity" with "the truths of God in [its] mind, beneficent objects in [its] heart . . ., and with a clear conscience unsullied by the past."[31]

The policies enacted in the name of actual settlers during the 1830s and 1840s must also be understood as a compromise between the Whig and Jacksonian visions of national growth. Where the former advocated a national destiny of carefully paced, qualitative development through time, the latter envisioned more rapid, quantitative progress across unsettled space: what Jackson termed "extending the area of freedom."[32] The selective creation of land entitlements incrementally extended and

[29] Hietala, *Manifest Design*, pp. 272. According to Hietala, the "epic quality of the pioneers' adventures len[t] sanctity to American expansion and obscure[d] the actual dynamics of empire building." Hietala refers more to rhetorical reliance upon popular myth than to the formal embedding of that myth in Jacksonian public policy (pp. 256–8). On rhetoric as a behavioral component of congressional decisionmaking, see Ronald L. Hatzenbuehler and Robert L. Ivie, *Congress Declares War: Rhetoric, Leadership, and Partisanship in the Early Republic* (Kent, OH: Kent State University Press, 1983).

[30] On the construction of social problems, political leaders, and enemies, see Murray Edelman, *Constructing the Political Spectacle* (Chicago: University of Chicago Press, 1988). See also Samuel P. Huntington, *Political Order in Changing Societies* (New Haven, CT: Yale University Press, 1968), pp. 140–3, regarding the need of states to foster a "new social consciousness" in addition to new public policies for political modernization to occur.

[31] John L. O'Sullivan, *Democratic Review*, VI (November, 1839), p. 427, cited in Major. L. Wilson, *Space, Time, and Freedom: The Quest for Nationality and the Irrepressible Conflict 1815–1861* (Westport, CT Dreenwood Press, 1974), p. 108. O'Sullivan, an ardent Jacksonian Democrat, coined the phrase "manifest destiny."

[32] Wilson, *Space, Time, and Freedom*, pp. 12, 108.

consolidated American territorial claims and facilitated the population of the public domain while allowing Congress to equivocate on national land policy, neither abandoning its general sales policy nor adopting the universal homestead policy that increasingly was being agitated.

A stunning example of the Government's construction of the settler ideal in expansionist Jacksonian public policy is found in the Florida land law of 1842, less euphemistically known after its passage as the Armed Occupation Act. The act entitled a particular category of actual settlers – civilian men willing to inhabit and improve tracts south of Gainesville while bearing arms against "marauding" Indians – to grants of 160 acres of land on the condition that they persevered in their efforts for at least five consecutive years. Inspiration for the law stemmed from the United States' misfortunes in the Second Seminole War. Despite the Army's dedication in a contest that more "resemble[d] the pursuit of wild animals than a warfare with human beings," in which "the triumphs of success [we]re mingled with pity, not far removed from contempt, for an inglorious foe,"[33] the United States was forced to terminate its expensive and bloody campaign against Florida's black and Native American residents without achieving victory.[34] Secretary of War John Spencer thus turned to the idea of sending civilians to Florida, a proposal that had been floating in Congress since its introduction in 1839 by Thomas Hart Benton. Spencer argued that since it was no longer expedient to go to the trouble and expense of keeping a large military establishment there,

---

33 "Report of the Secretary of War," *CG* (27/2), Dec. 1, 1841, Appendix, pp. 11–16.

34 As Virginia Peters has detailed, the series of wars fought in Florida during the nineteenth century are commonly termed the Seminole Wars because Native Americans by that name made up the majority of the aboriginal people involved. However, dissident Creeks from Georgia and members of other decimated tribes living in the territory were also involved in those conflicts, as were numerous blacks who lived in Florida in harmony and kinship with the territory's Native Americans. Spanish records dating from 1688 document the presence of escaped English slaves in Florida, a group of whom petitioned the Spanish government for their freedom and were granted it in 1730. Others also had fled from slavery in the United States to live under the protection of the Spanish government and had children who were born to freedom. Still other black Floridians had been emancipated by the British for fighting in their forces against the Americans or had been acquired by the tribes through purchase or as trophies of war. According to Horsman, the "hostilities" in Florida were for some congressmen not just an effort to dispossess the Native Americans of areas desired by white settlers, but a "confrontation between the colored and white races of the earth." Virginia Bergman Peters, *The Florida Wars* (Hamden, CT: Archon Books, 1979), pp. 11–12, 189–90; Reginald Horsman, *Race and Manifest Destiny: The Origins of American Racial Anglo-Saxonism* (Cambridge, MA: Haward University Press, 1981), pp. 204–5.

the "occupation of the peninsula of Florida by a hardy and armed body of men" would be the "most effectual means of preventing any hostile incursions by the Indians."[35] Some senators agreed, reasoning that such an "agrarian policy" would encourage "poor and destitute, but vigorous, energetic, and hardy men, who were filled with enterprise" to go to Florida to "grapple with the Indian, and root him out" for the sake of the land they settled on, which they would love "the more because they had to fight for it."[36] Other members of Congress were appalled, and denounced the proposal as a "new-fangled mode of allowing the lands of the Government to plundered" and a "fraud on the public." Majorities of both chambers voted to approved it.[37] Thomas Blake, then commissioner of the General Land Office, applauded the Armed Occupation Act's beneficent reincarnation of the citizen-soldier. The new law "presented to the enterprising and industrious citizen a strong inducement to seek a home in a country represented to be of good climate and unsurpassed fertility, and affording abundant facilities for obtaining a competency and independence with comparatively little labor."[38]

---

[35] Letter from the secretary of war to David Levy, Representative of the Florida Territory, April 26, 1842, printed in *CG* (27/2), p. 503. Levy had the letter from Spencer inserted into the record to protest President Tyler's announcement of "the final termination of the Florida war," which "claim[ed] before the nation the *éclat* of an achievement which ha[d] not been performed." Levy did not object to the settlement proposal, but was horrified that the United States would leave Florida "to the possession of the enemy" after seven years of struggle, annual expenditures of millions of dollars, and "a sacrifice of life unparalleled in the history of wars." Senator Caleb Cushing of Massachusetts responded that while he could understand Levy's duty to represent the interests of his constituents, there had never been a *war* in Florida; the Government had merely engaged in "hostilities." The idea of a war was simply ludicrous: "[t]he United States, an enlightened nation of 17,000,000 inhabitants, declaring war against 80 Indians!" *CG* (27/2), p. 504.

[36] Remarks of Senators William Preston of South Carolina and Louis Linn of Missouri, August 1, 1842, *CG* (27/2), p. 818.

[37] Remarks of Representatives Francis Granger of New York and William Johnson of Maryland, July 18, 1842, *CG* (27/2), pp. 765, 764; House passage (by a vote of 82 to 50), July 18, 1842, p. 766; Senate passage (by a vote of 24 to 16), August 1, 1842, p. 818; "An Act to provide for the armed occupation and settlement of the unsettled part of the peninsula of East Florida," August 4, 1842, *U.S. Statutes at Large*, vol. V, pp. 502–4.

[38] "Annual Report of the Commissioner of the General Land Office," December 1, 1842, H.doc. 18 (27/3) 419, p. 4. A bill "to authorize the occupation and settlement of the Oregon Territory," which proposed to entitle white males over the age of eighteen who settled on and cultivated Oregon land for a minimum of five years to 640 acre tracts, was also introduced in the Twenty-seventh Congress but was dismissed as "indelicate" in the face of treaty negotiations with Great Britain. See the remarks of Senator Linn, August 31, 1842, *RD* (27/2), pp. 736–7. Linn continued to urge that the United States

The rancorous debate preceding the passage of the Armed Occupation Act in the House revealed the Government's reliance upon Jacksonian moral and gender stereotypes. Samuel Stokely of Ohio argued that there was nothing novel in the Florida bill's proposal to grant land to settlers, for the same had been done for the soldiers of the War of 1812 and for Revolutionary veterans before them. Outraged by Maryland Representative William Johnson's accusation that the purpose of the bill was to provide men with arms and ammunition "to turn sportsmen, and range at pleasure over a vast domain in pursuit of game" rather than kill Indians, Stokely noted that the bill neither proposed to establish a "bounty for a parcel of idle loafers" nor even to provide munitions or supplies. The clause authorizing the Government to furnish rations and arms had been stricken out. Replacing it was language granting an additional 160 acres of land to *wives* willing to travel to Florida – a provision that "would have the most salutary influence in effecting a permanent settlement; for the presence of their families would bind the settlers to the soil." After Stokely "narrated some instances of heroism displayed by females in the early settlement of the Western country, which had a most happy effect in stimulating the courage and enterprise of their male relatives," John Pope of Kentucky attributed Johnson's attack on the bill to his having "gone off half-cocked against the provision in favor of the women." The final version of the bill neither provided arms for Florida's new, presumptively male settlers nor added any benefits for the wives who might accompany them. It would not pass in the House until several amendments proposed by Johnson were voted down, including one that would have required the secretary of war to issue a formal proclamation, approved by the president, conceding that "armed settlers, men, women, and children ... [we]re more available troops than the gallant army of the United States."[39]

The Armed Occupation Act's deployment of civilians as a kind of paramilitary force represented the failure of previous Federal efforts to acquire Florida for white citizens. Despite several decades of military efforts, the Government had neither eradicated Florida's people of color nor removed them to the trans-Mississippi West. It made no difference

should assert its rights by encouraging settlement in Oregon in the next session of the Twenty-seventh Congress, but again the question of the treaty was raised.

39 *CG* (27/2), pp. 764–6. The Armed Occupation Act did provide for the transfer of land rights to the heirs of settlers who died either before five years had passed or before their patents (land titles) were issued.

to Federal policymakers that many of the people they sought to elimi-
nate were the descendants of the territory's original inhabitants, who had
been born to freedom long before the United States existed and whose
agrarian existence was essentially similar to the one they promoted for
the actual settler. Not surprisingly, the targets of the Armed Occupation
Act found the Government's behavior as bewildering as it was deceptive.
Captured Seminole Chief Coacoochee poignantly summed up the situation on July 4, 1841, a year before the Armed Occupation Act was passed:

> I was once a boy; then I saw the white man afar off. I hunted in these woods,
> first with a bow and arrow, then with a rifle. I saw the white man, and was told he
> was my enemy. I could not shoot him as I would a wolf or a bear; yet like these
> he came upon me; horses, cattle and fields he took from me. He said he was my
> friend; he abused our women and children, and told us to go from the land. Still
> he gave me his hand in friendship; we took it. Whitlst taking it, he had a snake
> in the other; his tongue was forked; he lied and stung us. I asked but for a small
> piece of these lands, enough to plant and to live upon, for a spot where I could
> place the ashes of my kindred, a spot only sufficient upon which I could lay my
> wife and child. This was not granted me. I was put in prison.[40]

John Sprague, then an Army lieutenant in Florida, noted the irony of
Coacoochee, "a man whose only offence was defending his home, his
fireside, the graves of his kindred, stipulating on the Fourth of July for
his freedom and his life." Ironic or not, the bands of Coacoochee and
Chief Hospetarke, a group of some 290 Native Americans and blacks,
boarded the brig *Saratoga* and embarked on the first leg of their journey
to Arkansas in November 1841, shortly before the Government's next
round of assaults on the territory's original residents would begin via the
Armed Occupation Act.[41]

General Land Office Commissioner Richard Young's 1847 proposal
to expand the terms of the Preemption Act of 1841, which had established preemption rights for squatters only upon the surveyed lands of
the United States, was also permeated by the ideology of the white male
actual settler. "In regard to the existing laws on the subject of the right

---

[40] Chief Coacoochee to Colonel Worth, July 4, 1841, cited in Peters, *The Florida Wars*, p. 212.

[41] Sprague, cited in Peters, *The Florida Wars*, p. 213; see also pp. 218, 252. The Armed Occupation Act did result in white relocation in Florida. By the 1840s, newcomers were
penetrating central Florida via the St. Johns River and other routes, with steamboat
traffic soon linking settlements. James M. Denham, *"A Rogue's Paradise: Crime and Punishment in Antebellum Florida, 1821–1861* (Tuscaloosa: University of Alabama Press, 1997),
pp. 48–9.

of preemption, in favor of prior settlers upon the public lands," Commissioner Young asserted,

I respectfully recommend that they be so amended and modified as to embrace the case of every *bona fide* settler who has gone, or may hereafter go, upon any portion of the public domain with a view to acquire a home for his family; and that the privilege be extended as well to the *unsurveyed* as the surveyed lands, in all cases where such settlements may be made after the Indian title shall have been extinguished.

A policy thus liberal towards a very large class of our fellow citizens cannot fail to produce the most beneficial results. It will facilitate the settlement and improvement of the frontier portions of the country, raise up a hardy race of backwoodsmen for its protection against the encroachments of our Mexican and Indian neighbors, afford them the means of improving their condition in many respects, and, above all, to educate their children, and will impress those patriotic frontier-men with deeper feelings of regard for their government, when they find that they are no longer in danger of losing their hard earned improvements by being brought into competition with a more wealthy class of citizens at the land sales.[42]

Young's proposal to make preemption rights effectively universal undoubtedly was influenced by problems in the implementation of the 1841 legislation, for it had not stopped the land frauds prevalent in the 1830s. Many people had figured out how to take advantage of the provisions of the existing preemption laws to hold land without making improvements on it in anticipation of selling it to latecomers, just as the larger capitalist speculators were doing.[43] Young's racist invocation of the virtues of America's "*bona fide* settlers," "hardy backwoodsmen," and "patriotic frontier-men" nonetheless speaks volumes about the attitudes of contemporary Federal actors toward the so-called encroachments of inferior Indians and Mexicans upon U.S. territory[44] – and thereby upon the designs of the American state. By the time Commissioner Young presented

---

[42] "Annual Report of the Commissioner of the General Land Office," December 13, 1847, S.exdoc. 2 (30/1) 504, p. 29 (emphasis in the original).

[43] Gates, *Public Land Law Development*, p. 240; see also "Frauds Committed Under the Preemption Laws," communicated to the Senate, March 10, 1836, *ASP, Class VIII, Public Lands*, vol. VIII, pp. 535–40. Contemporary public demand for a universal homestead policy of free land grants likely also figured in Young's proposal. See below.

[44] Concerning race, expansion, and the Mexican War, see Horsman, *Race and Manifest Destiny*, pp. 208–48; Smith, *Civic Ideals*, pp. 205–6; David J. Weber, "'Scarce More Than Apes:' Historical Roots of Anglo American Stereotypes of Mexicans in the Border Region," in *Race and U.S. Foreign Policy in the Ages of Territorial and Market Expansion, 1840 to 1900*, ed. Michael L. Krenn (New York: Garland Publishing, Inc., 1998), pp. 89–101.

his annual report in late 1847, the expansionist gropings of a growing nation had resulted in the annexation of Texas, the colonization and acquisition of Oregon, and a declaration of war on Mexico that shortly would result in the addition of an area of more than 500,000 square miles to the United States, if not the entire Mexican republic.[45] That there would be striking disparities between the expansionists' glorious expectations and their actual achievements would later become manifest.[46] For the moment, though, America's destiny – and the destiny of entitlement as a Federal policy practice – had yet to be realized.

Movement Toward Universalism, 1847–1862

With the Ten Regiments Act of 1847, Congress returned to a familiar mode of raising enlistments – programmatic entitlement – to ensure that the nation possessed an Army capable of winning the Mexican War.[47] Enacted nine months after combat began, with President Polk determined to bring the war to a rapid conclusion and Congress still bitterly divided over his request for $2 million to settle U.S. "difficulties" with Mexico,[48]

---

[45] James K. Polk ran for president in 1844 on a Democratic platform that called for the "re-occupation" of Oregon and the "re-annexation" of Texas, as if both areas already belonged to the United States – an optimistic assessment at best. Charles Sellers has observed that the overt manifest destiny theme contained in Polk's inaugural address "barely hinted at the audacious course of policy" that was to be the result of Polk's territorial enterprise. Even as the treaty was being negotiated that would convey what is now California, Nevada, Utah, most of New Mexico and Arizona, and part of Wyoming and Colorado to the United States, Polk believed the entire Mexican republic to be within reach. Sellers, *James K. Polk, Continentalist, 1843–1846* (Princeton, NJ: Princeton University Press, 1966), pp. 213ff; Kirk H. Porter and Donald Bruce Johnson, *National Party Platforms 1840–1964* (Urbana: University of Illinois Press, 1966), p. 4; David M. Potter, *The Impending Crisis: 1848–1861* (New York: Harper Torchbooks, 1976), pp. 1–6.

[46] Hietala, *Manifest Design*, pp. x, 255–72.

[47] Having provoked the war with Mexico in the face of vociferous opposition from northern Whigs shortly after Congress had declared its aversion to conscription, Polk was forced to rely heavily upon volunteers to fight the war. The wartime force included a temporarily enlarged regular army of about 42,000, some 12,000 militiamen from the gulf states, and 61,000 U.S. volunteers, most of them from the South and West. John Whiteclay Chambers II, *To Raise an Army: The Draft Comes to Modern America* (New York: Free Press, 1987), p. 36.

[48] Polk's formal admission that the United States should pay for cessions of Mexican land in his "Two Million Dollar Bill" had not only acknowledged that the war in the Southwest was one of territorial aggrandizement, but also afforded an opportunity for divisions in the Democratic Party over national policy to come to the fore. David Wilmot, a Democrat from Pennsylvania, caused the first session of the Twenty-ninth Congress to end in stalemate by critiquing the president for not acting more openly, then proposing his famous

the act offered 160 acres of land to all noncommissioned officers, musicians, and soldiers who would march "to the seat of war" and serve for at least a year or until the end of the conflict, whichever came first.[49] As was the case with the War of 1812 veteran's land bounties, the Army's officers were excluded from benefits, and land warrants could not legally be transferred or sold. For the first time, however, the tracts promised under the Ten Regiments Act could be located anywhere on the public domain rather than only in military districts.[50] The act thus abandoned the Government's hope that military land bounties would establish a "screen" of veterans on the edges of an expanding frontier. It also gave veterans entitled to acreage a new option reminiscent of commutation in 1783: that of forgoing land benefits in order to receive $100 in U.S. Treasury scrip bearing 6 percent interest. Although demobilized veterans chose land warrants over Treasury scrip by a ratio of 30 to 1,[51] the act's

amendment to the bill: "that, as an express and fundamental condition to the acquisition of any territory from the Republic of Mexico ... neither slavery nor involuntary servitude shall ever exist in any part of said territory, except for crime, whereof the party shall first be duly convicted." Far more than the "distraction" Polk deemed it, Wilmot's Proviso raised the curtain on the sectional conflict that would end in the Civil War. See *CG* (29/1), pp. 1217; Potter, *The Impending Crisis*, pp. 18–29; Stephen Skowronek, *The Politics Presidents Make: Leadership from John Adams to George Bush* (Cambridge, MA: Belknap Press of Harvard University Press, 1993), pp. 168–74.

[49] "An Act to raise for a limited Time an additional military Force, and for other Purposes," February 11, 1847, *U.S. Statutes at Large*, vol. IX, pp. 123–6. The act entitled those serving for less than twelve months to 40 acres of land.

[50] Some of the debate over the Ten Regiments Act focused on the fact that the land bounty provision had been appended to the bill for the increase of the Army. Senator Benton believed this move had been designed to thwart his long-awaited graduation proposal, since land giveaways coupled with war expenses would hamper any efforts to reduce land prices. A new justification presented for excluding regular Army officers from the benefits of the act was that nonassignable warrants rendered career officers unable either to sell bounty lands or live on them, whereas noncommissioned officers could settle where they pleased and "make the grant administer to the necessities of [themselves] and [their] famil[ies]." Benton said that the only reason for distinguishing between volunteer and regular officers was that the former could vote. See the remarks of Senators Benton and Badger of North Carolina, Jan. 19, 1847, *CG* (29/2), pp. 205–6. Congress would briefly revive its previous practice of banning the sales of military land bounty warrants in the act of 1850, then explicitly reject it again in the so-called Assignment Bill of 1852. See James Oberly, *Sixty Million Acres: American Veterans and the Public Lands before the Civil War* (Kent, OM: Kent State University Press, 1990), pp. 18–21.

[51] Oberly, *Sixty Million Acres*, pp. 11–12. As Oberly notes, the warrants were worth $200 at face value, given the current Government minimum price of $1.25 per acre. Despite the fact that the warrants were technically unassignable, they were quickly dumped on the market to be bought and resold by speculators. More than 88,000 warrants for more

offer of money in lieu of land formally reversed the Government's long-standing position that land benefits were inherently different from cash. Absent the pretense that land grants would convert military veterans into frontiersmen, the moral virtue ascribed to the citizen- soldier in law was decoupled from that of the "actual" settler.

Although Army officers were omitted from benefits under the Ten Regiments Act, its land bounty provisions nonetheless revitalized the claims of the dissatisfied officers of the War of 1812, who began to lobby Congress in earnest for benefits. They believed that the state had treated them inequitably in refusing to entitle them to land bounties like the War of 1812's soldiers, and they demanded that the situation be remedied.[52] Given the well-known trajectory taken by Revolutionary veterans' pensions, the notion of retrospective rewards for military services performed decades earlier was not novel.[53] Neither was the idea of enacting benefits in honor of the nation's citizen-soldiers, whose successes in Mexico had shown once again that a republic could "prosecute successfully a just and necessary foreign war with all the vigor usually attributed to more arbitrary forms of government."[54] Nor would it prove impossible

than 13,000,000 acres of Federal land were issued under the Act of 1847. Gates, *Public Land Law Development*, pp. 270–3.

[52] Note that all veterans of the War of 1812, officers and soldiers, were aggravated that they had not received pensions like the veterans of the Revolution and were actively pressing Congress to enact them. They would not be granted until 1871 (see the later discussion).

[53] Retrospective awards were so far from novel, in fact, that they then could be – and would long continue to be – considered a norm, largely because early entitlements tended to be so selective that they generated subsequent demands for inclusion. Cf. Oberly, *Sixty Million Acres*, p. 14. Oberly's assertion that granting land "not simply as a recruiting device to attract young men to military service but rather to reward old men" for services performed decades earlier was a "new idea" is correct only insofar as it pertains to land benefits per se. Little more than a decade earlier, Congress had enacted general pension legislation for the widows of Revolutionary officers and soldiers in the Pension Act of July 4, 1836, effectively placing the capstone on the supplementary Pension Act of 1832, which had expanded the Revolutionary pension system to the extent of generating some 24,000 new claims. By late 1834, more than fifty years after the end of the Revolution, there were approximately 40,000 Revolutionary pensioners receiving cash benefits. Hence the statutory reorganization of the Pension Office recommended by Secretary of War Cass in 1833, as well as its move to the newly created Department of the Interior in 1849. Congressional action in 1843 had added responsibility for the implementation of military land bounty laws to the duties of the commissioner of pensions. See Chapter 4 and William N. Glasson, *Federal Military Pensions in the United States*, ed. David Kinley (New York: Oxford University Press, 1918), pp. 80–91.

[54] President Polk informed Congress in his annual message of 1848 that victory in Mexico had proven that citizen-soldiers could be as effective as the veteran troops associated with a standing army. December 5, 1848, cited in Hietala, *Manifest Design*, p. 207. As Hietala

for Congress to establish retrospective land entitlements for the officers, notwithstanding the fuss over earlier proposals, once the War of 1812's *militiamen* and their survivors – a group including hundreds of thousands of voters – joined the chorus of demand for bounty lands after decades of silence. Those veterans of the second war for independence were part of "the only class of officers and soldiers who ha[d] not in one way or another secured some mark of remembrance from the Nation." Congress would have to grant them land benefits "to wipe away the reproach incident to th[at] discrimination."[55] After the Fugitive Slave Act was passed, the slave trade abolished in the District of Columbia, the New Mexico and Utah territories organized, California admitted to the union, and land grants established for settlers in Oregon,[56] Congress finally acted to satisfy the 1812 veterans' complaints. Statutes enacted in 1850, 1852, and 1855 progressively proffered more and more land to the nation's veterans until all men who had served for a minimum of fourteen days in any American war since 1775 became legally entitled to 160 acres of the public domain.[57] Including the Ten Regiments Act of 1847, the enactments of the Mexican War era gave away six times as much land as previous legislation for the veterans of the Revolution and the War of 1812 combined, or over 61 million acres.[58]

It would be easy to conclude that just as victory over Mexico was "a fitting climax to the quest for empire that had begun with the Revolution

recounts, there was a notable discrepancy between Polk's positive postwar assessment of America's military men and his observations during the war.

55 "Soldiers of the Late War," petition referred to the Senate Committee on Military Affairs, Thirty-first Congress, cited in Oberly, *Sixty Million Acres*, p. 16; see also pp. 14–17 for a discussion of veteran lobbying in 1848–50.

56 For an account of the complex politics of slavery and territorial expansion that led to the Compromise of 1850, see Potter, *The Impending Crisis*, pp. 64–120. The Oregon Donation Act is discussed later.

57 The act of September 28, 1850, entitled all officers and soldiers who had served for nine months in any U.S. war since 1790, including the Indian wars, and who had not previously received land, to unassignable warrants worth 160 acres; those who had served for four months received 80 acres and, for a month, 40 acres. The act of March 22, 1852, rendered all military bounty warrants that had been or would be issued assignable; authorized persons entitled to preemption rights to use bounty warrants in lieu of cash; and extended benefits to militiamen called into service after 1812. Finally, the act of March 3, 1855, provided bounties for all who served for a minimum of 14 days (or less for those who had engaged in battle) since 1790, as well as Native Americans, chaplains, and short-term veterans of specific battles, and for the officers and soldiers of the Revolution or their widows and minor children. *U.S. Statutes at Large*, vol. IX, pp. 520–1; vol. X, pp. 3–4, 701–2.

58 Oberly, *Sixty Million Acres*, p. 21.

and independence,"[59] so too were entitlements distributing large portions of that empire to the citizenry. The Mexican War had been a stunning military success (at least in the eyes of expansionists), and President Franklin Pierce had been elected on a platform proclaiming that war "just and necessary."[60] The inclusive land bounty laws enacted in the wake of that war surely represented an acknowledgment that certain veterans had been "unfairly treated in a material and political way" compared with others who fought to establish the nation.[61] However, military men were by no means the only citizens agitating for land. Even as congressional majorities enacted bounty laws between 1850 and 1855 in an effort to equalize the nation's treatment of its veterans, they also deliberately, and very selectively, ignored many other citizens' claims of need and right. If the public land policy of the 1840s and 1850s was moving away from revenue generation toward the goal of providing for the public welfare,[62] it still remained to be seen just whose welfare actually would be recognized.

---

[59] Hietala, *Manifest Design*, p. 213. Hietala observes that by the close of the Mexican War, "the United States possessed a continental empire as well as an elaborate ideology to sanction it." The distribution of Federal land entitlements reinforced that ideology both instrumentally and symbolically. Increases in its pace and scope during the 1840s had as much to do with justifying the American state's aggressive territorial expansionism as with satisfying citizen demands for land.

[60] Porter and Johnson, *National Party Platforms*, p. 17.

[61] Oberly, *Sixty Million Acres*, p. 29.

[62] Scholars have long disagreed over precisely which enactments signaled that this shift had taken place. To Arlene Zahler and Roy Robbins, the Preemption Act of 1841 signified that Congress finally regarded the settlement of the public domain as more desirable than the revenue that might be generated from it. Oberly, by contrast, locates a shift toward utilizing the public lands for public welfare in the bounty land legislation of the Mexican War era, because it entitled many citizens to outright grants rather than purchase rights. According to Michael Lanza, the Homestead Act of 1862 completed the transformation in thinking about the public lands from a source of revenue to a catalyst for settlement. Gates, however, denied that the Homestead Act was the capstone of an increasingly liberal land policy, arguing that "its adoption merely superimposed upon the old land system a principle out of harmony with it; . . . until 1890 the old and the new constantly clashed. Zahler, *Eastern Workingmen and National Land Policy*, pp. 120–1; Robbins, *Our Landed Heritage*, p. 91; Oberly, *Sixty Million Acres*, p. 24; Michael L. Lanza, *Agrarianism and Reconstruction Politics: The Southern Homestead Act* (Baton Rouge: Louisiana State University Press, 1990), p. 10; Paul Wallace Gates, "The Homestead Law in an Incongruous Land System," in *The Public Lands: Studies in the History of the Public Domain*, ed. Vernon Carstensen (Madison: University of Wisconsin Press, 1963), p. 317. It must be noted that beyond fostering the well-being of individual settlers during this period, Federal land policies also favored timber dealers, cattle graziers, mining interests, and speculators and heavily subsidized the corporate development of western transportational facilities,

The saga of Dorothea Dix's failure to secure Federal land grants as a source of support for the indigent insane is undoubtedly this period's best-known (and most often recounted) story concerning the public lands and Federal social provision. Dix repeatedly memorialized Congress between 1848 and 1854 in the hope of convincing the nation's legislators to provide land that could be sold for the relief and institutionalization of poor, insane citizens. She eventually succeeded in getting both the House and the Senate to approve a bill for that purpose, only to have it vetoed by President Pierce. In his veto message, Pierce argued that it was unconstitutional for the Federal Government to become "the great almoner of public charity throughout the United States." Pierce also professed concern about the impact of Dix's proposal as a policy precedent: "Whatever considerations dictate sympathy for this particular object apply in like manner, if not in the same degree, to idiocy, to physical disease, to extreme destitution. If Congress may and ought to provide for any one of these objects, it may and ought to provide for them all."[63] Despite the well-known precedents already set by Federal pension and land benefits, Pierce's veto was upheld.

Contemporary efforts by advocates of a national homestead policy would come to be far more significant than Dix's efforts on behalf of the mentally ill. As it originally was envisioned, homestead was to be an essentially universal entitlement, whereby the public domain, held in trust by the Government, would be delivered to its rightful owners: all of "the People."[64] Ever since Thomas Hart Benton's graduation/donation proposal and organized labor's early efforts in the 1820s, the demand for land reform, or free land grants for settlers, had become more insistent.

especially railroads. See Robbins, *Our Landed Heritage*, pp. 159–68; Gates, "The Homestead Law"; and Mark W. Summers, *The Plundering Generation: Corruption and the Crisis of the Union, 1849–1861* (New York: Oxford University Press, 1987), pp. 98–115, 151–3.

[63] James D. Richardson, *A Compilation of the Messages and Papers of the Presidents 1789–1897* (Washington, DC: Bureau of National Literature and Art, 1901), vol. V, p. 249; *CG* 33/1, p. 507; see also Seaton W. Manning, "The Tragedy of the Ten-Million-Acre Bill," *Social Services Review* 36 (1962): 44–50; Thomas J. Brown, *Dorothea Dix: New England Reformer* (Cambridge, MA: Harvard University Press, 1998), pp. 148–214. Pierce's arguments against the bill also were articulated in the Senate.

[64] Thomas Devyr, George Evans, et al., "To The People of the United States," *Working Man's Advocate*, July 6, 1844, reprinted in Commons, *Documentary History of American Industrial Society*, vol. VII, pp. 293–305. Advocacy of a universal homestead entitlement did not necessarily imply a societal consensus over who, precisely, "the people" were. This became particularly obvious as homestead bills began to be debated seriously in Congress. See the later discussion.

Pressure mounted when the implementation of the 1841 Preemption Act neither satisfied the West nor aided individual settlers to the degree that many had anticipated it would. As graduation bills favoring the actual settler resurfaced in Congress, George Henry Evans and his newly organized National Reform Association published a manifesto insisting that the only solution for the sufferings of eastern workingmen was a national land policy that provided an alternative to wage labor.[65] National Reform was ridiculed at first, but after organized labor gathered in New York City under the banner "Let's All be Unhappy Together" to adopt the principles of land reform at its Industrial Congress of Workingmen in October 1845, the conservative press began to take the movement seriously enough to call it a menace.[66] President Polk advised Congress in December 1845 that the price of inferior Federal lands should be graduated and reduced so that "worthy citizens" unable to pay higher rates might buy them,[67] but the continuation of a program of land *sales* (albeit at reduced prices) was considered no remedy for the low wages, long work hours, job insecurity, and urban social conditions decried by National Reform. Only a national-level, egalitarian, universal entitlement to free land would suffice. January 1846 found newspapers across the country advocating land reform, while handbills urging "Vote Yourself a Farm" were plastered on the walls of New York City and reprinted and distributed far and wide.[68] Horace Greeley, the prominent Whig and New York *Tribune*

---

[65] Zahler, *Eastern Workingmen and National Land Policy*, p. 41. See also Devyr et al., "To The People of the United States"; Lewis Masquerier, *Sociology: or, the Reconstruction of Society, Government, and Property* (New York: published by the author, 1877); and Sean Wilentz, *Chants Democratic: New York City & the Rise of the American Working Class, 1788–1850* (New York: Oxford University Press, 1984), pp. 335–43, 369–70, 383–4. Zahler's 1941 volume remains the preeminent scholarly account of the land reform movement.

[66] Zahler, *Eastern Workingmen and National Land Policy*, pp. 42–3. Earlier in 1845, the editor of the *Working Man's Advocate* had congratulated fellow reformers on the "improved tone of the aristocratic press," reminding them that in 1829 they had been called the "spawn and vomit of garrets and cellars" and "a party emerging from the slime of th[e] community." Cited in Commons, *Documentary History of American Industrial Society*, vol. VIII, p. 39.

[67] Annual Message to Congress, *CG* (29/1), Appendix, p. 7. Expansionism had been a more prominent issue in the 1844 presidential campaign than public land policy. The Democratic platform was somewhat cryptic on the subject, opposing "laws lately adopted" and any law favoring distribution while advocating that "the proceeds of the Public Lands ought to be sacredly applied to the national objects specified in the Constitution." Porter and Johnson, *National Party Platforms*, p. 4.

[68] The circular or handbill drew upon sources ranging from Poor Richard to the Bible to the principles of the American Revolution to denounce political parties and capitalists

editor who had coined the phrase "Go West, young man" in the wake of the Panic of 1837, determinedly took up the cause on the eve of the Mexican War,[69] and petitions for free land and homestead bills began to inundate Congress.[70]

This impulse toward universal land grants clearly drew as much strength from the bottom up as from the top down. It attested to the

and extend the natural rights–based arguments of early reformers in favor of making the public lands free to actual settlers alone. "Are you an American citizen? Then you are a joint-owner of the public lands. Why not take enough of your property to provide yourself a home? Why not vote yourself a farm?" . . . Are you endowed with reason? Then you must know that your right to life hereby includes the right to a place to live in – the right to a home. Assert this right, so long denied mankind by feudal robbers and their attorneys. Vote yourself a farm. . . ." Reprinted in Commons, *Documentary History of American Industrial Society*, vol. VII, pp. 305–7; see also Zahler, *Eastern Workingmen and National Land Policy*, pp. 20–31, 43, 46. Zahler observed that the land reformers thus effectively transformed what had been a derogatory label earlier attached to them (the "vote yourself a farm party") into a powerful slogan.

[69] Greeley, who had been studying land reform for some time, articulated his position in the newspaper on January 23, 1846: "Every day's reflection inclines us more and more to the opinion that the plan of holding and settling the Public Lands of our Union proposed by the little band who have taken the name of 'National Reformers' is the best than can be devised. . . . [It] would rapidly cover the yet unappropriated Public domain with an independent, substantial yeomanry, enjoying a degree of Equality in Opportunities and advantages such as the world has not seen." *New York Weekly Tribune*, cited in Roy Marvin Robbins, "Horace Greeley: Land Reform and Unemployment, 1837–1862," *Agricultural History* 7 (1933): 25. See also Greeley's *Hints Toward Reforms, in Lectures, Addresses, and other Writings* (New York: Fowlers and Wells, Publishers, 1854, 2nd ed.), pp. 311–17. Greeley introduced a homestead bill after he was elected to the House in 1848, but it was quickly tabled. He spent the rest of his brief time as a member advocating congressional reform, publishing exposés of a congressional mileage reimbursement scam and drunken members voting extra compensation to House employees who plied them with liquor. Greeley then returned to the *Tribune* and land reform after Zachary Taylor's 1849 inauguration and "hideously vulgar" ball. Glyndon G. Van Deusen, *Horace Greeley: Nineteenth-Century Crusader* (Philadelphia: University of Pennsylvania Press, 1953), pp. 126–30.

[70] See, e.g., *CG* (29/1), Jan. 9 and Mar. 9, 1846, pp. 172, 473; see also George M. Stephenson, *The Political History of the Public Lands, from 1840 to 1862: From Pre-emption to Home-stead* (New York Russell & Russell, 1917), pp. 116–17; Zahler, *Eastern Workingmen and National Land Policy*, pp. 132–4; Robbins, *Our Landed Heritage*, p. 105. As Stephenson indicates, the question of which member of Congress had the "extraordinary distinction" of being the "father of the homestead bill" has long been debated. Robert Smith, a representative from Illinois, actually introduced a resolution in 1844 asking the Committee on Public Lands to inquire into the expediency of legislation donating eighty acres of land to every actual settler, and an amendment to a graduation bill embodying the homestead principle was proposed in 1845.

It is interesting to note that Andrew Johnson's July 1846 homestead proposal attempted to condition the receipt of land benefits upon the outcome of both means and morals tests. Had his bill passed, applicants would have been required to furnish reliable evidence concerning their poverty, character, and marital status. *CG* (29/1), p. 1077.

existence of a genuine opening for the development of a broader welfare rights philosophy in the United States in the mid-1850s. The moral vocabulary that had emerged from the artisan and workingmen's movements of the Jacksonian era fused natural law and civic republicanism in an urgent call for a new conception of property that would realize the equal rights of all citizens.[71] The creation of universal Federal land entitlements in response to this call made sense both theoretically and politically. Manifest destiny and the settler ideal were well ingrained in American political culture and public policy, and land acquisition and development were as central to national efforts at continental expansion as they were to subsistence-based arguments for social minima. State actors could create land entitlements with relative ease compared to monetary entitlements, and there were strong positive relationships between expansionism, land ownership, population growth, and the fortunes of the new western states.

Congress's enactment of generous veterans' land entitlements in the early 1850s in the face of its continued rejection of homestead proposals outraged westerners and advocates of land reform. The Ten Regiments Act of 1847, passed prospectively by an overwhelming majority of Congress to raise Army enlistments, had been one thing, but the retrospective post hoc bounty measures of 1850–5 were quite another. It was widely appreciated that military land grants historically had not led to settlement but rather to speculation. Most veterans were either unable or unwilling to go west to secure lands with their own warrants, and sold them for cash to capitalists and land and money brokers, who used them to acquire large portions of the public domain. Westerners were convinced that military land bounties diminished the value of school lands, deprived the public land states of income from Federal land sales, and frustrated wholesale increases in the population that constituted their source of national political power. They complained bitterly, both in and out of Congress, about their states being "patched up," "papered," and "shingled over" by nonresidents holding veterans' land warrants. Rampant nativism probably explained the western-dominated Senate committee on Public Lands' vehement condemnation of the homestead proposal in 1850, but that committee's declaration that hardy men had no need of gratuitous gifts from the Government must have appeared incredibly

---

[71] Elizabeth Bussiere, *(Dis)Entitling the Poor: The Warren Court, Welfare Rights, and the American Political Tradition* (University Park: Pennsylvania State University Press, 1997), pp. 23–46; see also Wilentz, *Chants Democratic*.

unprincipled given Congress's enactment of retrospective military land bounties that same year.[72] Land reformers considered Congress's passage of the Assignment Act of 1852, which rendered the act of 1850's bounties salable, permitted veterans to locate their claims upon land valued at more than the minimum price and granted land to militiamen, an absolute slap in the face. Greeley, for one, derided the "illustrious" Senate for denying benefits to the landless and then voting "that the speculators in Bounty Warrants should go at it with a perfect looseness henceforward."[73]

---

[72] "Report to accompany bills S. Nos. 8, 38, and 85," S.rp. 167 (31/1) 565. Andrew Johnson was among those who noted the discrepancy between congressional attitudes toward the enactment of a homestead policy and military land bounties. Defending homestead against the objection that the public lands had been pledged for the payment of the public debt, he pointed out that Congress hadn't regarded that such a pledge tied its hands when it had disposed of large portions of the public lands to war veterans. "Speech on the Homestead Bill," July 25, 1850, in *The Papers of Andrew Johnson, Volume 1, 1822–1851*, ed. Leroy P. Graf and Ralph W. Haskins, (Knoxville: University of Tennessee Press, 1967), pp. 559–60.

Note also that Congress passed the categorical Oregon Donation Act in September 1850, which granted land to white Americans, half-breed Indians, and persons of other nationalities intending to become American citizens over eighteen years of age who had resided on and cultivated Oregon public lands for at least four years. Single persons were entitled to 320 acres and married persons to 640 acres. The act also promised half of these amounts to similar persons arriving in Oregon between December 1, 1850, and December 1, 1853. This benefit scheme was extended to settlers of the Washington Territory in 1853, and land grants of 160 acres were established for persons settling in New Mexico before 1858. As Gates noted, the Government used grants of public land in the 1840s and 1850s retrospectively to reward particular Americans and immigrants for settling certain areas, and prospectively to direct them to areas unlikely to draw population without a bounty attached or to attract them to danger spots such as Florida. Land entitlements were not established in California, which apparently needed no such stimulus to settlement, or in Utah, which due to criticism of the Mormon community was not included in the public land system until 1869. *Public Land Law Development*, pp. 388–90.

[73] Stephenson, *Political History of the Public Lands*, pp. 118–22; Robbins, *Our Landed Heritage*, pp. 112–16; Gates, *Public Land Law Development*, pp. 271–3, 278–9; Greeley, *New York Weekly Tribune*, January 24, 1852, cited in Robbins, *Our Landed Heritage*, p. 114. Other congressional actions disposing of the public lands such as the railroad right-of-way act passed in 1852, which granted all railroad corporations 100-foot rights of way through the public domain (as well as the rights to use timber and acquire additional land), also infuriated advocates of land reform. Greeley argued that the homestead principle was antithetical to railroad subsidies. See Robbins, *Our Landed Heritage*, p. 165. The House did pass a watered-down homestead bill for the first time in May 1852, perhaps because the debate over it was "the stalking horse for political disquisitions bearing on the Presidential question" of that year. Stephenson notes that numerous congressmen opposed to it were afraid to have their negative votes recorded. *Charleston Courier*, cited in Stephenson, *Political History of the Public Lands*, p. 145.

Regardless of its repeated failures in Congress, the idea of a universal homestead entitlement continued to gain momentum. It had gone from being a "wild and visionary" notion to one that was increasingly popular and legitimate,[74] despite the cries of conservatives who branded it "deluded" and "socialistic."[75] The Free Soil and Free Democratic parties had included land reform planks in their 1848 and 1852 platforms.[76] Petitions from individuals and groups of citizens asking for land continued to flood Congress, where homestead bills were repeatedly introduced. Many northern Whigs and progressive Democrats had already been won over to the homestead idea by 1850. Moreover, homestead was increasingly being advocated because of sectional concerns. Given its positive implications for western migration and settlement, the West was essentially unanimous in favor. As the unprecedented waves of immigrants entering the United States in the early part of the decade began to allay fears in the North Atlantic manufacturing states that free western land would drain off their supply of labor, interest in homestead legislation as a means of developing western markets also arose in the North and East.

In other quarters, however, opposition to the homestead idea was strengthening. As Robbins's analysis has revealed, southern hostility toward homestead proposals emerged as it became clear that western expansion could only mean the extension of a nonslaveholding, small-farm frontier and forms of development favoring the industrial East. Southerners also feared that land giveaways might attract immigrants who would increase the free-state population and reduce Federal land revenues enough to justify an increase in the tariff.[77] Eastern speculators

---

[74] Andrew Johnson's observation in 1850, *CG* (31/1), Appendix, p. 950.

[75] See Zahler, *Eastern Workingmen and National Land Policy*, pp. 150–3, for a sampling of epithets from contemporary newspapers. Interestingly, more than one southern newspaper coupled a sectional argument against land reform with the accusation that it would be unfair to the nation's military veterans. According to Zahler, the Athens, Georgia *Herald* called homestead a "wholesale robbery of the old states and the soldier." The Richmond, Virginia, *Enquirer* likewise found it "unfair to poor holders of bounty warrants and harmful to the South" (p. 152).

[76] See Porter and Johnson, *National Party Platforms*, pp. 13–14, 18–20. As Hibbard noted, the basis of each party's argument in favor of homestead was slightly different. Where the Free Soilers essentially embraced a labor theory of value to argue that undeveloped land should be free because it was worth no more than the price of developing it, the Free Democrats echoed the land reform principle that individuals had a natural right to the soil. *A History of the Public Land Policies* (New York: Macmillan Company, 1924), pp. 356–8.

[77] On average, despite the general sales policy, only 6 percent of Federal revenues were derived from land sales between 1851 and 1862. Gates, *Public Land Law Development*, p. 392.

joined the South in opposition out of apprehension that a universal program of western land grants might diminish their profits from the public domain.[78] The battle to enact a universal Federal entitlement to land in the early to mid-1850s thus increasingly pitted regions of the country against each other. That there were sectional interests involved did not, of course, mean that arguments for and against the homestead proposal were not attempted on the basis of principle. Representative Thomas Averett of Virginia, for example, contrasted the homestead bill with the precedent of the military land bounties to argue that, in contrast with veterans, the homestead bill's proposed beneficiaries would have performed no public service whatsoever. He moreover asserted that the U.S. Government acted as fiduciary guardian for a public domain that belonged to all of the people, and portrayed the House's 1852 homestead bill as inappropriate if not unconstitutional class legislation that would take property belonging to the entire nation and selectively give it to a favored segment of the community. "What right have we," Averett asked, "to classify our people?"[79]

Congressional debates over the homestead proposal in the 1850s were centrally concerned with the classification or categorization of Americans, for legislative arguments over who should be entitled to Federal land grants were essentially arguments about who should be counted as citizens. Free blacks posed the most obvious questions with respect to who constituted "the people" of the United States for public policy purposes, because representatives urging race-based exclusion from land benefits could not dismiss free blacks as legal property, as they could slaves. Nor, in some cases, could they easily deny them citizenship, at least at the state level, for although some states had reformed their constitutions to deny citizenship to people of color, reflecting the increasingly hostile racial climate of the early to mid-nineteenth century, free blacks were considered citizens and enfranchised in several northern states.[80] Land ownership, moreover, was as central in contemporary black American political

---

[78] Robbins, *Our Landed Heritage*, pp. 107–9, 171–3, 177. See also Potter, *The Impending Crisis*, pp. 391–2. According to Lanza, the South was not completely united against homestead legislation, for some believed that homesteading would appropriately dispose of marginal public land that failed to sell even after the Government lowered its minimum price. *Agrarianism and Reconstruction Politics*, p. 8.

[79] *CG* (32/1), April 1, 1852, pp. 1018–19. Averett went so far as to warn his colleagues that gratuitous homestead entitlements for those who had performed no public service would cause "every one of the 200,000 land warrant holders, for services in the Mexican War," to "repel the insult you thus offer them, at the polls."

[80] Regarding black citizenship in the 1850s, see Smith, *Civic Ideals*, pp. 253–8.

thought and action as it was in that of whites. Numerous free blacks of means had migrated, bought property, and formed communities of their own in the old Northwest and West.[81]

Thus it was that Pennsylvania Representative Hendrick Wright tried to justify amending the 1854 homestead bill to entitle whites only to land with arguments about the *relative* worthiness of potential homestead recipients. His reasoning echoed the logic earlier employed by the Senate to restrict the benefits of the Pension Act of 1818 to veterans of the Continental Army and Navy. Wright explained that he had no prejudice in regard to color, nor was he the enemy of the negro; he simply "love[d] the white man more." Pennsylvanian John Dawson, chair of the Agriculture Committee reporting out the bill, clearly agreed with the proposed racial restriction but declared Wright's amendment redundant, for it had never been "contemplated for a moment that the black population of th[e] country should be put on an equality with the white population" in the enjoyment of the bill's benefits.[82] Opponents of the amendment pointedly asked how a homestead program legitimately could exclude from its benefit scheme persons who were recognized as citizens by some of the sovereign states, some of whom were veterans who had fought to establish the nation.[83] To this Dawson replied that the "literal and legal meaning

---

[81] Edward Magdol, *A Right to the Land: Essays on Freedmen's Community* (Westport, CT: Greenwood Press, 1977); Stephen A. Vincent, *Southern Seed, Northern Soil: African-American Farm Communities in the Midwest, 1765–1900* (Bloomington: Indiana University Press, 1999); see also James Oliver Horton and Lois E. Horton, *In Hope of Liberty: Culture, Community, and Protest Among Northern Free Blacks, 1700–1865* (New York: Oxford University Press, 1997).

[82] *CG* (33/1), Feb. 28, 1854, pp. 503–4. Wright responded to Dawson's charge of redundancy by pointing to the diversity of opinion regarding black citizenship. He argued that the language of the bill should be utterly clear with respect to its intended beneficiaries so that Congress's intent would be unmistakable in the event of judicial interpretation of the statute.

[83] Representative Thomas Davis of Rhode Island argued: "We are now preparing a bill which is large, liberal, and just, and in its spirit contemplates the improvement of all classes of the community, and in God's name why should this class be excluded? Why should we indulge in the prejudices of the gentleman from Pennsylvania? ... In our state, and in other States, the colored man is just as much a citizen as the whitest man there.... I know that these men make good citizens. They are industrious, and they should be left to occupy the soil which their fathers have cultivated, and which they have cultivated; which, for the last one hundred years, they have done more to develop than any part of our countrymen; and to defend which they shed their blood during the Revolution. These things should not be forgotten, and that very territory is the joint result of that labor and that contest. These colored men ... have contributed as much as any people of this country to secure it; and it is the cruelest injustice to shut them out

of the word citizen" in the U.S. Constitution meant "nothing more and nothing less than a white man," anticipating Chief Justice Roger Taney's majority opinion in *Dred Scott* v. *Sanford.*[84] Though the racially exclusive homestead bill of 1854 ultimately failed to become law, the Supreme Court's 1857 decision in *Dred Scott* that blacks were not citizens within the meaning of the Constitution, and possessed no rights that white men were obligated to respect, ensured that they would not immediately be among those benefiting from the Homestead Act that was enacted in 1862.

Issues of gender, age, marital status, immigrant status, and other ascriptive characteristics also figured prominently in debates over the 1854 bill's qualifying criteria in intersecting ways. Members of Congress clarified early on that the language of the bill's first section, granting homesteads to "persons" who were heads of families and U.S. citizens, meant both male and female persons, but it was implicit in their discussion that female heads of families were widows. Amendments thus were proposed to ensure that single men and women would also benefit from the proposed law, with natural rights arguments made to bolster the deservingness of single women.[85] The age of proposed beneficiaries was also debated. Some argued for benefits to persons younger than twenty-one years of age on the grounds that women often married young and militia service was required of eighteen-year-old men, but concern was raised over granting land to minors who still might be under the legal control of their parents. The notion of granting homesteads to poor European immigrants and "lazy fellows and loafers" was also questioned. Observing that the public domain had been obtained by "violent solicitation" – "whipping

from it; a wrong beyond which you cannot go.... I trust that this committee, who are legislating for the people of the United States, will not adopt this invidious principle. I say, sir, that the colored man can go there under that bill, because he is a citizen of the States, and every citizen of a State has the rights of every citizen of all the States. I know that this principle is violated in one half of the States of the Union, but it is nevertheless true and sound." *CG* (33/1), Feb. 28, 1854, p. 504.

[84] *CG* (33/1), Feb. 28, 1854, p. 504; 60 U.S. 393 (1857).

[85] "If a female desires to possess a home, and is willing to conform to the requirements of the law," asserted Representative William Barry of Mississippi, a Yale-educated attorney, "there is no reason why she should be an alien to the justice or the charity of her country. If she is unfettered by marriage ties she has the same natural right to be provided a home from the public domain that the unmarried man of the same age has. And if she is a widow, though under the age of twenty-one, the reason is still stronger in her favor." *CG* (33/1), Feb. 28, 1854, p. 503. Barry's differentiating description of the homestead bill as "justice or charity," echoing the debate over the 1818 Revolutionary pensions, suggested that the exact nature of Federal entitlements as legal or political claims had yet to be resolved.

and flogging the Native Americans, and browbeating the Mexicans" –
Senator John Thompson of Kentucky asked his colleagues whether, in
distributing the spoils, one-half of the nation would "turn round and say
to the other half, you smell of the nigger, and you shall not have any
of the land; we will give it to the foreigners, and you shall not take a
particle?"[86]

The homestead proposal was facilitated by the Thirty-third Congress's
passage of the divisive Kansas-Nebraska Act in 1854. In the long run, it
would also be fundamentally reshaped by its consequences. In opening
new territory to settlement, the act simultaneously repealed the Missouri
Compromise and the Indian Intercourse Act of 1834, which had guaranteed the region to Native Americans,[87] exacerbating the sectional schism
that was already brewing over slavery.[88] In many respects, it constituted
a political point of no return. Greeley called the Kansas-Nebraska Act a
"death-blow" to northern "quietism and complacency," for it cried "Sleep
no more!" to "all who had fondly dreamed or blindly hoped that the Slavery question would somehow settle itself."[89] As land claimants subsidized
by pro- and antislavery organizations rushed to "bleeding Kansas," a new
coalition formed to oppose an extension of the South's "peculiar institution" in the West. Many southerners came to identify the homestead proposal as an essentially abolitionist measure, equating a universal policy of

---

[86] *CG* (33/1), p. 947.

[87] The United States had sent Commissioner of Indian Affairs George Maypenny to try
to convince the Indians to get in line with the "new order of things" the previous year,
but they refused to agree to absolute removal. Not surprisingly, the treaties Maypenny
negotiated failed to keep aggressive settlers and speculators off of newly reserved Native
American lands, just as earlier ones had. George Fitzhugh observed in his contemporary
defense of slavery that "[t]he Indian, like the savage races of Canaan, is doomed to extermination, and those who most sympathize with his fate would be the first to shoot him
if they lived on the frontier." Competition with the naturally superior Anglo-Saxon of
Fitzhugh's theory would also have exterminated blacks freed from the protections of slavery. Prucha, *American Indian Treaties: The History of a Political Anomaly* (Berkeley: University
of California Press, 1994), pp. 241–2; Paul Wallace Gates, *Fifty Million Acres: Conflicts over
Kansas Land Policy, 1854–1890* (Ithaca, NY: Cornell University Press, 1954), pp. 1–47;
Fitzhugh, *Sociology for the South, or, the Failure of Free Society*, 1854, cited in Horsman, *Race
and Manifest Destiny*, p. 273.

[88] As Potter noted, it was ironic that the slavery issue became divisive in an area where
most residents cared little about it. More than any else, the friction that arose in Kansas
in the early 1850s had to do with conflict over land claims. See *The Impending Crisis*,
pp. 199–207.

[89] *Recollections of a Busy Life* (New York: J. B. Ford and Company, 1868), p. 294; see also
Wilson, *Space, Time, and Freedom*, p. 180.

free land with free soil.[90] The polarization of both the homestead and slavery questions and prohomestead and proslavery forces quickly became so complete that one senator characterized Congress's policy options as "giv[ing] niggers to the niggerless, or land to the landless."[91] Although the final march toward the enactment of the Homestead Act had begun, the advent of the Civil War would mean that the long-awaited law would be passed by a Union Congress engaged in fighting a war between the states. Initially, that Congress would create a selective entitlement for white northern loyalists only, rather than a universal entitlement for all Americans.

Domination by the southern and eastern interests guaranteed that the homestead proposals of 1854–8 would all stall out,[92] but with speculators effectively shut down by the Panic of 1857 and congressional elections approaching, land reform advocate Galusha Grow of Pennsylvania put forward another homestead bill in early 1859.[93] Horace Greeley and the

[90] See, e.g., remarks of George Julian of Indiana, *CG* (31/2), Appendix, pp. 136; Eric Foner, *Free Soil, Free Labor, Free Men: The Ideology of the Republican Party Before the Civil War* (New York: Oxford University Press, 1970), pp. 28–9, 54–5; and Lanza, *Agrarianism and Reconstruction Politics*, pp. 6–8. Potter notes that southern opposition to homestead effectively backfired in that it placed the South in a position "not only of defending slavery but also of resisting progress. In effect, by blocking the dynamic economic forces which were at work in the North and West, the South impelled the proponents of those forces to join in a coalition, which might not otherwise have materialized, with the antislavery forces. The logical vehicle for such a coalition [would be] the Republican party." *The Impending Crisis*, p. 392.

[91] Benjamin Wade of Ohio, Feb. 25, 1859, *CG* (35/2), p. 1354. Wade was responding to Georgia Senator Robert Toombs's accusation, with regard to the Cuban annexation plan, that "land for the landless" most exercised "the patriotic bosoms of Free Soilers" in the Senate whenever a question arose that they were afraid to meet. "We are for land for the landless, not niggers for the niggerless" became a popular campaign slogan in Iowa in 1860. Eugene H. Berwanger, *The Frontier Against Slavery: Western Anti-Negro Prejudice and the Slavery Extension Controversy* (Urbana: University of Illinois Press, 1967), p. 131.

[92] A graduation bill succeeded instead of a homestead measure in 1854, immediately depreciating the price of public land in proportion to the length of time it had been on the market. With land that had remained unsold for more than thirty years reduced to a price of 12.5 cents per acre, one of the greatest land rushes in American history ensued. Congress also passed the Old Soldier's Bill in 1855, granting 160 acres to anyone previously unrewarded with military bounty lands who had served for more than fourteen days in any American war since 1775. Public land sales had generated 48 percent of the U.S. Government's annual income in 1836; by 1853, land receipts accounted for only 2 percent of Government revenues. Income from land sales rose in 1854–6 but fell back to 2 percent in 1861 and a mere three-tenths of 1 percent in 1862. Gates, *Public Land Law Development*, pp. 184–96, 278; see also Oberly, *Sixty Million Acres*, pp. 20–53.

[93] See Robert D. Ilisevich, *Galusha A. Grow: The People's Candidate* (Pittsburgh: University of Pittsburgh Press, 1988), pp. 175–97, 204, 210–12.

newly formed Republican Party hailed the measure as a "new Declaration of Independence" and the beginning of a new era, warning advocates of slavery, railroad grants, and military bounty land warrants that it was time to step aside and "give the settlers a chance," but they had spoken too soon: the bill was tabled in the Thirty-fifth Congress.[94] Its reintroduction in the House a year later, coupled with a homestead bill of Andrew Johnson's in the Senate, provoked yet another bitter, racialized debate in which southern Democrats accused homestead of being nothing more than a political engine instituted to abolish slavery and encourage foreign immigration.[95] A diluted compromise bill finally passed in both houses of the Thirty-sixth Congress in May 1860,[96] but it was vetoed by President James Buchanan, whose voluminous objections included the argument that honest poor men neither needed nor wanted charity.

Homestead advocates lost no time in lambasting the president for contradicting his inaugural promises. Buchanan had pledged to help the actual settler, and new states and territories, by "furnishing them a hardy and independent race of honest and industrious citizens, ... secur[ing] homes for our children and our children's children, as well as for those exiles from foreign shores who m[ight] seek in this country to improve their condition and to enjoy the blessings of civil and religious liberty." Despite Buchanan's assertion that emigrants who became citizens should be recognized and "entitled, under the Constitution and laws, to be placed on a perfect equality with native-born citizens," the nativism in his homestead bill veto message was clear.[97] He found it inadvisable to proclaim to foreigners that they could have a free farm, and fretted that if the homestead bill passed, the United States would find "numerous actual settlers from China and other Eastern nations enjoying its benefits

---

94 Robbins, *Our Landed Heritage*, pp. 177–8; *New York Tribune*, February 9, 1859, cited in Zahler, *Eastern Workingmen and National Land Policy*, p. 169; and Robbins, "Horace Greeley: Land Reform and Unemployment," pp. 38–9; *CG* (35/2), Feb. 17, 1859, pp. 1074–6.

95 See the remarks of James Mason of Virginia, *CG* (36/1), pp. 1634–5; and, generally, the debate recorded on pp. 1293ff., 1506–12, 1552–6.

96 As Lanza notes, the voting pattern of the twenty House members from the southern public land states on the 1860 homestead bill was interesting: three voted in favor, six voted against, and the other eleven representatives did not vote. By contrast, all of the House members from the southern slave states as well as the entire Southern membership of the Senate voted against the bill. *Agrarianism and Reconstruction Politics*, pp. 8–9.

97 James D. Richardson, *A Compilation of the Messages and Papers of the Presidents 1789–1897* (Washington, DC: Bureau of National Literature and Art, 1910), vol. V, pp. 434, 611–13.

on the great Pacific Slope." Buchanan also pronounced the homestead legislation discriminatory, arguing that it would benefit new settlers more than the ones who had first settled the frontier and foreigners more than American nationals. His complaint that conferring an exclusive "boon" on "cultivators of the soil" would discriminate against "respectable" artisans and laborers suggests that he recognized the problems that selective entitlements typically caused, but the argument was curiously out of step with the homestead movement's universalist impulse and the myth of the virtuous settler.

Although the Thirty-sixth Congress's attempt to override Buchanan's veto failed, the homestead proposal remained on the congressional agenda until after Abraham Lincoln had been elected, the South had seceded, the United States Congress had become the Union Congress, and Galusha Grow had been chosen as speaker of the House. The homestead bill and Justin Morrill's agricultural college land-grant bill, also previously vetoed by Buchanan, became the centerpieces of the domestic Republican program that came before the Thirty-seventh Congress. That Lincoln had pledged himself to the enactment of a homestead bill shortly before his inauguration, advocating the division of "the wild lands into small parcels so that every poor man m[ight] have a home,"[98] made another presidential veto seem unlikely.

Homestead nonetheless encountered numerous obstacles in the Union Congress. Eastern Republicans, worried about the financial exigencies of the Government as it embarked upon a new war, argued for a revival of the general Federal policy of revenue generation through land sales. Not surprisingly, an attempt also was made to graft a new military land bounty scheme onto the homestead bill.[99] Concerned that the opportunity to pass a national homestead law might be lost, House Speaker Grow left the rostrum on February 21, 1862, to revive historic arguments in favor of land grants for citizens. He denounced military land bounties as discriminatory policy that favored the soldier on the battlefield while ignoring the brave conquerors of the wilderness.[100] Grow also dismissed

---

[98] Lincoln, cited in Ilisevich, *Galusha Grow*, p. 211.

[99] See Leonard P. Curry, *Blueprint for Modern America: Nonmilitary Legislation of the First Civil War Congress* (Nashville: Vanderbilt University Press, 1968), pp. 102–5. The fate of proposals to grant Union veterans land benefits is discussed later.

[100] *CG* (37/2), pp. 909–10. Grow said (p. 910): "Whatever disposition Congress may evince to reward the patriotic devotion of the soldier, relieve his sufferings and provide for his future while living, or to wreathe his grave when dead, will meet my hearty coöperation.... But there are soldiers of peace – that grand army of the sons of toil,

the idea of reserving the public domain as a basis of Federal credit, observing prophetically that the "standard of credit with a nation is not the amount of unproductive property that it may possess, but the *ability of its people to pay taxes.*"[101]

The homestead bill passed in the House a week later by an overwhelming margin of 107 to 16, including a section that guaranteed cash and land bounties to men enlisting in Union forces.[102] The Senate voted to enact the bill by a vote of 33 to 7, but only after amending it to excise the military land bounty provision and add the critical qualifier that the nation would not provide homesteads to rebels. Only those citizens and citizens-to-be who had "never borne arms against the United States Government or given aid and comfort to its enemies" would be entitled to land. The House initially refused to accept those terms, but after a conference that "satisfied everyone's dignity," a bill essentially similar to the Senate's version was passed by both chambers. The Homestead Act was signed by President Lincoln on May 20, 1862, consummating, at least for certain Americans, the "long struggle for the land for the landless."[103] In its discrimination against black Americans and white citizens of the Confederacy, the Homestead Act was not the universal entitlement that many originally had envisioned.[104] As implemented, the act would fall

whose lives, from the cradle to the grave, are a constant warfare with the elements, with the unrelenting obstacles of nature and the merciless barbarities of savage life. Their battle-fields are on the prairies and the wilderness of your frontiers; their achievements, felling the forests, leveling the mountains, filling the valleys, and smoothing the pathway of science and civilization in their march over the continent. While we provide with open hand for the soldier on the tented field, let us not heap unnecessary burdens upon these heroes of the garret, the workshop, and the wilderness home."

[101] *CG* (37/2), p. 910 (emphasis in the original). The first national individual income tax had been enacted the previous year.

[102] *CG* (37/2), Feb. 28, 1862, p. 1035.

[103] *CG* (37/2), May 6, 1862, p. 1951; "An Act to secure Homesteads to actual Settlers on the Public Domain," May 20, 1862, *U.S. Statutes at Large*, vol. 12, pp. 392–3; Grow, cited in Ilisevich, *Galusha Grow*, p. 211. Explicitly excluding southern rebels (and, implicitly, people of color), the Homestead Act granted, for a small filing fee, up to 160 acres of surveyed public land to any person who was the head of a family or who had arrived at the age of twenty-one years; who was a U.S. citizen or who had filed his declaration of intent to become one; and who would reside upon and improve said land for five years, though the land could be bought by the homesteader for the government minimum price after six months' residency.

[104] Legal restrictions banning the receipt of Federal land grants by blacks and southerners would be formally lifted five years after the Homestead Act's passage. Some observers have taken this to imply that the initially exclusionary terms of the act were not significant. Yet, those terms embodied contemporary struggles to define the meaning of

even further short of the expectations of those who had fought for its en-actment.[105] Nonetheless, the Thirty-seventh Congress finally had voted many Americans a farm.

Reconstruction Redux: The Civil War, Its (Union) Veterans, and Selective Entitlement

By the time the Civil War began, the United States had a firmly estab-lished history of national-level social provision rooted in the entitlement of certain categories of Americans who served the purposes of the state as it sought to claim, protect, and expand its sovereignty over an im-mense portion of the North American continent. Programmatic entitle-ment was an ingenious legislative solution to the problems of building and consolidating a nation of unprecedented size and diversity. Estab-lishing tangible links between the military and civil society and between civil society and representative institutions, the pensions and land grants enacted between 1776 and 1862 mobilized citizens both physically and ideologically, helping to legitimate ambitious efforts at state and nation building, and contributing to the political incorporation of a rapidly ex-panding polity.[106] Simultaneously distributive, redistributive, and regu-latory in their creation of substantive benefits tied to legal categories of deservingness, America's original entitlement programs would have an enduring influence on the scope and direction of Congress's constitu-tional authority, the contours of Federal social policy, and the meaning of American citizenship.

In addition to the entitlement programs established on the spending side of the U.S. budget, it is important to note that entitlements were also created in the exemptions and deductions that were part of the first national income tax established by the Thirty-seventh Congress in 1861.

American citizenship. They also demonstrated Congress's facility in categorizing and selectively entitling particular citizens to benefits as national needs arose. Note that the Morrill Act, which granted states 30,000 acres of public land for each senator and rep-resentative for the purpose of establishing agricultural and mechanical colleges, also categorically barred Confederate states from receiving its benefits until Reconstruction. "An Act donating Public Lands to the several States and Territories which may provide Colleges for the Benefit of Agriculture and the Mechanic Arts," July 2, 1862, *U.S. Statutes at Large*, vol. 12, pp. 503–5.

[105] Gates, "The Homestead Law."

[106] Though more limited in scope, the many private bills passed by Congress to establish benefits for individuals and groups between the founding and the Civil War almost certainly produced these effects as well.

As Robert Stanley's illuminating analysis has demonstrated, an income tax was not proposed and enacted during the Civil War simply because of its potential to generate new revenues and reallocate tax burdens. It was established because it could serve the multiple centrist purposes of a relatively uncohesive state that was attempting to organize itself and achieve autonomy.[107] In addition to requiring the expansion of Federal internal revenue administration and creating a national-level forum for decision making by congressional committees, revenue administrators, and courts, the income tax was an extraordinarily flexible congressional policy tool. The establishment of exemption levels facilitated a precise targeting of the social class of the taxpayer. Deductions allowed the manipulation of the meaning of "income," inviting bargaining in an administrative setting[108] and further legal categorization of "worthy" citizens and behaviors. Congressional and Supreme Court action would move the personal income tax in and out of the Federal statute books during the late nineteenth century. Nonetheless, the structural provisions of the Civil War income tax, including its special exemptions and deductions, would come to constitute the foundations of the modern income tax established by the Sixteenth Amendment, paving the way for the extraordinary growth of tax expenditures – particularly selective ones – during the twentieth century.

Some of today's best-known (and most beloved) tax deductions can be traced directly to the Thirty-seventh Congress's 1861 decision to delegate the "details" of the new Federal income tax, including the definition of taxable income, to the secretary of the Treasury. Congress was generally agreed that fairness dictated that the net, not gross, income of citizens should be taxed, but income tax advocates were unsure how to write the appropriate legislation. As Rhode Island Senator James Simmons remarked, "I thought of putting this word 'net' in; but I could see so many ways of evading it that I thought it better to let the Secretary of the

---

[107] *Dimensions of Law in the Service of Order: Origins of the Federal Income Tax, 1861–1913* (New York: Oxford University Press, 1993).

[108] Stanley, *Dimensions of Law*, pp. 243–4. Exemptions explicitly free part of what statutes define as income for a given year, usually that amount considered a "subsistence minimum." Some deductions are also used to calculate taxable income, refining gross income to economic net by subtracting from gross receipts the expenses and losses incurred in the pursuit of income. Others deductions are established by Congress for purposes of attaining particular social or economic policy goals. C. Harry Kahn, *Personal Deductions in the Federal Income Tax* (Princeton, NJ: Princeton University Press, 1960).

Treasury prescribe his rules, and let the bill cover all incomes."[109] The 1861 and 1862 Federal income tax laws specified only that national, state, and local taxes would be deductible in the calculation of taxable income, but interest paid on indebtedness was made deductible in 1864. This provision of the 1864 Tax Act was the origin of the home mortgage interest deduction, a contemporary selective entitlement that benefits only those citizens financing the cost of purchasing a home (despite widespread belief that it is the product of twentieth-century law enacted in the name of "housing policy"). The Civil War–era income tax code actually attempted to equalize the situations of homeowners and renters by making the cost of rental housing tax deductible in 1863. That provision was not transmitted into the modern income tax, however. It expired along with the Civil War income tax and was not revived in the Federal income tax of 1894.[110]

Distinct patterns emerge when the entitlements created between 1776 and 1862 are considered in terms of their type, their degree of selectivity, and the timing of their establishment.[111] *Military veterans* received two kinds of monetary benefits: disability pensions and service pensions. Disability pensions typically were enacted either prospectively or soon after the onset of a major military engagement, then later adjusted to be more generous as needs or demands arose. Service pensions, by contrast, with the exception of the half-pay enactment extracted from the Continental Congress during the Revolution, were legislated and then expanded after wars were won – usually long after. Land grants for military veterans

[109] *CG* (37/1), July 29, 1861, p. 315.
[110] American taxpayers were first required to report separately the home mortgage and other consumer interest they paid in 1963. All interest on indebtedness paid by individuals remained deductible until the Tax Reform Act of 1986, which established a gradual phaseout of all interest-related tax deductions *except* the deduction allowed for home mortgage interest. "An Act to provide increased Revenue from Imports, to pay Interest on the Public Debt, and for other Purposes," August 5, 1861, *U.S. Statutes at Large*, vol. 12, p. 309; "An Act to provide Internal Revenue to support the Government and pay Interest on the Public Debt," *U.S. Statutes at Large*, vol. 12, pp. 473–4; "An Act to amend an Act entitled 'An Act to provide Internal Revenue to support the Government and pay Interest on the Public Debt,' approved July first, eighteen hundred and sixty-two, and for other Purposes," *U.S. Statutes at Large*, vol. 12, p. 723; "An Act to provide Internal Revenue to support the Government, to pay Interest on the Public Debt, and for other Purposes," June 30, 1864, *U.S. Statutes at Large*, vol. 13, pp. 281–2; Edwin R. A. Seligman, *The Income Tax: A Study of the History, Theory, and Practice of Income Taxation at Home and Abroad* (New York: Macmillan Company, 2nd ed., 1914), pp. 511–12.
[111] The disability pensions established in February 1862 for Union veterans of the Civil War is discussed later.

were established both before and during military engagements as inducements to enlistment. They were also created retrospectively, either as post hoc rewards for service or because of pressures to augment existing benefits. Always categorical and often highly selective when debated and enacted, veterans' benefits repeatedly generated controversy in and out of Congress due to their putatively disparate treatment of different classes of citizens (though the wisdom of establishing disability benefits per se was never in doubt).

With the exception of the aid created by the terms of the income tax in 1861, all of the programmatic entitlements established for *civilians* in the early to mid-nineteenth century involved land (despite their obvious fiscal implications).[112] Perhaps as a consequence, they followed a somewhat different trajectory with respect to their inclusiveness than veterans' benefits did. Some land entitlements were quite selective, like the original preemption measures advantaging particular classes of squatters, the Armed Occupation Act's land grants for men willing to settle on and defend land in Florida, and the grants for the settlers of Oregon and Washington. These benefits specifically were intended to reward only those civilians willing to move into and occupy peripheral regions where the nation's claim to dominion was tenuous, and even to act as a paramilitary force.

By contrast, the increasingly general and increasingly prospective preemption laws passed by Congress in the 1830s and 1840s constituted a discernible shift toward the creation of universal social benefits. The impetus behind these laws gained even more force in the homestead movement, as land entitlements became widely envisioned as a form of public welfare and as a basic commitment of the state to its citizens. The combined forces of the *Dred Scott* decision and secession resulted in the Homestead Act's exclusion of people of color and southern rebels from its benefits. Nonetheless, the principle of universal social provision was still on the table in 1862, and it effectively became embedded in American law when the *Southern* Homestead Act was passed by the radical

---

[112] Untangling the question of whether Federal land grants were simply an indirect way of providing citizens with property that they could sell for ready cash rather than migrate and engage in subsistence farming is beyond the scope of this study. This question was nonetheless implicit, if not even explicit, in the recurrent congressional arguments pitting the virtues of the actual settler against the speculator who bought up land rights, and it has influenced a large portion of the scholarship related to westward expansion and the public domain.

Thirty-ninth Congress in 1866 to add former Confederates and freedmen to the subset of the citizenry already entitled to land. The act was the first piece of American national legislation to prohibit discrimination on the basis of race or color in its interpretation or implementation. Its first section read: "[n]o distinction or discrimination shall be made in the construction or execution of this act on account of race or color."[113] The language had been proposed by George Julian of Indiana, chair of the House Committee on Public Lands, who took aim at the Supreme Court and the Democratic Party to explain that

[i]n consequence of the Dred Scott decision, and the power of latter-day Democracy in debauching the public sentiment of the country, it is not generally understood that black men have any rights in relation to the public domain of the country.... I believe it is now unknown to multitudes of white men, even in the northern States, that colored men have any rights under the homestead law. We ought to make that fact known to black and white, so that the multitudes of landless people may understand what are their rights of acquiring homesteads.[114]

Despite such convictions as Julian's, the primary motivation behind the enactment of the Southern Homestead Act was not a desire to create an egalitarian society or even an egalitarian public land system. The Union Congress's urge to punish the former Confederacy, especially southern planters, clearly was key to the passage of the act. So, too, was contemporary sentiment against corporations and land speculation, and the widespread belief that landownership and self-help would be the basis of economic survival for freedmen and poor southern whites.[115] The act

---

[113] "An Act for the Disposal of the Public Lands for Homestead Actual Settlement in the States of Alabama, Mississippi, Louisiana, Arkansas, and Florida," June 21, 1866, *U.S. Statutes at Large*, vol. 14, pp. 66–7.

[114] *CG* (39/1), Feb. 7, 1866, p. 716. Julian was an abolitionist and long-standing advocate of land reform. He was also in favor of enfranchising women. In 1868, prior to the ratification of the Fifteenth Amendment, he proposed a sixteenth amendment to the U.S. Constitution establishing equal, citizenship-based voting rights that could not be denied on the basis of race, color, or sex. See George W. Julian, *Political Recollections, 1840–1872* (Chicago: Jansen, McClurg, & Co., 1883), p. 324 (reprinted Miami: Mnemosyne Publishing, 1969).

[115] Lanza, *Agrarianism and Reconstruction Politics*; Robbins, *Our Landed Heritage*, pp. 210–12; William Cohen, *At Freedom's Edge: Black Mobility and the Southern White Quest for Racial Control, 1861–1915* (Baton Rouge: Louisiana State University Press, 1991), pp. 51–3; Robert H. Bremner, *The Public Good: Philanthropy and Welfare in the Civil War Era* (New York: Alfred A. Knopf, 1980), pp. 99, 118–19. Had it not been for executive reluctance, the Union Congress might well have enacted legislation granting confiscated rebel land to Union veterans and loyal poor citizens of all races. Confiscation was dreaded in the South and was a significant factor in prolonging the Civil War. The Confederate

promised land for "homestead actual settlement" only in the states of Alabama, Mississippi, Louisiana, Arkansas, and Florida. Its implementation was deeply flawed, in ways that worked against the poor and people of color, who were least able to avail themselves of benefits.[116] Nonetheless, the Southern Homestead Act extended the line of earlier policies entitling civilians to land in a radically inclusive direction. In principle, and to a degree in practice, both selective and universal, citizenship-based entitlements stood as Federal policy precedents as the nation was reunited and Reconstruction ensued, and the now famous system of benefits for veterans of the Civil War began to take shape.[117]

Not surprisingly, the outbreak of the war had led immediately to congressional consideration of military disability benefits. The Thirty-seventh Congress's enactment of disability and survivors' pensions in July 1862 was in many ways similar to the passage of earlier statutes establishing such benefits for U.S. veterans. Historic arguments were invoked regarding the injustice of discriminating between classes of military veterans, but to no avail: the 1862 program once again distributed pensions according to rank, with disabled officers receiving the greatest benefits.

Congress's last appeal to the people of the South in 1865 railed against "surrender and submission to the will of the conqueror," an "arrogant foe" that would not only confiscate the property and estates of the vanquished "rebels," but divide and distribute them "among our African bondsmen." Failure, asserted the Confederate Congress, "will compel us to drink the cup of humiliation even to the bitter dregs of having our history written by New England historians" (cited in Robbins, *Our Landed Heritage*, p. 212).

[116] Lanza, *Agrarianism and Reconstruction Politics*; Cohen, *At Freedom's Edge*, pp. 52–3.

[117] The Civil War pension system recently has been chronicled by Theda Skocpol in her widely acclaimed book *Protecting Soldiers and Mothers: The Political Origins of Social Policy in the United States* (Cambridge, MA: Belknap Press of Harvard University Press, 1992). Rich accounts are also found in Stuart McConnell, *Glorious Contentment: The Grand Army of the Republic, 1865–1900* (Chapel Hill: University of North Carolina Press, 1992); and Ann Shola Orloff, *The Politics of Pensions: A Comparative Analysis of Britain, Canada, and the United States, 1880–1940* (Madison: University of Wisconsin Press, 1993). See also Orloff, "The Political Origins of America's Belated Welfare State," in *The Politics of Social Policy in the United States*, ed. Margaret Weir, Ann Shola Orloff, and Theda Skocpol (Princeton, NJ: Princeton University Press, 1988, pp. 37–80; Orloff and Skocpol, "Why Not Equal Protection? Explaining the Politics of Public Social Spending in Britain, 1900–1911, and the United States, 1880s–1920," *American Sociological Review* 49 (1984): 726–50; and Heywood T. Sanders, "Paying for the 'Bloody Shirt': The Politics of Civil War Pensions," in *Political Benefits: Empirical Studies of American Public Programs*, ed. Barry S. Rundquist (Lexington, MA: D. C. Heath, 1980), pp. 137–59. All of these works draw upon two early-twentieth-century works that assayed the Civil War pension system in detail: William Glasson's seminal *Federal Military Pensions* and John William Oliver, "History of Civil War Military Pensions, 1861–1885," *Bulletin of the University of Wisconsin*, no. 844, History Series 4(1) (1917).

Like its predecessors, the new program initially limited benefits to men actually injured in combat and the dependents of men who were killed, but these categories would later expand. The projected cost of the Civil War disability benefits was also grossly underestimated, just as earlier pension expenditures had been, though the legislators enacting the 1862 law obviously had no way of knowing so at the time.[118]

In other ways, the Pension Act of 1862 broke new ground. To begin with, it was more generous and more inclusive than the disability legislation of earlier wars had been, both with prespect to the categories of veterans it covered (Army and Navy alike, including regulars, volunteers, militia, and the marine corps) and with respect to the people it counted as veterans' dependents: not just widows and orphans, but, for the first time in American history, also mothers and orphaned sisters. In addition, the legislation was more prospective than ever before, extending disability benefits forward in time indefinitely to the veterans of future American wars.[119] Finally, and most critically, the 1862 Pension Act, by virtue of the conflict it was enacted in, selectively entitled only veterans of *Union* military service to disability benefits. Though the law would be expanded and extended enormously over time to include new categories of veterans and survivors, this exclusion of southern insurgents would never be eradicated from the statute books of the reconstructed nation. Enacted by a Union Congress for loyal citizens only, the "wisest" and "most liberal pension law ever enacted" by the U.S. Government[120] would never aid Americans who served on the wrong side of the state, no matter how many years passed after the nation's reunification. Its exclusion of disabled Confederate officers and soldiers made obvious sense in 1862, when they effectively were citizens of another nation at war with

---

[118] *U.S. Statutes at Large*, vol. 12, pp. 566–9. The act was passed in large part because the July 1861 statute authorizing the president to accept the services of volunteers, which had included language entitling disabled veterans and their survivors to the same benefits conferred on persons in the regular military service, was not explicit enough. Glasson, *Federal Military Pensions*, pp. 124–5; Oliver, "History of Civil War Military Pensions," pp. 6–8. Note also the enactment three days later of the Militia Act, designed to facilitate Federal drafting and help guarantee blacks emancipation in exchange for Union service, potentially a "giant step along the road away from *Dred Scott* and toward abolition and citizen status." Mary Frances Berry, *Military Necessity and Civil Rights Policy: Black Citizenship and the Constitution, 1861–1868* (Port Washington, NY: Kennikat Press, 1977), p. 43.

[119] Glasson, *Federal Military Pensions*, pp. 127–9.

[120] Characterizations of the 1862 pension law by the U.S. secretary of the interior and commissioner of pensions, cited in Oliver, "History of Civil War Military Pensions," p. 9.

the United States. That the Government staunchly refused to extend its generosity to these men long after they had been restored to American citizenship, however, denying them the benefit of its historic commitment to support its disabled veterans, signified that the former rebels continued to be considered veterans of another nation for Federal policy purposes.

The actors involved in the passage of the July 1862 Pension Act thoroughly understood the substantive and symbolic power of selective entitlement. They had demonstrated this only a few months earlier, when they discontinued paying Federal pension benefits to over 2,000 southern veterans of earlier wars and their survivors. By the terms of legislation enacted in February 1962, all persons who had taken up arms against the United States, or who had in any way encouraged or sympathized with the rebels or their cause, were striken from the pension rolls by the secretary of the interior – an action ratifying the commissioner of pension's 1861 decision to suspend payment of pensions in the eleven Confederate states. Though these benefits later were restored, complete with arrears payments for those who could prove unabated loyalty to the Union and who were willing to swear their allegiance to the United States, some aged men and women lost their pension benefits, and the pension system was not operational in every southern state again until 1872.[121] Doubtless it made good tactical sense for the Union government to cut off sources of financial assistance to those in rebellion, especially given the dire condition of the Federal treasury and the fact that some Union soldiers had not been paid for several months in early 1862. Yet, the termination of southern veterans' benefits in 1861 presumed that all southern veterans were disloyal to the Union. The war obviously did not alter the fact that the disenrolled southern veterans previously had served the nation and qualified for benefits. Nor did it alter the life conditions of pensioners who were disabled, old, poor, and/or widowed. What instead had changed was the state's perception of their deservingness. Rescinding the most sacred of America's public benefits, Union actors revealed their belief that the authority to entitle selectively encompassed the power to *disentitle* selectively when circumstances warranted, no matter how legitimate recipients' claims, previously recognized by the state and its laws, might have been.

---

[121] Act of February 4, 1862, cited and discussed in Oliver, "History of Civil War Military Pensions," p. 7, and Glasson, *Federal Military Pensions*, p. 127.

Many of the men who volunteered or enlisted in the Union's forces anticipated that they would be given land grants, as had veterans of other American wars.[122] After all, policy precedents for such grants extended back to the nation's founding. The enactment of extremely generous retrospective land bounties for veterans of the Mexican War (and indeed all prior wars) was also very recent history, and contemporary political campaigns and party platforms featured promises of land for veterans. As noted previously, however, the question of establishing military land grants for men serving in the Civil War had become caught up in the politics of the homestead question. Congressional attempts to include a Union veterans' land bounty provision in the Homestead Act of 1862 failed, as did all of the military land bounty proposals made in Congress after the Homestead Act was enacted.[123]

By many accounts, the idea of granting land only to actual settlers, whether civilians or veterans, had become deeply ingrained, to the extent that after the war, newspapers often carried such notices as "Soldiers who served in the late war have no privileges connected with the homestead law which are not enjoyed by all persons."[124] Though a desire to preserve both the ideology and policy of universal provision for all settlers was almost certainly a factor in Congress's decision not to provide land bounties to Union veterans, the secretary of war's estimate that veterans' land grants would require more than 360 million acres of land, or an area eleven times the size of Ohio, may have been dispositive.[125] Legislation

---

[122] This paragraph draws upon Dixon Wecter, *When Johnny Comes Marching Home* (Cambridge, MA: Riverside Press, 1944), pp. 205–6, and Gates, *Public Land Law Development*, pp. 281–3.

[123] These included, as noted earlier, proposals to entitle Union veterans to homesteads on confiscated Confederate lands or to use the confiscated lands as a means of establishing homes for Union veterans disabled in the conflict. See the *Annual Report of the Secretary of the Interior*, 1864, cited in Oliver, "History of Civil War Military Pensions," p. 14.

[124] Wecter, *When Johnny Comes Marching Home*, pp. 205, 206.

[125] Note, however, that the land granted to western railroads in the 1850s, 1860s, and 1870s totaled about 180,000,000 acres, an area larger than the entire Old Northwest. According to Wecter, the fact that enlistees had been paid cash bonuses was also a factor in Congress's refusal to create Union veterans' land grants after the Civil War, yet land grants had been awarded in addition to cash enlistment bonuses in previous wars. The Grand Army of the Republic, the largest of the Union veterans' organizations, issued resolutions in the 1880s and 1890s articulating the notion that Union veterans had some sort of preemptory claim to the national domain. They also launched some remarkable policy proposals, including Union veteran ownership of Yellowstone National Park, but none of them were entertained seriously. Robbins, *Our Landed Heritage*, p. 215, 223; Wecter, *When Johnny Comes Marching Home*, p. 205; McConnell, *Glorious Contentment*, pp. 156–7.

enacted in 1870, 1872, and 1873 established special privileges for Union veterans *within* the framework of the Homestead Act,[126] but, in contrast to the policy path taken after previous wars, land benefits beyond the acreage promised to ordinary homesteaders were not forthcoming from Congress.[127]

Generosity for the veterans who had preserved the nation would come instead in monetary form, through a massive expansion of the pension system. The trajectory taken by that expansion was familiar. As Dixon Wecter observed, the patterns of Civil War veterans' claims and pension enactments were virtually identical to those of earlier wars. First came claims and legislation related to wounds, illness, or (in the case of survivors) death suffered while in the service. Claims and laws related to newly recognized infirmities, postwar declines in the health of pension beneficiaries, and losses in earning power followed. Last came claims and legislation predicated upon war service independent of disability or financial need, with the minimum time in uniform required to qualify for pension benefits falling all the while.[128] The initial wave of the pension system's expansion began before the war was over, when in 1864 Congress established higher rates of compensation for pensioners with certain severe permanent disabilities and extended benefits to the widows and

---

[126] The acts of July 15, 1870, April 4 and June 8, 1872, and March 3, 1873, authorized honorably discharged Union veterans to homestead on 160 acres of double-minimum priced areas reserved for railroads (civilians could only homestead on 80 acreas); count their years served in the military toward the five years homesteaders were required to live on their claims in order to receive title, though one-year residency was still a condition; and locate the balance of their homestead claims, if they originally had not located all 160 acres, anywhere within the public domain. (The Homestead Act was not amended to allow civilians to locate their claims on unsurveyed public lands until 1880.) Gates, *Public Land Law Development*, p. 282.

[127] Responding to voters who were upset that tribal lands often ended in the hands of speculators or railroad magnates instead of being included in the public domain and dedicated to homesteading, the House attempted to reestablish bicameral congressional control over the fortunes of the tribes and their possessions. In 1875, Congress extended the benefits of the Homestead Act to Native Americans willing to leave their tribes and settle on the public lands. The restriction that they could not sell lands claimed under the Homestead Act for five years was intended to induce them to commit themselves to farm life and, moreover, to renounce their heritage of political and cultural autonomy in favor of a more civilized, white form of citizenship. As an additional inducement to assimilation, Native American males continuing to live on reservations were made subject to the new requirement that they labor "at a reasonable rate" in return for Federal subsistence benefits – an early form of "workfare." Smith, *Civic Ideals*, pp. 318–20.

[128] *When Johnny Comes Marching Home*, p. 250.

children of black soldiers. Subsequent amendments included more specific disabilities under the program's qualifying criteria and empowered
the commissioner of pensions to set intermediate rates for injuries not
specified in the original law. They also proffered benefits to the dependents of deceased Union veterans even if their mothers had remarried,
and extended the time limit on filing pension claims.

Every Congress that met between 1865 and 1873 shaped a disability
pension law more liberal than its predecessors, as if to prove President
Andrew Johnson's assertion that "a grateful people will not hesitate to
sanction any measures having for their object the relief of soldiers muti-
lated and families made fatherless in the efforts to preserve our national
existence."[129] After prolonged congressional consideration and debate,
the Arrears Act of 1879 dramatically increased the aid available to disabled Union veterans and their survivors by backdating the start of all
pensions to each veteran's respective discharge date or date of death.
Those awarded benefits at some point after the war became entitled to
receive, in a lump sum, all of the monies they would have received had
they been granted benefits immediately upon death or discharge. Simultaneously retrospective and prospective in its explicit application to both
existing and new claims, the Arrears Act resulted in an immediate explosion of Federal disability pension claims, payments, and expenditures.[130]
The Dependent Pension Act of 1890 further liberalized the system by extending benefits to all honorably discharged Union veterans with at least
ninety days' service with mental or physical disabilities rendering them
incapable of manual labor, regardless of the source of those disabilities or
the veterans' financial situation. Strictly speaking, the act did not create a
service pension, but over time it essentially became one due to generous
construction by pension administrators.[131]

Some scholars attribute the growth of the Civil War pension system
(beyond early increases in claimants and costs due to rising numbers

---

[129] Cited in Oliver, "History of Civil War Military Pensions," p. 19; see also p. 35.

[130] Glasson, *Federal Military Pensions*, pp. 129–77; Oliver, "History of Civil War Military
Pensions," pp. 14–82. It must be emphasized, as Stuart McConnell has pointed out, that
the Arrears Act did not actually constitute a wholescale revision of the 1862 Pension
Act, for it did not remove service-related death or disability as the basic criterion for
entitlement, alter basic pension rates, or provide for new categories of persons. Rather,
it gave additional benefits to those who already had qualified for pensions and encouraged new claimants to come forward, resulting in a "stampede" on the Pension Office.
Glorious Contentment, pp. 146, 149.

[131] McConnell, *Glorious Contentment*, p. 153; Skocpol, *Protecting Soldiers and Mothers*, p. 129.

of casualities) to increasingly tight electoral competition between Republicans and Democrats. Theda Skocpol, for example, asserts that the enlargement of the pension system "reflected the changing competitive strategies of the major political parties" at the end of Reconstruction, when a revived Democratic Party vied with Republicans for control of the presidency and Congress, and politicians recognized that increasingly more inclusive legislation "maximized possibilities for using pensions to recruit voters." Ann Shola Orloff likewise characterizes the Civil War pension establishment as "an excellent example of the sort of policies generated by the operations of patronage democracy," pointing to the potential of an expanding system for mobilizing the electorate.[132] Partisanship and electoral concerns were undoubtedly key to the explosion in benefits from the late 1870s on. Yet, other developments seem to have exerted considerable influence on the pension system's evolution *before* then, during its initial, and arguably most critical, growth period.

Note, first, the Union Congress's passage of several statutes in the 1860s that entitled the last surviving veterans of the *Revolution* to bonus pension monies. The twelve men remaining on the pension list who had fought for independence were granted an extra $100 annually in April 1864 as a sign of special national recognition. With only five of the Revolutionary patriots still living in early 1865, Congress increased their benefits to $300 per year during the remainder of their lives. By June 1867, the last of the soldiers on the Revolutionary pension rolls had died. In 1868, however, Congress located and pensioned two new men as Revolutionary soldiers at $500 per year, until the last known survivor of the nation's original war, Daniel Bakeman, passed away on April 5, 1869, at the age of 109 years, 6 months, and 8 days. The widows of Revolutionary soldiers and sailors also received a pension rate increase in 1868.[133]

Congress turned next, in 1871, to the establishment of a new service pension program for the Americans who had ensured the nation's victory in its *second* war for independence: the veterans of the War of 1812 and their survivors. The Pension Act of 1871 granted benefits to all surviving soldiers and sailors who had served for at least sixty days in the War of 1812 and were honorably discharged, or who had received personal mention by Congress for specific services during the war, and to their widows, provided that they had been married prior to the treaty of peace

[132] Skocpol, *Protecting Soldiers and Mothers*, p. 115; Orloff, "Political Origins," p. 46.
[133] Glasson, *Federal Military Pensions*, pp. 92–3.

and had not remarried, without the requirement of poverty or disability. The effect of this unqualified service pension measure, as Glasson put it, "was promptly felt." Though there were few War of 1812 pensioners left on the disability rolls in 1871, some 32,000 new service-based pension claims were received within the eight months following the pension law's passage, of which some 25,000 came from veterans and 7,000 from widows.[134] No claims were allowed from citizens of the former Confederacy, who were barred from receiving benefits under the 1871 law regardless of whether they or their deceased spouses or fathers had served in the War of 1812.

What inspired Congress to acknowledge some of the nation's elderly military veterans during and immediately after the Civil War, to the extent of establishing an entirely new pension program for the veterans of the War of 1812 and their survivors almost a half-century after that conflict ended? Multiple reasons for the enactment of the 1871 Pension Act suggest themselves. Though not so numerous as to constitute a large percentage of the population, the large number of claims by men presented immediately after the law's passage suggests that electoral concerns might have been a factor. Petitions and other forms of lobbying might also have mattered, for although the ranks of the United Brethren of the War of 1812 were thinning with the passage of time, some War of 1812 veterans had continued to argue for service pensions after receiving land bounties in the 1850s, invoking the inclusive 1832 Revolutionary service pension law as precedent.[135] The existence of a large budget surplus rooted in high protective tariffs might also have been a factor,[136] given pervasive sectionalism and the desire to punish the South evinced in the pension law's exclusion of former rebels and rebel sympathizers. Members of Congress might also have felt a degree of fraternity with the aged soldiers, since

[134] Glasson's figures indicate that there were a total of 727 War of 1812 survivors and widows on the Federal pension rolls in 1871. That number climbed to 20,127 in the following year, then to 23,319 in 1873. *Federal Military Pensions*, p. 109–113.

[135] Oberly, *Sixty Million Acres*, pp. 35, 44–5. Oberly notes that "the lasting accomplishment of the United Brethren was to make veterans' fraternal organizations respectable and no longer perceived as subversive – the way Americans saw the old Society of the Cincinnati" (p. 53). A War of 1812 service pension bill was on the congressional agenda when the Revolutionary veterans' benefits were established in 1864 but was tabled at the end of the session.

[136] See Jill Quadagno, *The Transformation of Old Age Security: Class and Politics in the American Welfare State* (Chicago: University of Chicago Press, 1988), p. 37; Skocpol, *Protecting Soldiers and Mothers*, p. 114.

Union veterans held over 30 percent of the seats in the Fortieth and Forty-first Congresses.[137] None of these potential reasons for the passage of the 1871 Pension Act, however, explain Congress's sudden interest in identifying and rewarding a dozen aged veterans of the American Revolution in 1864.

That interest must be seen to demonstrate the extent to which contemporary Federal actors appreciated the symbolic power of categorical benefits. Congressmen and presidents understood that in addition to conferring national benefits, pension laws carried strong messages about citizenship and martial manhood. The timing of the new benefits was striking. The April 1864 law granting bonus pension monies to surviving Revolutionary patriots came a mere five weeks after the passage of legislation strengthening the highly controversial Federal conscription system and extending it to southern blacks and foreign-born immigrants, and two weeks before a new draft was slated to take place if the 200,000 volunteers called for by President Lincoln did not materialize. The February 1865 law increasing the Revolutionary veterans' pensions was enacted in the middle of a bitter debate over the reform of the conscription system and the nation's inequitable enlistment bounty system. The new benefits extended to a handful of elderly veterans obviously were not broad-based entitlements. Nonetheless, the tangible reminders of the Revolution and its heroes stood as a testimonial to the citizen-soldier ideal, state authority, and nationhood in the first American war officially to counterpose volunteerism and conscription.[138] Substantively and symbolically, the pension monies linked the past, present, and future. Speaking on behalf of the new benefits for the "small band of revolutionary patriots, all that [we]re left of those brave and gallant men who acquired our independence," Indiana Representative John Law revealed Congress's deliberate

---

[137] Richard Franklin Bensel, *Yankee Leviathan: The Origins of Central State Authority in America, 1859–1877* (New York: Cambridge University Press, 1990), p. 406.

[138] As Chambers has persuasively argued, the relationship between conscription and volunteerism during the Civil War was complex. Often portrayed as the "spur" that inspired men to volunteer in order to escape being a "conscript," the northern draft primarily acted to persuade elected officials to "raise much higher bounties to entice men to enlist and thus avert the need for governmental coercion." While not successful militarily – some 92 percent of the men in the Union army were volunteers – the first national draft was nonetheless a significant political achievement, demonstrating the North's resolve to prosecute the war to victory even to the extent of centralizing state authority and refining the terms of national citizenship. Chambers, *To Raise an Army*, pp. 64, 57–65; see also James W. Geary, *We Need Men: The Union Draft in the Civil War* (Dekalb: Northern Illinois University Press, 1991), pp. 116–32, 162–74.

elision of the nation's formative conflict and the ongoing war between the states:

Shall these centurial heroes, these old and infirm veterans, live to see the day when the Republic, which was cemented with their blood, is broken in pieces and drenched in gore by the fraticidal hands of their children? God forbid.... If in this nineteenth century, with the intelligence and love of liberty which ought to influence our people, with the blood that has been shed to obtain that liberty, with the example of our fathers, and with the advice of Washington, who saw and dreaded the *"sectional feeling"* which has increased from year to year for the last thirty years, we, forgetful of his counsels, should rashly and wickedly permit our Union to be dissolved, what hope is there in the future, what prospect of success? ... None, none whatever.[139]

The Revolutionary pension benefits passed in 1867–9, and the new program of service pensions enacted in 1871 for the veterans and widows of the War of 1812, were also rhetorically powerful policies. The messages that they conveyed about patriotism and desert resonated in a context in which ex-soldiers and civilians alike struggled to make sense of the most devastating war that America had ever experienced. What was lacking at the end of that war, as Stuart McConnell has revealed, "was an explanatory myth: a story about the place of the Union veteran in the newly restored Union and, at a deeper level, a story about the new Union itself."[140] Federal policies benefiting the Republic's original patriots served as the foundation of that explanatory myth by reinscribing the aspirations and self-sacrifice of previous generations in collective memory and imagination. The 1871 Pension Act's exclusion of southern War of 1812 veterans also recast the meaning of American patriotism by making it clear that while military service to the nation was meritorious, only *sustained* loyalty to the state would be deemed deserving of public recognition in the form of tangible benefits. As one member of Congress put it, the Government could "afford to be just and generous to its defenders," but it could not afford "to pension men who fought for its destruction."[141]

---

[139] *CG* (38/1), March 4, 1864, p. 939. The bill passed swiftly and unanimously in both House and Senate. A list of the Revolutionary patriots – *notably, all northerners* – was printed in the *Congressional Globe* (p. 939).

[140] McConnell, *Glorious Contentment*, pp. 23–4.

[141] Remarks of Representative John Hawley of Illinois, *CG* (41/2), May 28, 1870, p. 3926. Horace Maynard of Tennessee's argument that there was "no principle of justice ... which would require the Government, or of policy which should induce the Government" to include disloyal old soldiers in the law's benefit scheme (p. 3927) indicated that at least some members of Congress still distinguished between legal and political claims when considering questions of entitlement.

The Pension Act of 1871 had numerous consequences. First, its creation of new selective categories of desert and reward reinforced the efficacy of programmatic entitlement as a policy practice. As was the case with earlier pension laws, the act's classifications immediately were challenged. This shifted the focus of political conflict from broader questions about public welfare and the allocation of public benefits and costs to demands for the expansion of specific program categories – demands that eventually were satisfied in 1878.[142] Second, the precedent of granting monetary entitlements to veterans on the basis of service alone was revived after decades of congressional resistance, opening the door to claims for service pensions from veterans of the Mexican and Indian wars that would culminate in the passage of new categorical pension laws beginning in the late 1880s and early 1890s.[143] Finally, through the 1871 Pension Act's exclusion of disloyal southern veterans of the War of 1812 (until its amendment in 1878), northern veterans became constructed politically and legally as the only legitimate successors to the heritage of those who had founded and expanded the contours of the nation. This fueled the efforts of pension attorneys and the ideological campaigns of newly formed Union veterans' organizations like the Grand Army of the Republic, and undergirded, if not ordained, the massive expansion of the Civil War pension system for Union veterans after Reconstruction. More than acquisitiveness, lobbying, the economics of surplus, or party politics, it was *public policy* that helped to transform the terms of the pension debate in the early to mid-1870s. Federal policy encouraged

---

[142] Legislation passed in 1878 by commanding majorities of both House and Senate reduced the War of 1812 service requirement from sixty to fourteen days; lowered the evidentiary requirements for pension claims; dropped the condition that widows be married before the treaty of peace to allow pensions to be provided to widows unborn when the war was fought (though remarriage remained as a disqualifier); and abolished the requirement of loyalty during the Civil War. The law also explicitly granted new benefits to widows of Revolutionary soldiers. Glasson, *Federal Military Pensions*, pp. 110–11.

[143] Soldiers disabled in wars with Native American tribes, and the dependent relatives of veterans killed in those conflicts, received pension benefits under the general disability pension law passed by Congress in 1862. Pensions were enacted for all Mexican War veterans of sixty days' service and their widows in 1887, provided that such persons were at least sixty-two years of age or disabled. Loyalty during the Civil War was not a requirement, but disabilities could not have been incurred then. A pension measure benefiting veterans who had served for at least thirty days in the Indian wars of 1832–42 and their widows (provided that they had not remarried), regardless of loyalty during the Civil War, passed in 1892. Both the Indian and Mexican pension programs were liberalized early in the twentieth century. Glasson, *Federal Military Pensions*, pp. 114–19.

a burgeoning conception of Union military service as a debt that never could be repaid, and an understanding of programmatic entitlements for Union veterans and their survivors as the moral and legal rights of those who had preserved the nation.[144]

The Civil War pension system indeed constituted an "unabashed system of national public care" for the "deserving core of a special generation."[145] But it did not constitute the political origins of social policy in the United States, nor did it possess serious potential for expansion into a universal egalitarian system of social provision. Though more widely dispersed and generous than the Federal benefits that had come before, the Civil War pension system nonetheless was still fundamentally and deliberately exclusionary. It represented a major extension, rather than a negation, of Congress's historic practice of selective legal entitlement, and a rejection of the principle of universal entitlement embraced in the general preemption and homestead legislation of the mid-nineteenth century. An American welfare state undeniably had begun to form, but it was not a welfare state premised upon the ideal of equal national citizenship, nor even upon citizenship or social provision per se. Rather, it was one organized around the preferential treatment of particular categories of citizens who served particular Federal purposes through the establishment of programmatic rights, often at the expense of disfavored others. The distance between this basis for state organization and early American political and constitutional principles suggests that the capacity of national authority in the United States was in large part built at the expense of its character. Twentieth-century events would force episodic reconsideration of the American state's foundations, but efforts at reform would reshape, rather than fundamentally recast, the policy legacy of selective entitlement inherited from the nation's formative years.

[144] See McConnell, *Glorious Contentment*, pp. 153–65, for an illuminating discussion of the Union veterans' attitudes concerning the nature of Federal pensions.

[145] Skocpol, *Protecting Soldiers and Mothers*, p. 151.

6

Entitlements and the Constitution
of the American Nation

> It requires a steady, clear-viewed, thoroughly informed historical
> sense, therefore, to determine what was at any given time the real
> character of our political institutions. To us of the present day it
> seems that the Constitution framed in 1787 gave birth in 1789 to
> a national government such as that which now constitutes an in-
> destructible bond of union for the states; but the men of that time
> would certainly have laughed at any such idea, – and for the English
> race, as I have said, every law is what those who administer it think
> that it is.
>
> Woodrow Wilson, 1898[1]

The constitutional moment of 1789 involved a principled rejection of the
organizational qualities of the eighteenth-century European state: standing armies, centralized taxing authorities, the denial of local prerogatives,
and burgeoning castes of administrators.[2] Yet, the exigencies of American
nation building tested the strength of the Framers' convictions and found
them wanting. The diffusion of sovereignty across a federal system of regional and local jurisdictions served for most of the routine operations
of governance, but as members of the Continental and Confederation
Congresses had learned, a highly decentralized institutional order posed
severe challenges with respect to consolidating, expanding, and maintaining control of a sprawling empire and its population. To effectively wage
war against domestic and foreign nations, defending and extending its
territorial claims at the periphery while maintaining some semblance of
internal unity and coherence, the new U.S. Government required more

---

[1] *The State: Elements of Historical and Practical Politics* (Boston: D. C. Heath & Co., 1898, rev.
ed.), p. 463.
[2] Stephen Skowronek, *Building a New American State: The Expansion of National Administrative
Capacities* (Cambridge: Cambridge University Press, 1982), p. 20.

authority at the center. That authority needed to be coupled with new mechanisms for organizing the people as members of a national political community founded upon popular sovereignty, representation, and constitutional rights – mechanisms by which Congress could attend to citizens' concerns and invest them in the activities of the nation.

Legal entitlements were a logical choice for legislators trying to establish central authority and achieve some measure of command and effectiveness. Members of the Continental Congress recognized that their creation of selective veterans' benefits meant that America's repudiation of the *organizational* characteristics of European states would not be accompanied by a sustained rejection of European state *practices*. Yet, they also perceived that the creation of land and pension benefits would work to ensure the development of a military force capable of achieving national independence. Engaged in a formative conflict that would last for eight years and require over 100,000 men in arms, they had few if any other viable policy options at their disposal. If capitulating to "interest" would guarantee success in the Revolution, then they would have to capitulate.

The Congresses that were bound to fulfill the statutory commitments of 1776 through 1780 faced major political and institutional problems. By the end of the Revolutionary war, the national debt was enormous and national resources were seriously lacking. Neither money nor land was readily available for satisfying the claims of the Army's officers or soldiers or, for that matter, the many other creditors of the United States. Policy alternatives were again few. Congress's decisions to commute the veterans' pensions into lump-sum payments in 1783, and to render their land warrants salable in 1788, undoubtedly appeared to be reasonable compromises from the perspective of beleaguered state actors. Those compromises were not, however, what the veterans knew to be due them. Having met the military service requirements established for them in the nation's original pension and land bounty legislation, and trusting, with the encouragement of public law, that their claims were both legitimate and of special moral significance, the veterans believed themselves to be deserving of far better treatment. Their belief had everything to do with the "rights tied to reasons" logic at the heart of their pension and land entitlements. Their reliance upon those rights would not disappear simply because the condition of the nation was less than optimal. From their perspective, the fact that pensions and land grants were technically creatures of statute, and thereby subject to legislative change, was largely irrelevant.

The Continental Army veterans' continued expectations, along with the hopes and expectations of other veterans not originally entitled to Revolutionary pension or land benefits, posed grave dilemmas of governance for the U.S. Government. The ratification of the Constitution had not eliminated or even altered the adjudication of claims as a congressional practice and obligation. Just as citizens had presented their concerns to national and state legislative bodies before 1789, they continued to press their declarations of right and need upon the U.S. Congress after 1789. Americans had faith, rooted in both historic practice and constitutional text, that their representatives would be receptive and responsive to their petitions. Required to render judgment about debt and legal obligation, Congress had to find ways to provide fair consideration and payment to citizens with meritorious claims, yet at the same time guard the limited assets so necessary for the accomplishment of other national purposes. It was a difficult balancing act to achieve from the start.

As Congress worked to define and activate its institutional role through the development of internal structures and procedural rules, the 1800s and 1810s brought about a confluence of factors and forces that reoriented the nation's horizons and rendered new forms of governance possible. The public domain was expanded radically. The national debt was reduced and then transformed into a surplus, and a second war for independence was fought and won. Unresolved cultural anxieties about the nature and virtue of the Republic surfaced, coupled with new dreams of commercial development and expansionism, and colored by evolving social structures of race, gender, and class. Energized by colonial policy feedbacks and Congress's obligation to recognize the people's claims, a politics of interest emerged. Military veterans, squatters on the public domain, victims of natural disaster, deranged Army officers, and even state and territorial legislatures prayed for tangible forms of congressional assistance. In lieu of responding to constituents' innumerable memorials, petitions, and claims on an individual, ad hoc basis, Congress hit upon the idea of attending to the demands of certain groups en masse, through the establishment of *programmatic* benefits for categories of worthy citizens. Federal actors might have been divided over the validity and wisdom of internal improvements in the early years of the nineteenth century, but neither constitutional scruples nor contemporary notions of propriety sufficed to bar congressional majorities from creating entitlement programs in the names of America's patriots and settlers.

Legal entitlement was an ingenious legislative solution to multiple thorny problems of national governance. The establishment of benefit programs for military veterans and civilians provided early U.S. Congresses with a means of necessitating and justifying, both instrumentally and symbolically, the growth and development of national institutions, including the military, the treasury, the public domain, and a fledgling bureaucracy. It also facilitated the penetration of those institutions into the life of the nation. Entitlement programs allowed Congress to represent a growing constituency of unprecedented size and diversity, and to forge novel, unmediated relationships with preferred citizen-clients that bypassed closer affiliations with institutions and party leaders at the state and local levels. Entitlements also offered Congress a means of simultaneously achieving a variety of policy goals, from establishing territorial dominion in the face of other nations' claims, to the removal and extermination of indigenous peoples, to continental expansion. America's first entitlement programs did not create a centralized welfare state during the formative years of the nation, or result in central state building that was unremitting or uniform. Nonetheless, the selective entitlements enacted by a new government of limited ability and authority provided avenues for future reconstructive assaults on the nation's original decentralized institutional order and initiated the United States into the ways of fragmented, categorical social policymaking. In creating programmatic benefits for groups of citizens in the late eighteenth and nineteenth centuries, the Federal government gradually gained and exerted an unanticipated measure of power, reifying preferred social arrangements through a legal discourse of citizen "difference" as it developed the capacity to extract and redistribute community resources, to act as fiduciary guardian, and to direct and monitor its chosen beneficiaries.

This is not to suggest that the entitlements enacted from the nation's founding through its reconstruction were the result of autonomous state action. If anything, they were equally the product of transformations in a political and constitutional culture that was exquisitely tuned to signals from the citizenry. Though the personal politics of petitioning and the legislative adjudication of claims eventually would give way to new mechanisms of mass politics and the judicial determination of legality, the Congresses that governed during the formative years of the nation faced popular expectations that were the legitimate inheritance of colonial legislative practice. In the wake of the War of 1812, many Americans supported the enactment of pensions for the patriots and frontiersmen whose efforts had established the nation. Pragmatically and ideologically invested in the citizen-soldier and the actual settler, they often framed their petitions and claims to Congress in terms invoking those mythical figures. When legislative tradition and the legal duty to be attentive to citizens' claims collided with ostensible limits on Congress's authority to define the public interest and distribute resources, the former won out. Neither federalism nor the terms of the Constitution's taxing and spending clauses stood in the way of Congress's creation of Federal entitlements as new forms of legal property.

That the advantages of establishing selective entitlements came at the price of generating a potentially dysfunctional politics was recognized even by the state actors of the 1780s, who discovered all too quickly that the exclusionary, redistributive nature of the Revolutionary officers' pensions ignited widespread conflict over the legitimacy of the Continental Congress's actions. The earliest years of American veterans' pensions indeed demonstrated how societal discord over discretionary benefits coupled with a lack of central fiscal and institutional capacity could effectively scuttle a national-level entitlement program. During the first part of the nineteenth century, however, the fledgling U.S. Government learned that conflicts arising over statutory limits of deservingness could serve as an asset instead of a liability, for they signified a shift in the locus of political and legal activity from the fundamental issue of establishing entitlements per se to more specific questions about *who* should qualify to receive particular entitlements and *why*. Once some citizens had been deemed entitled and had begun to receive pensions and land benefits from the nation, the programmatic boundaries separating the deserving from others generated struggles aimed at benefit category expansion, pathological attempts at inclusion by fraud, and demands for new legal categories of deserving, "qualifying" individuals and new benefit programs. In their invocation of the rights of deserving citizens, early American entitlements quickly came to be viewed as sacred obligations, conferring singular virtue and legitimacy upon both program beneficiaries and benefits that defied reconsideration. All of these feedback effects fueled the *expansion*, rather than the elimination, of categorical policies, which in turn required and justified the enhancement of national-level fiscal and administrative capacities.

The Continental Congress's decision to privilege the officers of the Continental Army both capitulated to one of the state practices *against* which the American Revolution was being fought and conceded upon the ideal of equal citizenship *for* which the Revolution was being fought. Although the enactment of officers' pensions served to keep the Continental Army together through the victorious completion of the war in 1783, social protest coupled with a lack of fiscal capacity allowed the government essentially to renege on its promises, facilitating a popular revival of the claims of national moral superiority that had incited the original movement toward independence. The extent to which the new American state could actually remain distinctive, however, remained to be determined, for the Continental Congress's statutory promise of exclusionary officers' pensions had established both a policy legacy and an aggrieved interest group that would lie in wait until the political and socioeconomic transformations of the War of 1812 era afforded opportunities for new beginnings. It was then, when a newly victorious and unabashedly expansionist national government decided to create a land grant program only for War of 1812 Army soldiers, and to revisit, reenact, and implement a pension program only for aged, poor veterans of the Continental Army and Navy, that the American state and American social policy began to take shape.

It is undoubtedly the case that the states, not the U.S. Government, exercised the primary role in terms of public functions and services from the founding through Reconstruction. State legal codes were indeed responsible for the organization and control of much if not most of American social and economic life. Early Federal governance was nonetheless very significant in the development of the nation. The notion that the early American state was a limited, underdeveloped, premodern shell at the center is simply inaccurate, as is the contention that the origins of American social policy lie in the developments of the Reconstruction or the New Deal. Legal entitlements have been a defining feature of American governance, and a constitutive element in the American polity, since 1776. Because the implementation of public benefit programs compelled the development of material, institutional, and psychic resources, early American entitlements were inherently nationalizing policies that shifted authority away from subnational entities toward the institutions of the U.S. Government, even as they shaped citizens' conceptions of themselves and others, and their view of the national government's role.

The Federal Government's reinvention of the Continental Congress's Revolutionary pension program in 1818 played a major role in molding the incentives, resources, and understandings of citizens and state actors. Picking up on past policy precedents as well as social and cultural imperatives, the Pension Act of 1818 established a new program of pension benefits for surviving veterans of the American Revolution. It was a curious hybrid, born of ambition and benevolence, anxiety and celebration, generosity and thrift. It did not extend pensions to veterans solely upon the basis of military service. Nor did it provide pensions for all American veterans (to the great unhappiness of those who fought in the War of 1812) or even for all Revolutionary veterans (to the outrage of the militiamen who had served in the war for independence). Instead, the 1818 law created pension entitlements *only* for veterans of the Continental Army and Navy who had served during the Revolution for at least nine months, who *also* were aged and poor, and who *also* were willing to declare their poverty publicly in a formal plea for the nation's help. Enacted retrospectively, some thirty-five years after the war, the Pension Act of 1818 was not aimed primarily at sustaining the U.S. military. Its passage nonetheless encouraged veterans of past and future conflicts, young and old, financially self-sufficient and not, to expect service pensions, to be disappointed when they were not forthcoming from a grateful Congress, and to petition and lobby almost incessantly for their enactment.

The policies established for the acquisition and disposition of the public domain were obviously essential to nation building. Warnings that the physical growth of the United States might outpace the development of its institutions or the definition of its purpose did not quell the desire of Americans in every state and section for land beyond the new nation's borders. As John Mayfield has suggested, the expansion of the Republic had been so swift and astounding by the 1840s that few even remembered the Antifederalists' warning that a democracy might not work when spread over a large territory. "Fewer still would have taken the warning seriously," for expansion and progress seemed destined to go hand in hand.[3] The creation of selective land entitlements for military veterans and certain civilians was an ideal policy strategy for a state determined upon a course of territorial aggrandizement because of those entitlements' dual instrumental and rhetorical possibilities. Coupling the allocation of public benefits to deserving citizens with a culturally resonant and very public rationale for doing so, land grants and preemption

---

[3] John Mayfield, *The New Nation 1800–1845* (New York: Hill and Wang, rev. ed., 1982), p. 207.

rights encouraged "qualified" settlers to appropriate and occupy territory where Federal ownership was tenuous, while they extended authoritative claims of national purpose into ideological space with a force that Hamilton's land sales plan never could have achieved.

The acquisitive exploits of the nation led by Jackson and Polk, and, for that matter, Jefferson, did not take place free of controversy. Objections were raised with respect to every aspect of expansionism, from the financial and human costs of territorial gain, to the morality of Indian removal and slaughter, to the destruction of the natural environment. Of all the questions raised by the prospect of national growth, the ones that were most intractable had to do with the effects that the disposition of an enlarged public domain would have on the balance of power between states, between sections, and between levels of government.

The disparate policy options regarding the public lands that emerged by the 1820s – cession, distribution, preemption, graduation, and homestead – essentially represented contending visions of what the operational realities of the American federal system should be. Proposals to cede Federal lands back to the nation's regional units of government, the states, reflected fears about centralization that might have constituted a return to a more confederate Republic had they succeeded. Distribution schemes advocated a sharing of power and resources between the U.S. Government and the states that ranged from a no-strings approach to a more conditional penetration of central policy goals (such as the congressional designation of Federal land revenues for particular purposes, including education and internal improvements). Preemption and graduation proposals implied even more Federal authority, reserving the public lands as a source of national revenue while allowing the Government to use squatters and legal settlers as paramilitary forces, and to reduce the price of lands in particular areas to guide and stimulate local development. Selective land grant programs and homestead entitlements represented even stronger mechanisms of Federal control that forged novel relationships between the nation and its citizens, promoting Federal policy purposes and competing with local allegiances. The working out of these proposals during the first half of the nineteenth century demonstrated all too clearly that acquiring a continent was one thing, and consolidating and governing it quite another. As it became undeniable that Federal policy in the territories was an expression of national goals that did not include slavery, the Framers' federal Republic discovered the depth of the divisions within it. Madison's hope that Americans would be able to live together as "fellow citizens of one great, respectable, flourishing empire"[4] was shattered along with the union, stifling the egalitarian impulses that recently had propelled a new vision of the social rights of citizenship, and urged universalism as a fundamental principle of American governance.

The Congresses that came to govern during the Civil War and Reconstruction of the United States inherited a policy legacy of selective, programmatic entitlement. Their actions demonstrated that they fully understood entitlement's instrumental and symbolic potential. The qualifying criteria precluding rebels and southern sympathizers from receiving homesteads and War of 1812 veterans' pensions would be dropped from the laws entitling citizens to land and pensions by the late 1870s. Those qualifiers nonetheless rendered vital programs, at a critical juncture in American political development, part of a new set of selective entitlements enacted for the morally worthy citizens of the Union. Like earlier selective benefits, these entitlements elevated the needs and deeds of some citizens to the national policy agenda while consigning others to subnational public and private systems of care.

By far the most overt of these entitlements was the extraordinary system of pension benefits established for Union veterans of the Civil War and their survivors, which mirrored the nation's earlier enactments in form but grew to an unprecedented scale. Selectively benefiting the men who had saved the Union and their relatives while ignoring, if not even penalizing, those who had served on the wrong side of the conflict, these pensions became a central fixture of the partisan politics aimed at asserting and maintaining control of the postbellum state. Like earlier pensions and land grants for those who had founded and sustained the nation, they were conceptualized and justified as the contractual rights of a morally worthy group of uniquely deserving patriots. Where earlier selective entitlements had sorted deserving from other military veterans according to such criteria as rank, length of service, or service in national-level forces, the Civil War pension system employed a geopolitical qualifier to make sure that disloyal southerners and other citizens who had not contributed to the Union's preservation would never receive Federal disability or service benefits, no matter how needy they might be.

Although it was never enacted, the introduction of Federal legislation that would have granted confiscated land in insurgent southern districts to Union veterans and loyal, poor citizens of all races demonstrated the

---

[4] *The Federalist*, no. 14, pp. 103–4.

extent to which some Federal actors were willing to employ the policy strategy of selective entitlement to reward certain citizens at the expense of disfavored others. A land confiscation bill actually passed in the House in the Thirty-eighth Congress by a close vote, only to be stopped before it reached the Senate by the U.S. attorney general, who ordered all property seized by Federal authorities returned to its former owners.[5] Undaunted, a majority of the Thirty-ninth Congress responded by passing the Southern Homestead Act of 1866, allocating 46 million acres of the public domain in Alabama, Arkansas, Florida, Louisiana, and Mississippi as free homesteads for settlers regardless of race or gender. For the first six months after its passage, the act's entitlements were restricted to freedmen, white Union loyalists, and unmarried women. Its benefits soon were extended to citizens willing to swear an oath of allegiance to the United States, opening up choice public lands to whites, and then repealed a decade later when most of the Federal lands had been disposed of. Nonetheless, the act briefly imposed a radical variant of the Jeffersonian agrarian vision. Enacted when the southern delegations were absent from Congress, the measure was as much an attempt at revenge on southern landowners as an attempt to create an egalitarian society in the South. It was an effort that evinced the flexibility of programmatic entitlement, particularly selective entitlement, as a policy device.

The Consequences of Policy Choice

The programmatic entitlements enacted from the founding of the Republic and through its Reconstruction undoubtedly seemed a constructive application of national authority to many of those who sought to build the new American state. They enabled a decentralized government of limited size and resources to achieve a number of distinctive goals, not the least of which was founding and expanding the "first new nation."[6] They helped to build and sustain national institutions, and guaranteed that the citizens of a vast republic were represented and supported. In conjunction with other policies, they worked to ensure that national governance was enabled, key legal concepts developed, and the

---

5 *CG* (38/1), pp. 874, 2253; Roy M. Robbins, *Our Landed Heritage: The Public Domain, 1776–1936* (Princeton, NJ: Princeton University Press, 1942), pp. 210–12.
6 Seymour Martin Lipset's phrase. *The First New Nation: The United States in Historical and Comparative Perspective* (New York: Basic Books, 1963).

federal balance maintained. America's early entitlements were a form of law "formed largely by the imperatives of action."[7] They embodied a dynamic, rather than static, view of property: one that encouraged people to tie their loyalties to the central state by taking positive action in the service of Government goals.[8]

Given their inherent flexibility and adaptability to a variety of policy problems, *selective* entitlements were quickly recognized as one of the Federal government's most powerful standard operating procedures. State actors of the 1780s understood that carefully targeted land grants and pension enactments simultaneously could secure the services of military leaders, direct their energies toward the nationalist purposes of the new American state, and strengthen the Government by justifying congressional revenue measures and rationalizing central administration. The implementation and extension of selective veterans' pensions and military and civilian land entitlements in the early nineteenth century furthered the growth of fiscal and administrative capacity at the center as presidents and members of Congress both expanded the contours of the nation and acquired a powerful means of responding programmatically to a growing electorate. These nineteenth-century pension and land entitlements created a new nexus between the citizens and their representatives in Washington while exacerbating subnational conflicts over cultural and economic interests. By the time of the Civil War, selective entitlements were the obvious vehicle for establishing a large-scale system of national public care for citizens who had preserved the Union. As with the earlier enactments, the issue was never just social welfare per se, but rather that of how programmatic entitlement could be used to further and justify the diverse goals of the government that sat at the center of a radically deconcentrated, federally organized state.

As America's first experience with national-level social programs so amply demonstrated, the implementation of selective entitlement policies was destined to be problematic. The Continental Congress's decision to reward some, but not all, military veterans with public benefits through the imposition of national redistributive obligations did not sit well with ordinary citizens. Had fiscal calamity and government reorganization not

---

[7] James Willard Hurst, *Law and the Conditions of Freedom in the Nineteenth-Century United States* (Madison: University of Wisconsin Press, 1956), p. 5.

[8] This stands in direct contrast to the Bismarkian welfare state's use of social benefits as a means of keeping workers passive.

afforded the nation a way to finesse reneging upon its original promises, contemporary protest over the legitimacy of veterans' entitlements might have been far more consequential in the long run. Instead, however, the highly discretionary, original pension and land bounty legislation stood as policy precedents and legal commitments awaiting the nationalistic fervor, treasury surplus, and swelling public domain of the post–War of 1812 years.

The passage of the categorical 1818 Pension Act was a defining moment in the institutional history of Congress, the evolution of American constitutionalism, American state formation, and the development of Federal social policy. It provided the U.S. Congress with the first of many lessons in creating new property and in the difficulty of establishing definitive eligibility criteria for an intended, restricted set of beneficiaries. Its gross underestimate of the number of entitled claimants and costs, coupled with an overly optimistic sense of future national fiscal capacity, also provided the first of many hard lessons in the realities of using the spending power to establish open-ended budgetary commitments. The need to process, verify, satisfy, and police increasingly detailed pension and land grant claims arising under Federal programs also necessitated the enhancement of national administrative capacities, increasing program costs as well as the size and role of the U.S. Government. Yet, these early problems in implementation did not lead to a turning away from programmatic entitlement as a policy device, but rather to the kind of short-run retrenchment or categorical reform that *presumed* and *depended upon* the existence and expansion of national institutions. The Government's inability to maintain its borders and enforce other national policies, such as its treaties with Native American tribes and its prohibition against squatting, spurred the establishment of additional Federal entitlements, as did its efforts at territorial expansionism through military and civilian actions that eventually culminated in the Civil War.

Public reaction to the nation's early pension and land entitlements foreshadowed future political upheaval in that conflicts were related to the degree of exclusivity that different programs proposed to entail. The intersection of powerful legal and political demands for particularistic benefits with equally compelling legal and political demands for egalitarianism put early legislatures in the difficult position of needing simultaneously to extend and constrain the generosity of the nation. The fact that pension entitlements were obviously redistributive in nature, drawing upon the financial resources of the national community to benefit a select subset of citizens, heightened the level of social and political antagonism over which citizens would get "what, when, and how." This was true at the time half-pay pensions originally were promised, when military pension programs later were enacted and enlarged by the U.S. Congress, and especially during periods when national budgetary adversity imposed a need for reductions in those benefits, since the policy justifications for entitling "deserving" veterans and their survivors to benefits did not disappear from collective memory when the funds required to pay for them did.

The politics of land entitlements differed somewhat from pension politics in that the former disbursed benefits acquired by purchase or through wars against other nations and presumptively inferior peoples. Yet, land entitlements also generated dissension and conflict due to questions arising over the selectivity of different enactments, the morality of the state's aggressive behavior, and the means and ends of utilizing the public domain. Federal actors recognized that policies involving the disposition of the public lands were central to the nation's future and to the political balance within it. As time went on, and partisan and sectional differences became more pronounced, they increasingly disagreed over the direction that land grants, preemption rights, and other land policies should take.

Battles over the establishment, expansion, and contraction of nineteenth-century Federal entitlement programs stimulated intergovernmental antagonism, sectional and partisan dissension, the formation of interest groups, interpersonal conflict, and lobbying aimed at demanding or retaining particular benefits. This firmly ensconced the locus of political activity along programmatic boundaries of desert and reward, and induced Americans of various stripes (entitled, unentitled, disentitled), and the state actors standing guard over public resources, to assume watchful roles. The consequences were not merely fiscal, for Americans became all too accustomed to, and invested in, the encryption of their relative worth in the state's categorical benefit schemes. Where a national community of relatively equal citizens might have evolved, the American polity had begun to be divided into multiple, overlapping, legally circumscribed categories of clients, claimants, and outcasts.[9]

---

[9] Ironically, attempts began in the 1990s to lure back some of the Native Americans whose lands were bought or expropriated because it was believed that their presence would facilitate state and local economic development. Community leaders in Oregon's Wallowa Valley, for example, tried to reattract the Nez Percé, forced out by the U.S. Army in the 1870s, in the hope that Native American–related tourism might replace the valley's dying

For a time, the homestead movement held out the promise of a fundamentally different, universal approach to legal entitlement as a Federal policy practice. Nascent visions of the social rights of citizens, however, could not be divorced from contemporary politics of race and gender, nor from the geopolitics of Reconstruction. Blacks, women, and Native Americans might have become citizens of the nation in theory, but the practical dimensions of their inclusion in the polity remained to be worked out, and the restoration of southerners to national citizenship served to impede the development of the radically inclusive America that "never was."[10] White southern males might have benefited from the terms of a liberalized homestead law, but genuine, full membership in the polity in the sense of martial manhood was contingent upon their behavior during the Civil War. The men who had fought for the Confederacy would never be recast as veterans of the nation or be entitled to the benefits established for those who had saved the Union.

The lesson to be taken from this history is not that national-level entitlement programs should never have been enacted in the United States, but rather that the overtly discriminatory *form* that they typically were enacted in during the late eighteenth and nineteenth centuries led toward some dysfunctional ends. As the original opponents of Revolutionary officers' pensions predicted, selective entitlements fostered the concentration and purposeful application of central state capacity to privilege particular interests at the expense of more collective concerns. The recurrent societal convulsions that ensued from Congress's creation of pension and land entitlements focused upon the boundaries of exclusionary Federal programs rather than upon the policy practice of selective entitlement itself. Both action and reaction tended to work against, rather than toward, a broad and equitable incorporation of citizens into the polity, obstructing the development of the kind of citizenship-based system of social provision that other democracies came to envision by the late nineteenth century. This developmental trajectory did not preclude the enactment of more global social benefits in the United States in the twentieth century. But neither did it prevent the perpetuation of illiberal categories of desert and reward after the "constitutional revolution" of the 1930s.

logging and ranching economy. "Expelled in 1877, Indian Tribe Is Now Wanted as a Resource," *The New York Times*, 22 July 1996, p. A1, col. 6.

[10] See Rogers M. Smith, *Civic Ideals: Conflicting Visions of Citizenship in U.S. History* (New Haven, CT: Yale University Press, 1997), pp. 286–346.

Indeed, as congressional deliberation and action repeatedly suggested during the first century of the nation's existence, the Government's authority to selectively entitle always implied a power to selectively *dis*entitle when claims of social or fiscal calamity could lend legitimacy to programmatic reform efforts. The United States' historic failure to embrace the most basic of guarantees for all of its citizens – a failure that recently resulted in the "end of welfare as we knew it" – is rooted not in the policy missteps of the Great Society, or in the compromises of the New Deal, or even in the divisive cataclysm of the Civil War, but in the original legal dimensions of American governance. To explicate this history is not simply to tell a new origins story about the development of the American social policy or the American welfare state, but moreover to direct much-needed attention to the role played by law and legal entitlement in shaping the past and present contours of the nation.

Index